THE GREAT STRIKE

THE MINERS' STRIKE OF 1984-5 AND ITS LESSONS

Alex Callinicos and Mike Simons

A *Socialist Worker* publication

Published April 1985
by Socialist Worker, PO Box 82, London E2.
Distribution by Bookmarks, 265 Seven Sisters Road,
Finsbury Park, London N4 2DE, England.
Jointly published as International Socialism 27/28 (1985).

ISBN 0 905998 50 2

Printed by Krips Repro, Meppel, Netherlands.
Typeset by Kate Macpherson Photosetting, Clevedon,
Avon. Design by Peter Court.

Photographs by John Sturrock, except for pages 69 and
173 (Keith Pattison), pages 81 and 160–1 (Ron
Richardson), page 86 (Martin Shakeshaft), pages 112–3
(John Harris), page 122 (Denis Doran), and page 147
(Stafano Cagnoni, IFL).

Socialist Worker is the weekly paper of the Socialist
Workers Party, which is one of a group of international
socialist organisations:

AUSTRALIA: **International Socialists**, GPO Box
1437N, Melbourne 3001.
BRITAIN: **Socialist Workers Party**, PO Box 82, London
E2.
CANADA: **International Socialists**, PO Box 339, Station
E, Toronto, Ontario.
DENMARK: **Internationale Socialister**, Vestergade 24,
1 tv, 8000 Arhus C.
IRELAND: **Socialist Workers Movement**, c/o 41
Herberton Park, Rialto, Dublin 8.
UNITED STATES: **International Socialist Organisation**,
PO Box 16085, Chicago, Illinois 60616.
WEST GERMANY: **Sozialistische Arbeiter Gruppe**,
Wolfgangstrasse 81, D–6000 Frankfurt 1.

CONTENTS

This book is very much a result of collective efforts. It draws heavily on the coverage of the miners' strike in **Socialist Worker**, some of which we wrote. We are grateful to Peter Clark, Tony Cliff, Chris Harman, Sheila MacGregor, and Peter Marsden for helping to improve a manuscript written at great speed. Also to the staff of **Socialist Worker**. Above all, this book would have been impossible without the assistance given us by the many miners who spoke to us before, during and after the strike. Unfortunately the National Coal Board's attempts to victimise militants mean that we cannot acknowledge the help we received from these miners by name. That is why the only miners named in the book are NUM officials. Our thanks to all who talked to us. The book follows the general analysis of the strike developed by the Socialist Workers Party: any errors of fact or of judgement are, however, our own.

Alex Callinicos
Mike Simons

12 March 1985

Alex Callinicos is a member of the Socialist Workers Party. His earlier publications include **The revolutionary ideas of Karl Marx** and **The Revolutionary Road to Socialism**, both published in 1983.

Mike Simons reported on the 1984–5 miners' strike as a journalist for Socialist Worker. He is a member of the Socialist Workers Party and the author of **Workers' power, not nuclear power**.

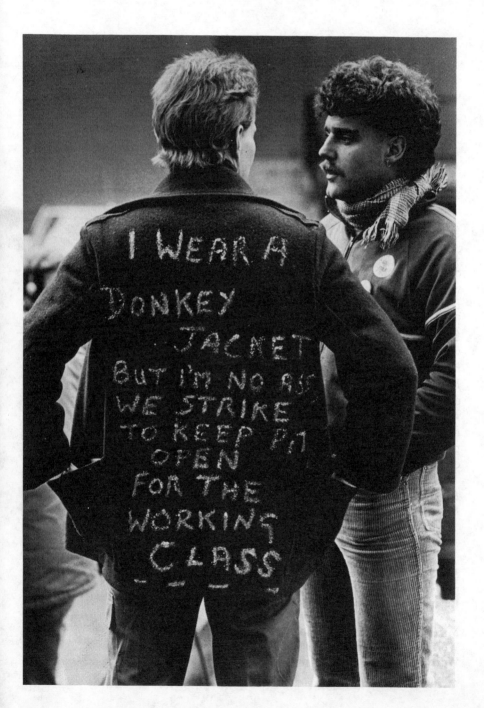

INTRODUCTION

ON 1 MARCH 1984 the National Coal Board announced that Cortonwood colliery in South Yorkshire would be closed. The miners and their families were horrified. They had been told that the pit would stay open for another five years. Entire villages such as Brampton depended on the pit as their only source of employment.

Susan Bradshaw, a miner's wife from Brampton, said: 'It was like a shock wave going through the village when the Coal Board said the pit would close in five weeks. People were really desperate because they knew that there were no other jobs to go to.'

Three days later the Cortonwood branch of the National Union of Mineworkers voted unanimously for a strike by the whole Yorkshire coalfield to stop the closure. No one realised that it would be the beginning of the longest major strike in the history of the British working-class movement.

Few people expected much to happen at all. In the years since Margaret Thatcher had become prime minister in May 1979 many communities like Brampton had been destroyed by closures. Millions of jobs had disappeared. The trade unions had mounted little resistance to the tidal wave of unemployment which swept through industrial Britain. Much the same was true of the labour movement in the rest of the western world. Many commentators, some of them socialists, had concluded that the industrial working class was finished.

How could the miners stand against the tide? Once they had humbled governments, in the great strikes of 1972 and 1974. But many believed the mineworkers' union was a shadow of its former self. In the three years since 1981 the NCB had got rid of 41,000 jobs in the face of no effective opposition. Arthur Scargill, the NUM president, had been humiliated in three successive national ballots when he tried to win strike action to save jobs.

Today's miners were different, many commentators argued. They had mortgages, cars, video recorders. The old fighting traditions of 1926 and 1972 were dying amid consumer affluence. Cortonwood would go without a fight, like all the other mines, factories and steel mills which had gone before it.

A year later, on 5 March 1985, the miners of Cortonwood marched defiantly back to work behind their branch banner. Across the coalfields tens of thousands of miners did the same. They had been out on strike for twelve months to prevent pit closures. For the closure of Cortonwood had unleashed one of the most epic struggles ever waged by workers anywhere.

Nothing like it had been seen since the General Strike of 1926. A. J. Cook, the miners' leader during that earlier struggle, told them: 'You have been fighting the legions of hell.' Again in 1984–5 the miners found the legions of hell arrayed against them. All the resources of the state were mobilised to defeat the NUM.

Mining community after mining community was invaded and occupied by paramilitary riot police seeking to protect the handfuls of scabs which the Coal Board gathered together in the hope of breaking the strike. The Department of Health and Social Security sprang into action and countless acts of meanness denied miners' families welfare payments in order to starve them back to work. One couple were denied funeral benefit to bury their son. The courts delivered judgement after judgement designed to weaken the strike, until in December they handed the union's funds to a Tory solicitor who declared: 'I *am* the NUM.' And through it all the press ran a campaign of misinformation and lies.

All this did not break the strikers and their families. With tremendous courage the men and women of the mining villages stood up to the worst that the state could serve out. The women especially were transformed — joining picket lines, travelling round the country speaking, organising soup kitchens, stiffening the backbones of wavering strikers. Rather than surrender, the mining communities did without. They gave up the blessings of affluence — cars, TVs, video recorders, furniture — and continued the struggle.

The heroism and determination of the miners and their families astonished the world and inspired millions. Many who did not regard themselves as socialists and who had been no great admirers of trade unionism began to see the miners as fighting, not just for themselves, but for all those who wanted to halt the devastation wreaked by the rule of Margaret Thatcher and her equivalents across the globe. In a crazy world where the gyrations of the money markets could make or break entire countries, at last a group of workers was prepared to stand up to the remorseless logic of capital. At last someone had refused to sit and accept the idea that workers should lose their jobs when what they produced was needed but not profitable. When the miners opposed the closure of 'uneconomic' pits they were standing up against a society which puts private profit before social need.

Yet they were, in the end, defeated. It was through no fault of their own. Ned Smith, the Coal Board's industrial relations director for most of the strike, told Channel 4 News on 4 February 1985 that the turning point for the NCB had not been the failure of the NUM to bring out the Nottinghamshire coalfield, where a majority of miners scabbed, but the refusal of the TUC to implement its decision to halt the movement of blackleg coal and oil. The trade union leaders' betrayal of the miners had ensured the strike's defeat.

The miners were beaten because union leaders like Norman Willis of the TUC and David Basnett of the General, Municipal and Boilermakers' Union failed to stand by them. This was encouraged by Labour Party leader Neil Kinnock, who sat on the fence throughout the strike, even-handedly attacking both police and pickets, refusing to stand by the miners' side. The strike's defeat was more than a tragedy. It was a crime.

But when the miners finally returned to work, a year after it had all begun, they did not slink back with heads hung in despair. They returned defiantly, with pride, banners flying and sometimes bands playing. They might have lost, but they weren't crushed. The Tories might have won, but at tremendous cost. They had been forced to spend £26,000 *per miner* to beat the strike, and had failed to break the miners' spirit or their organisation.

This is the story of that extraordinary struggle, of what will go down in history as the Great Miners' Strike of 1984–5. It tells what caused the strike, how it was fought, and why, in the end, it failed. It seeks to draw the lessons of the strike, so that, inspired by the miners' magnificent example, we can build on their achievements, and avenge their defeat.

1
THE STRIKE BEGINS

IN THE TWELVE MONTHS before the strike began the Coal Board had closed 23 pits and destroyed 21,000 jobs. Then on 1 March 1984 they announced the closure of Cortonwood — at just five weeks' notice.

The Cortonwood miners had been told their pit was good for another five years. The pithead baths had just been refurbished, and men were still being transferred to Cortonwood from the exhausted Elsecar Colliery. The NCB had been making a lot of noise about 'uneconomic pits', but Cortonwood was not one of these. According to a report made on the NCB by the Monopolies and Mergers Commission, Cortonwood came only 92nd on the list.

George Hayes, the South Yorkshire Coal Board director, gave an 'official' reason for the sudden decision. 'I selected Cortonwood,' he said, 'because there was no future there, not because it was the most uneconomic pit in the area — it wasn't.'[1]

As George Robertson, the NUM branch secretary at the pit, said, there were several reasons why they picked on Cortonwood. One was that Cortonwood's output matched exactly the cut in production that the NCB wanted to make.

But more importantly, there was the fact that Cortonwood had a reputation as a moderate pit. For several years it had taken workers from other pits that had closed. Cortonwood suited Maggie's purpose and they planned it to provoke us. She thought we wouldn't strike and she thought we wouldn't get support. She was wrong.

The Coal Board undoubtedly believed the men at the pit might accept the closure without a fight. And the closure of one Yorkshire pit, not through exhaustion, not even for economics, but at the whim of the area director, would be a devastating blow to the union.

More so because the Coal Board had said there was to be no time for the colliery review procedure, the local negotiations between unions and management that had closed so many pits. The closure of Cortonwood was a gauntlet thrown down to the NUM, signalling to NUM Area president Jack Taylor and the Yorkshire executive that they were superfluous to the Coal Board, that they were no longer needed to ensure the smooth running of the industry.

The Yorkshire miners' leaders understood that if they didn't fight now, they never would. No miner would choose to start a major strike in springtime, but the closure of Cortonwood left them no option. Besides, many miners were already pledged to strike because of other moves by the Coal Board over the previous few weeks. At Polmaise in Scotland, miners had been out since February in opposition to closure plans, while in Yorkshire itself four pits were out and a

strike was spreading through South Yorkshire in support of miners at Manvers who had been provoked by Coal Board attempts to sidestep the overtime ban imposed by the union in November 1983.

Sammy Thompson, the Yorkshire Area vice-president, decided that the time was come to go round the branch officials and appeal directly to the rank and file. He began ringing round his old contacts from the 1970s to arrange informal meetings. He told them what was going on in the Area, information that was impossible to get through official channels, and asked them to start pushing among miners at the pitheads for a strike.

On Saturday 3 March, Jack Taylor and Arthur Scargill addressed a packed meeting of militants at Askern. In an impassioned speech, the Yorkshire president said the South Yorkshire strike called in support of Manvers should be extended into an Area-wide stoppage over Cortonwood. Then on Sunday, the Cortonwood branch voted unanimously to call on the Yorkshire Area council, meeting the next day, to bring its members out.

But the strike was no foregone conclusion. Of the eleven pits in South Yorkshire, only four answered the panel's strike call. Flying pickets from these closed the rest. They then converged on Barnsley, where, despite a militant crowd of 500 miners outside the meeting, the Yorkshire Area council took four hours to decide. And when Jack Taylor addressed the miners outside after the meeting, he told them the strike call had been delayed until Friday to allow the delegates time to explain the case against pit closures to their members — something they should have been doing throughout the 18 weeks of the overtime ban!

During the week that followed, the unevenness of militancy throughout the union was to be shown up again and again, with some pits moving quickly towards a decision to answer the strike call while others hedged about. But though the intentions were confused, when it came to action the union went in one direction: forward.

Not all the officials had doubts about how things should be handled. Jack Collins, a senior Kent Area official, said: 'The fight came from the bottom, not the leadership . . . the only tactics we need is to let the men develop the strike.' He argued for flying pickets. 'If the miners are determined to stop work, that determination should be directed not only into their own coalfields but others as well.'

On Monday night Arthur Scargill addressed a rally of Polmaise miners who, just three weeks before, had been told by the Scottish

NUM that they'd have to strike alone. Scargill convinced the Scottish mineworkers' leaders to join Yorkshire and call their members out. Scottish NUM president Mick McGahey promised their action would have a 'domino effect' in the other coalfields. When asked about a ballot he replied: 'We are not dealing with a nicety. We will not be constitutionalised out of our jobs.'[2]

George Bolton, the Scottish NUM vice-president, declared 'I am absolutely convinced that by early next week we will have a national coal strike. The miners have had enough bullying.'[3]

The next day the Coal Board presented their plans for the next financial year to a meeting of the three mining unions. Output, they declared, would be cut by four million tons to just 97.4 million a year, the lowest level this century! The **Financial Times** noted that in the coming year it 'is important for the NCB [to] achieve a rapid rundown of capacity and manpower to a level of around 160,000. The present workforce is around 184,000.'[4]

But right-wing NUM leaders seemed more disturbed by the idea of flying pickets than NCB plans. Ray Chadburn, the right-wing Nottinghamshire president, declared: 'If we don't get the thing right there could be a bloody battle.' The right way to spread the strike, he said, was through a secret ballot. The last secret ballot in Nottinghamshire had produced a mere 19 per cent strike vote. Quite simply, those who called for a national ballot either before or at the NUM executive meeting on Thursday 8 March did so because they didn't want a strike.

As miners gathered to lobby the executive meeting, the government announced a massive hike in the severance pay available to miners. 'How much are you worth? Thirty thou? Forty thou?' middle-aged miners asked each other as they waited outside NUM headquarters. If the government hoped it would buy off the fight, they were mistaken.

Militants were angered by the affair. For years the miners had demanded early retirement and decent pensions, only to be told the money wasn't available. Now the money was there, but only if jobs were sold. And with more than 50 per cent of young people unemployed in many mining villages, it wasn't a popular offer.

Miners lobbying the NUM executive meeting took the redundancy offer as a sign that the government could be forced to back down. 'If they're offering this before we've come out, what will they offer when we really hit them' was the feeling.

The national executive meeting voted by twenty-one to only three to back the Yorkshire and Scottish strikes and to sanction action by any other Area under 'Rule 41' — which allows Areas to call strike action without a ballot providing they have the permission of the union's national executive first. The three votes against were Trevor Bell, secretary of the union's white-collar section COSA, Roy Ottey from the Power Group, and Ted McKay from the tiny North Wales Area. Bell had called for a national ballot, in which he was supported by Henry Richardson from Nottinghamshire and Sid Vincent from Lancashire — but neither of these voted against backing the strike.

After the destruction of thousands of miners' jobs since the Tories had come to office, and three abortive attempts by Arthur Scargill to get the union to stand up nationally to the NCB butchery of the coalfields, the battle was on.

In Yorkshire, the weekend brought elation as branch after branch backed the strike — followed by frustration as branch officials in most pits tried to bottle up and control the enthusiasm of their members. Hundreds of men packed the branch meetings. Houghton Main was typical. 'It was a great atmosphere, 900 men in the room. They called for pickets and hundreds volunteered, but then there was no call for them to all come out and get involved. They were told they'd be contacted when they were needed.'

But at Armthorpe a thousand miners packed the welfare club on Sunday to thrash out what to do. Rank-and-file miners argued that flying pickets should be sent out immediately. Some said the support for the day of action against the union ban at GCHQ had shown there was an anti-Tory mood to be tapped. Others warned that the Tory anti-union laws would be used to cripple a fightback and so should be defied from the start. Above all it was emphasised that rank-and-file miners arguing with other rank-and-file miners stood the best chance of winning solidarity action. If the strike was to be won, the thousand men at the meeting would have to be actively involved and not left sitting at home.

At the end of the meeting just eight miners opposed the flying pickets. This vote in the Armthorpe miners' welfare was to prove crucial.

Yorkshire may have been solid but the other coalfields looked uncertain. In Scotland, branch meetings at five pits solidly backed the strike, but at the rest of the Area's pits there was doubt. The Bilston Glen branch meeting ended in uproar as the branch officials refused to take a vote and instructed their members to join the strike.

Wales too looked doubtful. Out of the 28 pits, 18 voted not to strike. Emlyn Williams, the Area president, who moved the resolution on the national executive that sanctioned an Area-by-Area strike, was devastated. 'I've never known anything like it in 25 years,' he said. In Durham the majority of branches backed the strike and Tommy Callan, the Area president, warned that 'busloads of pickets' would deal with any pit that remained at work.

The national press on Monday 12 March, the day the strike was to begin, could barely disguise their glee. 'Revolt grows in pits strike' splashed the **Daily Star**. The **Financial Times** declared: 'The attempt to usher in national industrial action has virtually collapsed.' **Breakfast TV** were so eager to confirm the morning's headlines that they announced that Blair Hal colliery in Scotland was working normally. Unfortunately it had closed down years before!

But they had all reckoned without the pickets.

All the Scottish pits were shut on Monday morning except Bilston Glen. There, 300 worked the day shift but just 70 went in on the afternoon as a 200-strong picket took effect. An angry spokesman for the Coal Board's Scottish Area complained that 2,200 men had turned back at picket lines.

In South Wales too the pickets had a spectacular success. Only three pits worked on Monday. A miner at the threatened St John's colliery explained why the men there had voted against striking but stopped solidly when the pickets appeared: 'Until now we'd never failed to back a strike call. Scargill got a 95 per cent vote at this lodge. The men were prepared to come out on strike. They wanted to come out but they also wanted Yorkshire to stew.'

When the South Wales miners had voted overwhelmingly to strike against the closure of Lewis Merthyr pit a year earlier, Yorkshire hadn't backed them. Now it worked the other way.

Maerdy was one of the lodges that sent out flying pickets. As one miner said, the voting was 'a parochial response by rank-and-file miners here. Yorkshire started this strike but they didn't support us last year. I also believe it was a rejection of the Welsh leadership. The rank and file just said "bugger the leadership". When the men went out this morning they found the response was fantastic. When rank-and-file miners met rank-and-file miners on the picket line and the boys got the argument straight, it was a different ball game.'

A panic meeting of the Welsh NUM executive, called to talk about what on Sunday looked like disaster, found the flying pickets had turned the situation round within a couple of hours. As a miner from Maerdy said: 'The rank and file got the momentum up and the leadership caught up with it.' The pickets had saved the strike and were rapidly spreading it across the coalfields.

'HERE WE GO!' Miners after the NUM delegate conference which declared the strike official

2
TOWARDS CONFRONTATION

THE MINERS have been at the centre of all the great working-class struggles in Britain this century — the Labour Unrest of 1910–14, the General Strike of 1926, and the strike wave of 1970–4. The strike which has just ended has its roots in the miners' strikes of 1972 and 1974, which first humiliated and then caused the downfall of the Tory administration of Edward Heath.

The struggles against the Heath government were described by the labour historian Royden Harrison as 'the most extraordinary triumph of trade unionism in its long conflict with government':

> First they blew the Government 'off course'; then they landed it on the rocks. First, they compelled the Prime Minister to receive them in 10 Downing Street — which he had sworn he would never do — and forced him to concede more in 24 hours than had been conceded in the last 24 years. Then two years later their strike led him to introduce the three-day week — a novel system of government by catastrophe — for which he was rewarded with defeat at the General Election.[1]

The strike of 1972 was the first national action taken by the miners' union since their terrible defeat in the seven-month lockout of 1926. What launched them into battle — and to victory — after nearly fifty years of keeping their heads down?

The miners and Labour

The leaders of the miners' union reacted to the defeat of 1926 by concluding that industrial action was doomed to failure. Only the election of a Labour government, their union leaders argued, could solve the miners' problems by nationalising the industry. In 1945 such hopes were answered with the election of the first Labour government to have an overall majority in parliament. On 1 January 1947 the mining industry passed into state ownership.

The mineworkers' leaders argued for the next 20 years that an industry run by the National Coal Board was very different from one in private hands. NUM president Sidney Ford said in 1963: 'People who foster the idea that there are two sides in this industry with separate and conflicting interests not only do a great disservice to those who rely upon this industry for their livelihood, but their attitude serves to project a distorted image of nationalisation.'

In line with this approach, an elaborate structure of joint conciliation and consultation between the Coal Board and the NUM was set up. A joint statement by the NCB and the union declared: 'There is no justification whatsoever for stoppages or strikes, which not only delay the ultimate settlement, but also result in a loss of earnings for the workpeople and much harm to the industry.'

But nothing fundamental had changed. True, the mines were no longer controlled by private colliery owners intent only on short-term profit. Instead they were run — not by the miners — but by the Coal Board, which represented the interests of British capitalism as a whole.

For the first decade after nationalisation, these interests demanded the production of as much coal as possible. The rapidly-growing postwar economy still ran on coal: in 1947 coal provided more than 90 per cent of inland energy consumption in the United Kingdom. This coal was priced below what it would fetch on the market, in order to subsidise the profits of the rest of British industry. Miners were constantly exhorted to produce, first by the 1945–51 Labour government, then by its Tory successors.

Then in 1957 the demand for coal dropped dramatically. Cheap oil began to supplant coal as a source of energy. The NCB lost two of its main markets in the 1960s, after the discovery of North Sea gas and the replacement of steam by diesel engines on the railways. Coal dropped from 85.4 per cent of inland energy consumption in 1955 to 46.6 per cent in 1970.

To add to this, the 1950s and 1960s were a time of rapid mechanisation in the pits. The most important development was the spread of power loading, which involved coal-cutting and loading in one single mechanical operation. The proportion of coal which was power-loaded rose from 23 per cent in 1957 to 92 per cent in 1968. This meant that fewer miners could extract the same amount of coal, at a time when less coal was wanted anyway.

The result of these changes for the miners was catastrophic. In 1955 there were 698 collieries. By 1971 the number had fallen to 292. The number of miners went down from 698,700 to 292,000. More than four hundred thousand jobs went.

Those miners who did not leave the industry found themselves transformed often into what Mick McGahey called 'industrial gypsies', driven by closures from one pit to another, and often from one part of the country to another.

The leaders of the miners' union offered no resistance to the closures. 'Our only hope of government assistance lies in the return of a Labour government,' Sidney Ford told the 1962 NUM conference. In October 1964 such a government was elected. Its manifesto contained a pledge to maintain coal production at 200 million tons a year. But the new Prime Minister, Harold Wilson, and his cabinet were concerned to establish Labour as the 'natural party of government', as efficient administrators of capitalism. They were not centrally concerned to promote the interests of their working-class supporters. Trade unionists generally had to face wage controls and spending cuts. And the miners were confronted with the continued rundown of the coal industry, despite Labour's election promises.

Will Paynter, then NUM general secretary, said of his first meeting with Economics Minister George Brown in November 1964: 'It was clear then that they were going to put industry and power stations onto fuel oil and nuclear power.' This was confirmed in September 1965 when a target for coal production was fixed: 170–180 million tons by 1970. High-cost pits were to be closed however large their reserves of coal.

The Coal Board closed down another 200 collieries between 1965 and 1969 — one pit almost every week for four years.

The NUM leadership protested against this betrayal, but took no action to prevent the closures. A special conference debated whether or not to take industrial action in March 1968. Will Paynter, speaking for the national executive, denounced the idea, preferring instead to rely on 'the agitation and the pressure that we and the miners' MPs have been able to exercise upon the government.' Conference backed him.

The rise of the NUM left

The supine attitude of the miners' leaders towards the closures of the 1950s and 1960s was partly a consequence of their politics. The NUM was, until the early 1970s, dominated by right-wing Labour.

The power of the right wing nationally rested on the balance of forces in the coalfields. The miners' union has been described as 'a federation of trade unions, even a federation of pit villages, with an untidy organisational structure and overlapping and competing unions.'[2] Organisation emerged first at pit and county level, reflecting the differences between private employers and coalfields. The Miners' Federation of Great Britain was formed in 1889, bringing together the main county unions — and these county unions still held most of the power, as the partial disintegration of the MFGB after the 1926 lockout showed. Above all, the piecework payment system for face-workers meant that wages were negotiated locally.

The Second World War brought national bargaining over wages and output — and in 1944 the MFGB became the National Union of Mineworkers. 'The authority and government of the union' was given to the annual delegate conference. The change, however, was more of form than of substance. The county unions, renamed Areas, survived. Twenty in number today, they are legally registered trade unions with their own officials and funds. Voting at conferences and on the national executive is still decided at the Area level. The national union is still a federation of powerful Area unions.

The base of the left in the NUM after the war was concentrated in three Areas: Scotland, South Wales and Kent. These were the strongholds of the Communist Party, a tribute to its role in the miners' struggles of the 1920s and 1930s. The left was powerful enough to elect two Communist Party members in succession to the post of NUM general secretary, Arthur Horner (1945–59), and Will Paynter (1959–68). But the Communist Party did not offer a different strategy to that of the right wing. Vic Allen writes:

> The political divisions amongst miners reflected differences in emphases not basic attitudes. Communist Party members . . . in official positions around the coalfields continued to advocate continuity in the union's policy of co-operation with the NCB . . . The union revealed no significant sectional differences over the important issues which faced it. On the question of contraction it insisted that the decisions to close pits, when and where, were the prerogative of the management. The union intervened

only to facilitate the closures by assisting to alleviate the hardships which might result from them.[3]

But the subservience of the right and the impotence of the left did not mean that miners took no action to defend their interests. On the contrary, between 1947 and 1957 disputes in coal mining were 70.5 per cent of all industrial disputes, accounting for 21.9 per cent of the total number of strike days in those years. These were all unofficial disputes, and were usually over the locally-negotiated piece-rates paid to faceworkers.

Militancy was concentrated in certain coalfields — Scotland, South Wales, and, despite right-wing control of the Area union, in Yorkshire. These three coalfields, 'which together have accounted for no more than 54 per cent of the NCB's pits and provided employment for less than half the industry's wage-earners, have been responsible for over 85 per cent of work stoppages and restrictions in most post-war years.'[4]

There were big unofficial strikes in Yorkshire in 1955 and 1961 — and this partly reflected Communist Party influence. The Yorkshire NUM is divided into a number of 'panels' (four since 1967, eight before that) corresponding to the NCB areas. Delegates from the NUM branches in each of these areas meet regularly as the panel. In theory they are just a channel of communication for the Area executive; in practice, as Andrew Taylor puts it, 'at times they have acted as alternative union structures.'[5] The Doncaster panel was the stronghold of the left wing of the Yorkshire NUM in the 1950s and 1960s.

The Communist Party's strategy in Yorkshire was, however, focused less on unofficial militancy as a means of building up independent rank-and-file organisation among miners than as a base for winning control of the official machine. Don Baines, one early member of the Yorkshire left, explained: 'The main thing was to get people elected to vacancies in the Area and nationally where they could exert influence. Policies were secondary at that stage. The main task was to identify vacancies and identify candidates for them.'[6]

The Yorkshire left did achieve some electoral successes. But what brought it to power was a tidal wave of rank-and-file militancy culminating in the national strike of 1972.

A number of factors lay behind this explosion. The most important was the policies of the 1964–70 Labour government. Until the mid-1960s Yorkshire had been comparatively little affected by pit closures. But the Wilson government called in September 1965 for coal output to be concentrated in the most productive pits rather than, as previously, the most productive coalfields. Consequently, Yorkshire suffered from the wave of closures in the late 1960s. Previously, redundant miners had found it fairly easy to find jobs elsewhere. The economy was booming and unemployment low. But the Labour government presided in the late 1960s over a sharp rise in unemployment. Miners hit by closures began to feel that there was nowhere else to go.

The lengthening dole queues were simply one aspect of the Wilson government's attacks on workers. The rate of profit in British industry was much lower than in other Western capitalist countries. Faced with the decline of British capitalism, increasing competitive pressures from abroad, and, towards the end of the decade, the first signs of the world slump, the Labour government sought to reduce real wages and thus increase the rate of profit.

The NUM leadership no more opposed Labour's wage controls than it did the pit closures. Faced, however, with considerable rank-and-file anger provoked by wage controls, the miners' leaders looked for a way round the problem. Salvation seemed to come when the Coal Board proposed to replace piece-rate wages with a nationally-negotiated day wage. The result was the National Power Loading Agreement (NPLA), signed in 1966. The NPLA was a productivity deal, made possible by the rapid spread of power-loading underground — though many militants welcomed it as a way of getting unity in the union.

Under the NPLA, instead of faceworkers' wages being fixed by bargaining at pit and Area level over piece rates, a set of common task rates would be negotiated nationally. For the NUM leadership this had the advantage of giving them, rather than the Area unions, control over wage negotiations. Also, because NPLA was a productivity deal, wages could be increased without clashing with the Labour government's incomes policy.

Whatever the intentions of the Coal Board and the NUM leadership, the NPLA blew up in their faces. The agreement involved equalising wage rates across the coalfields. To prevent big increases which would have undermined Labour's incomes policy, this was done by giving faceworkers in the low-cost coalfields such as Yorkshire and Nottinghamshire far lower pay increases than their counterparts in high-cost coalfields. The late 1960s were a period of rapidly rising prices. Faceworkers especially saw their wages fall behind inflation. This was, moreover, a time when wages generally were rising rapidly. Miners' wages sank behind those of other workers: weekly earnings in coal mining were 122 per cent of average weekly earnings in 1956, 105 per cent in 1960, 99 per cent in 1966, and 89 per cent in 1970.

'The effect of the NPLA was to equalise pay, but in doing so, *low pay* was "nationalised" and the unforeseen effect of NPLA was to "nationalise" dissatisfaction over wages throughout the NUM.'[7] The miners were, as a result, united as never before — each pit, and each Area, focussed on the one demand: better wages for the industry as a whole.

Yorkshire was at the centre of this new militancy. The traditions of unofficial organisation and militancy among Yorkshire miners converged in the late 1960s with the politics of the Yorkshire left, bringing the emergence of a new generation of rank-and-file leaders.

These leaders — above all Arthur Scargill — were as much shaped by the aggressive militancy of the 1950s and 1960s as they were by the machine politics of the official left. Above all, they were willing to lead unofficial action and to organise openly in defiance of the Area and national bureaucracy. In 1967, Scargill, a delegate from Woolley pit near Barnsley and a Labour member of the Yorkshire left, formed the Barnsley Miners' Forum. It met monthly, and was open to militant miners throughout the Yorkshire coalfield. Vic Allen describes how the Forum worked:

> The Forum was held on Friday evenings at Barnsley Co-operative Hall and was attended by hundreds of miners who listened to speeches by Lawrence Daly, Michael McGahey, Emlyn Williams, Jack Dunn and others. For the first time many young miners heard arguments against pit closures, in favour of high wages and a shorter working week. Through this medium Scargill acted as a catalyst with a small group of Barnsley miners including Peter Tait, George Wilkinson, Ron Rigby and Don Baines. They met in a room of a Barnsley hotel where Roy Mason, who became Minister of Power in July 1968, often drank in an adjoining bar.
>
> Fairly quickly these miners developed a cohesion which had not been present before. They were competent branch officials who until now had struggled in the isolation of their branches. They had never controlled the Barnsley panel but collectively they began to discover that they could influence its proceedings. Within a relatively short period they controlled it in much the same way as the Doncaster one was controlled by Ian Ferguson, Jim Oldham, Owen Briscoe, Mick Welsh and

Tommy Mullany. These representatives of the Barnsley miners began to meet with the Doncaster ones to discuss policy and strategy.[8]

A national Miners' Forum representing the left in Scotland, South Wales, Kent and Yorkshire also began to meet regularly in 1967. Like the old Yorkshire left its strategy was primarily electoral. Its first success was the election of Lawrence Daly, an ex-Communist from Scotland, to succeed Will Paynter as general secretary of the NUM in December 1968.

Of far greater importance, however, was the final explosion of miners' frustration over low pay in October 1969. The catalyst was the NUM demand for a forty-hour week for surface workers. Surface workers were usually older miners, no longer fit enough to work underground, and paid far lower rates than faceworkers. The Coal Board's refusal to concede them a forty-hour week was the last straw for miners already pushed to the limit by closures and low pay. On 11 October 1969 a special meeting of the Yorkshire NUM Area council brushed aside the constitutional objections of the right-wing Yorkshire president, Sam Bullough, and voted for an unofficial strike.

Control of the strike was in the hands of the four Yorkshire panels. Arthur Scargill later described how they operated:

> We formed an unofficial strike committee . . . And the first thing we did was to ask ourselves . . . was every pit in Yorkshire out? And the answer then 'yes'. That was completely sewn up. Now what was the next step? Then the next step was to get out every other pit in Britain if we could. So we sent emissaries to Scotland and to Wales, because we didn't think we needed pickets, and asked them to come out . . . And then we launched pickets into Nottinghamshire and Derbyshire. We decided that the best way that we could produce an effective stoppage was to have a rapid mobile picket.[9]

The flying picket had been used on a limited scale in the unofficial strikes in Yorkshire of 1955 and 1961. The unofficial leadership of the 1969 strike now organised flying pickets systematically.

> We launched from the coalfield here squads of cars, minibuses and buses, all directed onto predetermined targets, with five, six, seven hundred miners at a time. Of course, the police were going to come, but they couldn't cover forty points at a time, without bringing the British armed forces in.[10]

At the strike's height, 140 pits in Yorkshire, South Wales, Scotland, and the Midlands were out. Scargill emphasised:

You've got to understand that this strike was totally unofficial. We were getting no assistance from the Area headquarters of the union, we had no financial assistance and were launching into that coalfield [Notts and Derbyshire] on our own, out of our own pockets, in a sense.[11]

This unofficial leadership was all the more impressive in comparison with the performance of the NUM left nationally. Lawrence Daly, the recently elected left-wing general secretary, called on the strikers to return to work. The South Wales Area executive opposed the strike, and Mick McGahey, the Scottish Area president, remained silent. The Coal Board met the miners' pay claim in full, but did not concede the 40-hour week for surface workers.

The unofficial strike of 1969 set the pattern for the great battles of the early 1970s. It showed that the miners could take national strike action and force concessions from the NCB. The passive acceptance of industrial decline had been finally broken. Above all, the impulse behind the strike came from below.

The strikes of 1972 and 1974

The miners were not alone in their militancy. The late 1960s saw a rising curve of class struggle. The Labour government's wage controls brought it into conflict with the powerful rank-and-file organisation which had been built up during the years of the postwar boom in a number of industries — cars, docks, engineering and shipbuilding, as well as mining. Workers, confident of their own strength thanks to the bargaining power given them by full employment, refused to accept the pay restraint Labour now sought to impose on them. The result was a rapid increase in strikes, most of them unofficial.

The response from the government was to draft anti-union legislation. The Labour government's move to outlaw unofficial strikes, the White Paper **In Place of Strife**, was forced back by opposition both inside and outside parliament — but after the Tories won the general election of June 1970 with Edward Heath as prime minister, the Industrial Relations Act became law in 1971. With strict limits on picketing and a special court to deal with trade unionists who broke the new law, the Tories were set on confrontation.

The test of their strategy was soon to come. There was a preliminary skirmish between the Tories and the miners in October 1970 when the Doncaster panel launched an unofficial strike which at its height embraced 116 pits. It was, however, less solid than its predecessor a year before, and soon crumbled. Then on 1 November 1971 the NUM imposed an overtime ban in support of its demand for pay increases in breach of the Tory pay limits. Miners voted, by 58.8 per cent in favour of a strike in a pithead ballot on 2 December — and on 9 January 1972 the first national miners' strike since 1926 began.

The union's national executive, now headed by Joe Gormley, whose election in 1971 kept the union presidency in right-wing hands, issued instructions for pickets to halt the movement of coal completely. Responsibility for different parts of the country was allocated to the various Areas. Yorkshire, for example, was given the power stations of East Anglia.

Rank-and-file organisation of the same kind as had led the 1969 and 1970 strikes, not the official leadership, stopped the movement of coal. Scargill later recalled:

We had every pit picketed on the first morning to get out the weekly-paid industrial staff members, who were not members of the Yorkshire NUM . . . After this we immediately switched our attack to every major coal depot and power station in the region . . . I was appointed spokesman of the Barnsley Area Strike Committee and also put in charge of picketing. We had a number of battles inside the Committee as to the best tactics to employ. We had a thousand pickets deployed into East Anglia, and we had a major battle inside the Strike Committee. The differences of opinion were whether we should concentrate the pickets on one target or whether we should dispatch them all over East Anglia to all the power stations. And the argument that won the day was the one to send them to Yarmouth, to Bedford, to Cambridge, to Ipswich, to Norwich, to all the different power stations. I said that this was stupid and would not prove successful. For three days we battled with police in the East Anglia area. Then we had a weekend Strike Committee meeting and changed the policy. I picked the phone up and called East Anglia HQ and said 'Move everything in onto Ipswich dock, move everything we can.' We produced a thousand pickets in an hour and a half on Ipswich dock, and stopped the dock in an hour. We left a token picket at the docks, moved on, and closed down the power stations one by one. Within two days we'd shut the whole of East Anglia.[12]

Tactics of this sort rapidly halted the movement of coal — but it was not simply the miners' achievement. Rank-and-file trade unionists in other industries observed the TUC guidelines requiring them to respect NUM picket lines. The success of the flying pickets reflected the strength and confidence of workers generally.

This was most evident in the turning point of the strike, the battle of Saltley gate. By the beginning of February the strike was hitting home, as a succession of power cuts showed. The last substantial stockpile of coke was at Saltley depot in Birmingham. Scargill himself commented afterwards: 'The [miners'] picket line didn't close Saltley, what happened was the working class closed Saltley.'[13]

Even 3,000 miners led by Scargill couldn't stop the coke lorries in five days of picketing. But on Tuesday 8 February Scargill addressed the East Birmingham district of the Amalgamated Union of Engineering Workers. 'We don't want your pound notes,' he told them. 'Will you go down in history as the working class in Birmingham who stood by while the miners were battered down or will you become immortal? I do not ask you — I *demand* that you come out on strike.'

The AUEW and the Transport and General Workers Union called their members in Birmingham out on strike the next day. On Thursday 10 February 100,000 Birmingham trade unionists came out, and 20,000 marched on Saltley. Scargill described what happened:

> Some of the lads . . . were a bit dispirited . . . And then over this hill came a banner and I've never seen in my life as many people following a banner. As far as the eye could see it was just a mass of people marching towards Saltley. There was a huge roar and from the other side of the hill they were coming the other way. They were coming from five directions; it was in a hollow, they were arriving from every direction. And our lads were just jumping in the air with emotion — a fantastic situation . . . I started to chant . . . : 'Close the Gates! Close the Gates!' and it was taken up, just like a football crowd. It was booming through Saltley: 'Close the Gates'. It reverberated right across this hollow and each time they shouted this slogan they moved, and the police, who were four deep, couldn't help it, they were getting moved in. And Capper, the Chief Constable of Birmingham, took a swift decision. He said 'Close the Gates' and they swung to. Hats were in the air, you've never seen anything like it in your life. Absolute delirium on the part of the people who were there. Because the Birmingham working class were there — not

as observers but as participants.[14]

Reginald Maudling, the Tory Home Secretary, explained in his memoirs the dilemma Saltley posed for the government:

> then then Chief Constable of Birmingham assured me that only over his dead body would they [the pickets] . . . succeed [in closing Saltley]. I felt constrained to ring him the next day after it happened to enquire after his health! I am sure the decision he took was a wise one, because the number of strikers involved was so great, and feelings were running so high, that any attempt by the relatively small body of police who could be assembled to keep the depot open by force could have led to very grave consequences. Some of my colleagues asked me afterwards, why I had not sent in troops to support the police, and I remember asking them one single question: 'If they had been sent in, should they have gone in with their rifles loaded or unloaded?' Either course could have been disastrous.[15]

Short of bringing in the army, which would have brought the danger of a much more generalised confrontation with the working-class movement, the closure of Saltley left the Tories with no alternative but to concede defeat. Heath found a means of surrender by appointing a Court of Inquiry into miners' wages which went a long way to meeting the miners' demands. Even so it took a meeting between Heath and the NUM executive at 10 Downing Street, where further concessions were made, to end the strike.

The miners had won a historic victory. It reflected a general class militancy unprecedented for fifty years. 1972 saw not only the miners' strike but also the first national builders' strike since the 1920s, and a wave of factory occupations by engineering workers in the Manchester area. And in July the Industrial Relations Act received a near fatal blow when unofficial strike action forced the release of five dockers' leaders imprisoned in Pentonville for picketing in defiance of the Tories' law.

But Heath was not ready to concede defeat. In the autumn of 1972 he imposed a statutory wage freeze, followed by two more phases of pay restraint. The economic situation had in the meantime changed dramatically. 1972 and 1973 were years of boom, not only in Britain but throughout Western capitalism. But by the summer of 1973 the signs of recession were evident, as inflation soared and profit rates shrank. Then in October 1973 war broke out in the Middle East, leading to the quadrupling of the price of oil. The oil crisis tipped the world economy into the first great slump since the 1930s.

This energy squeeze increased the miners' bargaining power. Coal was now a far more attractive source of energy than it had been in the era of cheap oil. At the same time, Heath realised that British capitalism could now be restored to profitability only by a far more savage reduction of workers' living standards than had previously been assumed. Concessions to the miners might unleash a tidal wave of wage militancy. The Tories set their face against a compromise over the miners' 1973 pay claim.

The NUM imposed an overtime ban on 21 November, and a strike ballot was called for 1 February 1974 only after protracted negotiations and when it became clear that the ban was not reducing coal stocks as much as had been expected. The Tories attempted to isolate the miners from other workers by introducing a three-day working week, ostensibly to save energy. The miners voted by an 81 per cent majority for strike action and the executive called the miners out from 9 February. Heath reacted by calling a general election. ·

The 1974 miners' strike took place amid scenes of great panic in the ruling class. Yet the strike was very different from that in 1972. It was tightly controlled from the top. Vic Allen explains the attitude of Gormley and other miners' leaders:

> It was clear that on this occasion they wanted to avoid the spontaneity of 1972, the relative autonomy of local strike committees and the confrontations. This time they wanted to control the strike from the national centre so they could determine tactics and regulate its scope. They planned from the outset to contain the strike and, in so far as it was possible, to give it a respectable image. The national officials wanted the success of 1972 but none of its abrasive tactics which so obviously made that success possible.[16]

One major reason for Gormley's insistence on controlling the strike was the general election. Heath wanted to make the central issue 'Who governs the country — the trade unions or parliament?' The Tories mounted a red-baiting campaign aimed especially at Mick McGahey, a member of the Communist Party who in 1973 had been elected vice-president of the NUM. Gormley was desperate to avoid doing anything that would embarrass the Labour Party in the general election. He even supported Heath's suggestion that the strike be suspended for the duration of the election campaign.

But the union executive rejected this proposal. Nevertheless tight control was imposed on picketing. Gormley said: 'The flying picket can just fly out of the window.' Largely it did. A six-man limit was imposed by the executive on the size of pickets, and the movement of coal was halted mainly because other trade unionists respected usually token NUM picket lines. There were no Saltleys in 1974.

The role of the left in the union was also different. The victory of 1972 had enabled them to wrest control of the biggest NUM Area, Yorkshire, from the right wing. In May 1973 Scargill humiliated two right-wingers in the election for Area president. In the autumn of 1973 another left-winger, Owen Briscoe, was elected Yorkshire general secretary. The left was no longer on the outside in Yorkshire. Scargill continued to adopt a very militant stance, arguing at the national executive for example that 'a general election will not solve anything.' But he and his allies did not make the same effort to encourage rank-and-file organisation and initiative as they had in 1972.

The general election saw Labour returned as the largest single party in parliament, and at the beginning of March Harold Wilson again became prime minister. He appointed a left-winger, Michael Foot, as Employment Secretary, and Foot conceded much of what the NUM had demanded. The miners had won again.

The 1974–9 Labour government and the incentive scheme

No workers' victory is permanent as long as capitalism continues to exist. Heath's strategy of frontal assault had failed. The Labour government offered a way of achieving the sme objective — reduced living standards and weakened workplace organisation — by other means.

The crux of the new strategy was to be the 'Social Contract' between the Labour government and the TUC. Rather than the state imposing wage controls on workers, the trade union leaders would enforce them on their members in exchange for legislation that favoured the labour movement.

The trade union leaders played a central role in bringing workers to acquiesce in these policies. The two main figures on the TUC left, Jack Jones of the TGWU and Hugh Scanlon of the AUEW, were the most important supporters of the Social Contract, ably assisted by Michael Foot, who invoked the 'red flame of socialist courage' in its defence at the 1975 Labour Party conference.

But the Social Contract permeated every level of the trade union movement. Under Heath there had been a political alternative to the Tories — Labour, a party created and sustained by the trade unions.

To stand out against Labour's *own* wage controls involved going much further politically. Moreover, the system was now in deep crisis. To fight for higher wages when profits were so low was to challenge the economic system of capitalism itself. In the absence of any real forces willing to fight for a socialist alternative, militants took their lead from the trade union leaders, and grudgingly acquiesced in the Social Contract.

Many workplace leaders were caught up in the policies of collaboration with the employers pursued by the trade union bosses. The introduction of 'workers' participation' in the car industry led to senior stewards and convenors being drawn into close co-operation with management. To this was added a steady erosion of workplace organisation. Productivity deals and the consequent decline of piece-work deprived the shop stewards of their basic role, to negotiate the rate for the job. Moreover, an increasing number of senior stewards and convenors became full-time negotiators and became distanced from the shop floor as a result. The sectional workplace organisation which had broken the Heath government was decaying at the roots.

The miners did not escape these changes. Indeed, the 1974 strike, firmly controlled from the top in the interests of the election of a Labour government, set the pattern of the Social Contract years. After the strike, the Labour government set out to draw the NUM into close collaboration with the Coal Board. A tripartite committee for the coal industry was set up, involving government, unions and NCB. The result was the national 'Plan for Coal', approved in October 1974, which envisaged £600 million of investment with the aim of creating 40 million tons of new capacity by 1985. 'Plan 2000', approved in early 1977, proposed to create four million tons of new capacity each year between 1985 and 2000.

As Andrew Taylor comments, 'The political function of this exercise was to secure the co-operation of the NUM, negating the possibility of industrial action.'[17] Gormley and the rest of the right-wing majority on the national executive were quite happy to go along with this. But now there was a much stronger and more militant left wing, whose stronghold was in Yorkshire. Scargill bitterly attacked the 'social con-trick': 'It is unprincipled on the part of certain leaders of the trade union movement to accept decisions, both political and economic, which undermine the living standards of those people they represent because we have a Labour government.'[18]

Average real wages fell by 2 per cent in 1974–5, 4 per cent in 1975–6, and 5 per cent in 1976–7, the biggest reduction for a century.

Miners were affected by this: their earnings were 125 per cent of those in manufacturing in 1975, but only 108 per cent two years later.

This led to rising militancy among miners and a problem for the NUM and the government: how to pay the miners more without destabilising the Social Contract?

The answer was a pit incentive scheme. The Coal Board had been pressing for one since 1974. The NPLA had failed significantly to increase productivity, which actually fell in the 1970s: output per man-shift was 2.44 tonnes in 1970–1, and 2.18 tonnes in 1977. The right wing on the executive also wanted an incentive scheme — for example, Len Clarke, president of the Nottinghamshire Area, whose members, mainly in low-cost pits, would benefit from any deal tying wages to output. Moreover, Phase 3 of the government's incomes policy, which came into force in 1977, permitted 'self-financing' productivity deals. As in the case of the NPLA, the miners' leadership sought a new pay system as a way of avoiding a challenge to Labour wage controls.

Opposition to such a deal came from the left. An incentive scheme, they argued, would set miner against miner, bringing back all the divisions between different pits and coalfields which had existed in the days of piecework. The 1977 NUM conference threw out a motion proposing local incentive schemes.

What followed was remarkable in the light of the attitude taken towards ballots and union democracy by the courts and the NUM right wing during the strike of 1984–5. Gormley and the right carried through a decision at the national executive in September 1977 to put the incentive scheme they had negotiated with the Coal Board to a ballot vote, in defiance of the conference decision. The Kent Area, with Scargill's support, went to the High Court for an injunction overruling this flagrant breach of the NUM rulebook. But the Vice-Chancellor of the High Court, Sir Robert Megarry, backed Gormley and the right. 'What the NEC is proposing to do is to hold a secret ballot of all members. This is the very essence of the democratic proces.' The Court of Appeal upheld Megarry's ruling. Lord Denning, the Master of the Rolls, called the ballot 'a far more satisfactory and democratic method than leaving it to the delegates of a conference who might not be truly representative in their individual capacities of the views of the various men they represent.'

So the ballot went ahead in October 1977. The scheme had the support of Tony Benn, the Energy Secretary, who said that it should be given 'a fair trial' since it was designed 'to avoid the evils of past piecework schemes, which set men against men and lowered safety standards.' The left campaigned vigorously against the scheme, especially in Yorkshire. Scargill called it an 'incentive to dig and let die'. To the consternation of the right wing, 55.75 per cent of miners voted against the scheme.

Far from accepting this result of 'the very essence of the democratic process', Gormley and the right wing had the national executive declare the ballot 'null and void' in November 1977. Areas were permitted to negotiate their own local incentive schemes, which Nottinghamshire and others rapidly proceeded to do.

Back to court the Kent Area went, this time accompanied by Yorkshire and South Wales. Surely the judges would stand by their earlier rulings, and grant an injunction banning the local incentive schemes? The High Court, in the person of Mr Justice Watkins, proceeded to stand on its collective head. 'The result of a ballot, nationally conducted, is not binding upon the National Executive Committee in using its powers in between conferences,' he ruled on 21 December. 'It may serve to persuade the Committee to take one action or the other, or to refrain from action, but it has no great force or significance.' In other words, ballots were OK when the executive won them, but not when they didn't.

The result was a stampede to sign incentive schemes. Even in Yorkshire a majority of miners voted in favour of such a scheme. As its critics had predicted, large gaps opened up between the pay different miners received. For example in the Doncaster panel in September 1978, incentive pay varied from £6.55 a week in one pit to £43.90 in another. The seeds of the divisions of 1984 had been sown.

There were other signs of the future. Scargill's role was changing. Instead of rejecting court interference in union affairs, he supported the court actions against the national executive, creating a dangerous precedent in the light of the judges' role in the strike of 1984–5. Moreover, he did not actively campaign against the incentive scheme in the Yorkshire Area ballot. A majority against the scheme in Yorkshire might have rallied the opposition to the national executive throughout the coalfields.

In the summer of 1978 the three Yorkshire rescue brigades came out on strike against unfair productivity bonuses, low pay rates, and long hours. At Armthorpe they pulled the whole pit out, and organised flying pickets which closed the whole coalfield in a couple of days. A hurriedly convened NUM Area Council condemned the strike. Scargill personally intervened to persuade the two weaker rescue brigades at

Rotherham and Wakefield to return to work, isolating the militants from Armthorpe.

The left-wing leadership in Yorkshire was drifting apart from the rank and file from whom they had sprung. Once the left won control of the Area in 1973 the Barnsley Miners' Forum had begun meeting less regularly. It stopped meeting altogether in 1976. Now that the left were in office, apparently they did not need to organise independently.

The miners were not immune from the general erosion of workplace organisation. The basic unit of the NUM is the pit branch (or lodge in some Areas). Each branch has a committee and four officers, the president, secretary, treasurer, and delegate. The branch secretary was usually a full-time official, and there was a tendency for the president and delegate also to spend much of their time at the surface, away from their fellow miners. Above all, as Scargill boasted in his election address for president, there were few strikes in Yorkshire between 1974 and 1983. The rank and file organisation which had created the flying pickets and led the strikes of 1969, 1970 and 1972 was becoming atrophied. The miners were to pay a terrible price for this in 1984.

The Thatcher government: back to confrontation

Margaret Thatcher became prime minister in May 1979. Since replacing Heath as Tory leader in 1975 she had stood for a radical right-wing attempt to shift the balance of class forces decisively in capital's favour. Thatcher's chief aim was to reverse the defeats inflicted by the miners and other groups of workers on the Heath government.

But the new Tory team had learned from the struggles of the early 1970s. They did not plan an immediate collision with the trade union movement. Rather than attempt to enforce wage controls, which had brought down both previous governments, mass unemployment would be used to discipline workers. Instead of the Industrial Relations Act, with its special register and court which acted as a visible target for opposition, the Tories would legislate piecemeal to widen the powers of the existing courts over the unions.

The new government knew from the experience of their predecessors that the decisive confrontation was likely to come in the public sector where they planned to use the cash-limits originally introduced by Labour Chancellor of the Exchequer Denis Healey to reduce wages and manpower, and to increase the profits of the nationalised industries. While in opposition they had drawn up plans to deal with this challenge. **The Economist** (27 May 1978) leaked a secret report drafted for Thatcher by Nicholas Ridley, a radical right-wing MP (now Transport Secretary).

In an annexe to the main report, Ridley and some of his co-authors considered how to deal with a 'political threat' from 'the enemies of the next Tory government' in a 'vulnerable industry' such as coal, electricity or the docks. According to **The Economist**, 'they would like a five-part strategy for countering this threat:

*Return on capital figures should be rigged so that an above-average wage claim can be paid to the 'vulnerable' industries.

*The eventual battle should be on ground chosen by the Tories, in a field chosen by the Tories they think could be won (railways, British Leyland, the civil service or steel).

*Every precaution should be taken against a challenge in electricity or gas. Anyway, redundancies in those industries are unlikely to be required. The group believes that the most likely battleground will be the coal industry. They would like a Thatcher government to: (a) build up maximum coal stocks, particularly at the power stations; (b) make contingency plans for the import of coal; (c) encourage the recruitment of non-union lorry drivers by haulage companies to help move coal where necessary; (d) introduce dual coal/oil firing in all power stations as quickly as possible.

*The group believes that the greatest deterrent to any strike would be 'to cut off the money supply to the strikers, and make the union finance them' . . .

*There should be a large, mobile squad of police equipped and prepared to uphold the law against violent picketing. 'Good non-union drivers' should be recruited to cross picket lines with police protection.

Thatcher's six years in office have followed with eerie precision the pattern laid out in the Ridley report. The Social Security Act 1980 slashed welfare payments to strikers' families, for example, though generally the Tories preferred 'salami' tactics to frontal assault, taking on the working-class movement 'one slice at a time'. One by one, groups of workers were picked off, isolated, and beaten.

First came state-owned British Leyland. In November 1979 the firm's Labour-appointed boss, Michael Edwardes, succeeded in sacking Derek Robinson, convenor of the vast Longbridge plant in Birmingham and a member of the Communist Party. Shop stewards' organisation had now been neutered in one of its strongholds.

Next came steel: the defeat of the Iron and Steel Trades Confederation in a bitter thirteen-week strike in early 1980 allowed the rapid rundown of the industry. The civil servants followed in 1981, and the health workers and train drivers in 1982.

One reason for these defeats lay in the role of the trade union bureaucracy. The TUC stood by while union after union was beaten by the Tories. In the summer of 1982 the TUC general council itself forced the train drivers' union, ASLEF, to surrender to British Rail.

But the trade union leaders had played much the same role in the early 1970s. The impulse to fight had come then from below, from the rank and file. Thatcher benefitted from the effect of five years of Labour government, from the erosion of shopfloor organisation. Militants no longer felt confident enough to fight independently of the union leaders. To this was added the effect of mass unemployment. For the first time since the 1930s the threat, and only too often the reality of the dole queue, faced every militant trade unionist.

There were exceptions. Above all, the Tories provoked a premature confrontation with the miners. On 10 February 1981 Derek Ezra, chairman of the NCB, told the miners' national executive that to meet government financial targets they would have to close up to fifty pits: twenty-three were to go immediately.

The government had miscalculated. South Wales struck and their flying pickets soon brought out other areas. The militant response in the coalfields took them by surprise. On 18 February Energy Secretary David Howell met the miners' leaders to announce the closure programme was withdrawn.

But the Tories' retreat was purely tactical. Howell explained four years later:

> Neither the government nor I think society as a whole was in a position to get locked into a coal strike . . . In those days the stocks weren't so high. I don't think the country was prepared, and the whole NUM and the trade union movement tended to be united all on one side.[19]

Thatcher had run away to fight another day.

The summer of 1981 saw riots in many inner cities, the result of mass unemployment and racism. And on display for the first time in a co-ordinated fashion was another component in the Ridley plan — paramilitary riot police squads. The Tories had been faced in 1972 with the choice between surrendering at Saltley and calling in the army. The formation of highly mobile police riot squads provided another option, which could be used with less explosive political consequences.

The riot police were not Thatcher's creation. The Special Patrol Group, the first of these squads, was formed by the Metropolitan Police under the 1964–70 Labour government, and the number of similar units, trained in riot control and the use of firearms, grew rapidly under Labour in the later 1970s. But the Tories poured more resources into the police after 1979.

On one estimate 11,000 trained riot police were available nationally. The problem of co-ordinating Britain's 43 police forces in the event of a crisis was solved by means of the National Reporting Centre at New Scotland Yard. The Centre was conceived on 4 April 1972, shortly after the humiliation at Saltley, at a meeting between the Association of Chief Police Officers and senior Home Office officials.

In the general election of June 1983 the Tories trounced a weakened Labour Party and the new centre-right SDP/Liberal Alliance. The formation of Thatcher's second administration marked, it can be seen in retrospect, a turning point. Politically she had been astonishingly successful. Her government had ridden out the highest unemployment since the 1930s without provoking large-scale working-class resistance or losing the next election.

Economically, however, the Tories had made comparatively little headway. Writing after the 1983 general election, Peter Riddell, political editor of the **Financial Times**, expressed the cool judgement passed on Thatcherism by the more intelligent representatives of big business: 'The Thatcher administration has yet to show that it can successfully manage, let alone reverse, Britain's long-term economic decline.'[20]

The previous winter **The Economist**, that other internal organ of the British ruling class, had summed up the problem of British, and indeed world capitalism:

> Wages are too high. 'Too high' means the level of wages relative to profits . . . By our calculations . . . , wages in the five largest capitalist economies are now between 8 per cent and 24 per cent higher than they ought to be if profits are to regain the share of national income they held [in the 1960s].[21]

The magazine calculated that, to give profits a 30 per cent share of British national income would require a cut in real wages by 19 per cent. Judged by these standards, Thatcher had been an abject failure. As **The Economist** observed on 11 June 1983, after her triumphant re-election:

> One reason why the Tories came home at a canter in this election
> is that in their first four years average earnings rose by thirteen
> percentage points more than prices, at a time when the real value
> of Britain's gross national product fell by four per cent.

The brunt of the recession had been borne by the unemployed;
workers in jobs had seen their real wages rise. Thatcher's political
triumph had been won at the cost of economic failure.

These factors explain why, in Thatcher's second term, the
Tories have moved more openly on to the offensive against the
working-class movement. Two disputes before the miners' strike
showed the way the wind was blowing. The struggle over the closed
shop at the **Stockport Messenger** in Warrington saw an anti-union
small businessman, Eddie Shah, backed by the Tory right, successfully invoke the 1980 Employment Act against one of the toughest
craft unions, the National Graphical Association (NGA). Then in
January 1984 Thatcher personally intervened to ban the civil service
unions at the GCHQ communications centre in Cheltenham.

But Thatcher did not aim to destroy the trade unions. The role
of the TUC had been essential in containing mass resistance to redundancies. What she wanted was a weaker, more bureaucratic, less
political trade union movement closely policed by the courts. Her
model was the trade unions in the United States, whose leaders have
passively acquiesced in the mass sackings and pay cuts imposed on
them under Ronald Reagan.

The US trade unions had not always been so timid. In the 1930s
and 1940s they had displayed enormous militancy. This has been
broken only by a concerted ruling-class offensive in the late 1940s and
early 1950s involving anti-union legislation (the Taft-Hartley Act)
and the systematic weeding out of militants under the guise of Senator
Joseph McCarthy's anti-communist crusade.

The Americanisation of the British trade union movement could
be achieved only by taking on and decisively defeating a powerful
group of workers. The obvious candidate was the miners. They were
the only major section of the working class to have successfully
resisted the rundown of their industry during Thatcher's first term.
Arthur Scargill, elected national president of the NUM after Gormley's
retirement in 1981, symbolised the aggressive militancy of the early
1970s.

The Tories had carefully laid their plans. Coal stocks rapidly built up, from 42.25 million tonnes in 1981 to 57.96 million tonnes two years later. Almost all that increase — nearly 14 million tonnes — took the form of stocks at the power stations.

The government did everything in its power to undermine the coal industry. The NCB's main domestic customer is the Central Electricity Generating Board. With Thatcher's blessing, the CEGB pressed ahead with a programme of increasing the electricity industry's reliance on nuclear power. The policy was justified by cooked figures which purported to show that nuclear power was the cheapest energy source. On a proper comparison, however, nuclear-generated electricity cost 3.2 pence a unit, and coal-fired electricity only 1.8 pence.

The CEGB took other steps aimed at weakening the miners. The price paid for coal used in the power stations lagged in 1979–84 behind the price of electricity, adding to the Coal Board's losses, and helping to create the impression that most pits were 'uneconomic'. In the 1970s a number of huge oil-fired power stations on the south coast which had been planned before the oil crisis were completed. They could have been converted to burning coal as well as oil. Instead, they were simply moth-balled — kept for use in the event of a coal strike.

The miners were squeezed from another direction as well. The 'Plan for Coal' had involved large-scale investment designed to extend the life of existing pits and create new capacity. Central to the investment programme is MINOS (Mine Operating System), a computer system whose aim is to monitor and direct all activities in the pit from a control room on the surface. The 'Plan for Coal' also brought the formation of 'super-pits', either through grouping together existing collieries (16 pits in the Barnsley area were gathered into three complexes centred on automated preparation plants at Woolley, Grimethorpe and South Kirkby), or through creating new pits, for example at Selby in North Yorkshire.

The introduction of new technology in the pits had enormous implications for the miners. MINOS vastly increases the power of management, allowing them to supervise production directly from the surface control room. The skills of faceworkers and underground craftsmen are increasingly devalued as more and more decisions can be taken on the surface.

The super-pits also meant that fewer men were needed to produce the same amount of coal. The Barnsley reorganisation meant that output could be raised by 21 per cent and manpower reduced by 20 per cent at the same time. The automation involved in MINOS also cut jobs. The planned manning levels for fully integrated MINOS plants are 53 per cent of current levels.

Crucially, the new technology made many existing pits 'uneconomic'. The introduction of MINOS was concentrated in the central coalfields of Yorkshire, Nottinghamshire and Derbyshire. The resulting productivity increases there meant the NCB would not need many of the pits in the 'peripheral' coalfields of Scotland, South Wales, Durham and Kent.

The Monopolies and Mergers Commission in its June 1983 report on the coal industry classified 141 of the 198 pits as 'uneconomic'.

Bradford University academics estimated that the combined effect of MINOS and the closures announced in March 1984 would be the loss of 100,000 jobs in five years. By March 1989 there would be 79,000 miners concentrated in 94 pits. One of the Bradford team, Jonathan Winterton, wrote in the **New Statesman**:

> The Bradford findings have been confirmed by Ian Lloyd, a Conservative MP who is Chairman of the Select Committee on Energy, and who has thus seen confidential NCB evidence. Asked on Yorkshire Television's **First Tuesday** programme last month whether the mining workforce could be reduced to 80,000 within five years, he said: 'Yes, something of that order.'[22]

The message was plain enough. The Coal Board had been able to cut 41,000 jobs between March 1981 and 1984 using the colliery review procedure. But this involved a lengthy process of inquiries and appeals typically taking 6½ months. The scale of job cuts now in the pipeline required a more frontal assault.

The stakes were high: should the government succeed, not only would the working-class movement have suffered a decisive defeat, but the surviving profitable super-pits could be sold off to private capitalists (an intention Industry Secretary Norman Tebbit unwisely let slip in March 1984).

Thatcher now selected those who would carry out the assault on the NUM. Ian MacGregor took over as chairman of the Coal Board at the beginning of September 1983. MacGregor had won his spurs as boss of the American mining multinational Amax and had inflicted a severe defeat on the American mineworkers' union when he succeeded in closing the Bel Air colliery in Wyoming. Appointed deputy chairman of BL by the Labour government, MacGregor had played a crucial role in the sacking of Derek Robinson in November 1979. Then, as chairman of British Steel, he presided over the destruction of 80,000 jobs.

As MacGregor's political overseer was a new Secretary of State for Energy, Peter Walker. He was the last Heath man in the cabinet, a skilful politician and a veteran of the 1972 and 1974 strikes. ' "Peter, I want you to go to Energy," Walker is said to have been told by the Prime Minister the day after the 1983 election. "We're going to have a miners' strike." '23

The Tories had drawn up their battle lines. How well prepared were the miners?

The state of the union

NUM president Joe Gormley announced his retirement in July 1981. Arthur Scargill was the left's candidate to succeed him. It was a walkover: neither of the two right-wing candidates, Trevor Bell of the white-collar section COSA and Nottinghamshire president Ray Chadburn, stood a chance. Even on Chadburn's home territory, the Notts Area council voted 15 to 9 in support of Scargill.

When the results were announced in December 1981 Scargill had won 70.3 per cent of the votes cast. Not surprisingly, both the press and many socialists expected the result to herald an all-out confrontation between the NUM and Thatcher.

Instead Scargill and militant miners suffered a succession of humiliating defeats, losing no fewer than three national strike ballots in little more than a year. The first came in January 1982, when miners succumbed to a massive Coal Board and Fleet Street propaganda campaign and threw out a call for strike action in support of the NUM's pay claim.

The left in the union put this setback down to a last act of treachery by Joe Gormley, who had written an article in the **Daily Express** calling for a 'No' vote in the ballot. But it soon became clear that there was more to it than that.

After the NUM conference in June 1982 the miners' leaders began to link the issue of pay to that of closures. Already in November 1981 the **Yorkshire Miner** had pointed out:

> The Coal Board is already halfway to closing the 23 pits on its hit list. Warnings in February that withdrawal of the list would be followed by salami tactics — picking off the pits one by one — have been fully borne out. The closures — or agreements to close — have been carried out under the colliery review procedure which every three months assesses a pit's 'viability'.

Carried out on a pit-by-pit basis, this avoids announcements of mass closures and stifles mass resistance of the type which happened in February.

To combat this piecemeal offensive, the NUM executive called a second ballot on whether to take strike action in October 1982. This time the issue was both opposition to pit closures and support for the union's demand for a 31 per cent pay increase. Scargill toured the country speaking to rally after rally in support of a 'Yes' vote. But again the miners rebuffed their leaders.

The Coal Board took this as the cue to press ahead with pit closures. Kinneil colliery in Scotland and Lewis Merthyr in South Wales became its targets. The Scottish and South Wales executives of the NUM launched campaigns in defence of the threatened pits.

When the tough Scottish Area director of the NCB, Albert Wheeler, announced Kinneil's closure on 17 December 1982, the Kinneil miners themselves staged a sit-in strike down the pit over Christmas, and then sent pickets out throughout the Scottish coalfield. But the Area NUM officials, Mick McGahey, George Bolton, and Eric Clarke, persuaded the Scottish executive and a delegate conference that they would be isolated from the rest of the NUM if they came out on strike.

The issue of closures exploded again in February 1983, when the NCB announced that Tymawr Lewis Merthyr and Blaengwrach would be shut. The Lewis Merthyr men occupied their pit, and pulled out 3,000 miners in the rest of the South Wales coalfield. After strike action had been endorsed at an Area conference, again against the executive's opposition, delegations fanned out from South Wales to miners' meetings throughout Britain. Yorkshire and Scotland voted to come out in support.

An emergency meeting of the miners' national executive took place on 3 March. Scargill argued that a national strike could be called under Rule 41, which allows the national executive to authorise Area strikes. He was overruled by the right wing, who insisted that a national ballot be called. The result of this ballot was disastrous — a 61 per cent vote against strike action.

The March 1983 ballot was a turning point for many militants. For the first time miners unaffected by closures had decided that those whose pits were threatened should not be allowed to fight back. Miners had voted other miners out of a job. One Yorkshire miner said that he and others like him began 'to see ballots as the way you stabbed your mates in the back in secret.'

But why were miners behaving like this? South Wales NUM president Emlyn Williams simply blamed the members: 'The Achilles heel of this union is the rank and file,' he told an Area delegate conference.

The real reasons for the collapse of solidarity were elsewhere. One major factor was the Area incentive scheme introduced in 1977–8 in defiance of a national ballot vote. The government censored the tables in the Monopolies Commission report which revealed the vast disparity in earnings between different pits and different areas. Figures obtained by **Socialist Review** showed average incentive earnings varying between £90 per week in North Yorkshire and £25 in Scotland in April 1983.[24]

These figures are Area averages, and so underestimate the disparity between different pits and faces. The incentive scheme had built into miners' wage packets the division between 'economic' and 'uneconomic' pits. At the rundown pits, which suffered poor geological conditions and were threatened with closure, incentive earnings were lowest. Meanwhile miners in the 'safest' pits in the central coalfields such as Yorkshire and Nottinghamshire enjoyed the largest bonuses.

It's hardly surprising that it should be the high-bonus coalfields such as Nottinghamshire and Midlands which consistently voted against strike action in the ballots of 1982–4 (see Table). The main exception was Yorkshire, with its traditions of militancy and a highly organised left.

Per cent for strike action[25]

Area	Members (approx.)	January 1982	October 1982	March 1983	March 1984
Cumberland	650	52	36	42	22
Derbyshire	10,500	50	40	38	50
S. Derbyshire	3,000	16	13	12	16
Durham	13,000	46	31	39	—
Kent	2,000	54	69	68	—
Leicester	2,500	20	13	18	—
Midlands	12,200	27	23	21	27
Nottingham	32,000	30	21	19	26
Lancashire	7,500	40	44	39	41
Northumberland	5,000	37	32	35	52
Scotland	11,500	63	69	50	—
Yorkshire	56,000	66	56	54	—
North Wales	1,000	18	24	23	36
South Wales	21,000	54	59	68	—
Colliery Officials	16,000	14	10	15	—
Cokemen	4,500	32	22	39	—
National Average		45	39	39	—

But the incentive scheme didn't just divide the miners. It helped to spark off a guerrilla war underground. In the first six months of 1983 there were 189 stoppages, mainly caused by bonus or disciplinary disputes arising from the drive to boost productivity. The previous year there had been 403 stoppages involving nearly 200,000 miners — which was more than a quarter of all reported industrial stoppages in Britain.

The guerrilla war in the pits didn't just manifest itself in the strike statistics. In 1982 the Coal Board told miners its pay offer was worth up to 9 per cent. A year later, the government's New Earnings Survey revealed that wages had risen just 3.6 per cent for faceworkers and 3.1 per cent for those on the surface — one of the lowest rises in the public sector. The discrepancy was due entirely to the clawback of bonus as the Board tightened up on productivity and discipline.

The harshest discipline in the pits for generations produced its most spectacular fightback with the Dodworth strike in September 1983 when the pit walked out for the fifth time in a month, demanding the reinstatement of George Marsh, a miner sacked for hitting an overman. After two weeks' unofficial action, flying pickets shut down the whole Barnsley coalfield for a week, until pressured to return by Jack Taylor, the Yorkshire miners' leader, with the support of the Area council.

Faced with the Coal Board's offensive, the NUM leaders took a new tack, and introduced a national overtime ban in November 1983. Their aim was to cut production, reduce the mounting stockpiles of coal at the power stations and pitheads, and remove some of the threat to marginal pits. They also hoped that the ban would restore some unity to the union by hitting incentive pay.

An overtime ban had been the prelude to a strike in 1972 and 1974. This time the miners' leaders were wary of another strike ballot. Scargill talked of the ban lasting twelve months.

And the ban held. Miners wanted to take *some* action against the ever more loudly trumpeted threats of the new NCB chairman Ian MacGregor to run the industry down, even if a majority weren't prepared to strike yet. The traditions of absenteeism and local disputes meant that miners were used to, and prepared to tolerate, the loss of wages involved.

MacGregor threatened to ballot the miners himself over the union's head, but backed off when he found the ban was solidly supported. The NCB then changed tactics. Colliery managers began to change shift times and meal breaks to minimise production losses. They also began sending men home on Monday morning because safety work normally done over the weekend hadn't been done.

The Coal Board's biggest breakthrough came at the end of January with the results of the race to succeed Lawrence Daly as NUM general secretary. Peter Heathfield, the left-wing Derbyshire Area president, got just 51 per cent of the vote in a contest with John Walsh, a right-winger hardly known outside his home Area of North Yorkshire, who campaigned *against* the overtime ban. The Coal Board believed from this that they could bring the overtime ban toppling down round Scargill's ears and close pits at the same time.

In Scotland they announced the closure of Polmaise. Two years earlier, Polmaise had been called the 'success story of the Scottish coalfield' by Albert Wheeler, the NCB Scottish Area director. It also had a reputation as Scotland's most militant pit — which is the probable reason why it was singled out. The Coal Board then flooded the nearby Bogside colliery and blamed the loss of the pit on the miners' overtime ban. Bogside's reputation for militancy was second only to Polmaise. And neither pit was on any 'hit list'.

The gauntlet had been thrown down, but the Scottish miners' leaders refused to pick it up. They accepted the closure of Bogside and left the Polmaise men to strike alone. The Scottish leaders had long ago taken a conscious decision that they wouldn't initiate any fight, but would wait for a lead from Yorkshire.

Meanwhile in Yorkshire the overtime ban had erupted into a rash of local disputes. The most significant was a strike at Manvers over meal breaks. Pickets from this pit closed Wath and Kilnhurst, which are linked to it, and went on the road calling for support from other pits in South Yorkshire. As one pit joined in the strike action, the pickets moved to other, until only Manton, right on the Nottingham-shire border, was still at work. After three days picketing, this too was closed. Rank-and-file militancy, with unofficial flying pickets, had paralysed a major part of the Yorkshire coalfield.

The union leaders had a choice. They could either dampen down the militancy or use it to launch a national strike against closures. In Yorkshire, it seemed they had chosen the former course when at the end of February, the NUM Area council voted decisively against escalating the overtime ban into a strike. But the Coal Board raised the stakes once more: on 1 March 1984 they announced the closure of Cortonwood.

Within days flying pickets were surging through the coalfields. The long-awaited confrontation between the miners and the Thatcher government had begun.

3
THE TRAGEDY OF NOTTINGHAMSHIRE

THE FLYING PICKETS in Scotland, Wales and Durham set the strike on solid ground, but Yorkshire pickets took the offensive. They weren't prepared to sit and wait for the next NUM executive meeting to order a national ballot. They knew the best chance of a national strike was if most of the coalfield was shut down anyway.

That first Monday morning, 12 March, 250 pickets from Armthorpe, joined by others from two other Doncaster area pits, Rossington and Hatfield, travelled to Harworth, the most northerly Nottinghamshire colliery. Geographically, it was only a few miles from Doncaster to Harworth but politically they were light years apart. In the 1970s, rank-and-file militants from the two areas used to meet. When Arthur Scargill was Yorkshire president he ensured that their paper, the **Yorkshire Miner**, was distributed in Nottinghamshire, but by March 1984 all that had long since broken down.

One Yorkshire striker described the picketing at Harworth: 'There were about 150 of us. We tried to get the morning shift to stop but the officials at the pit encouraged them to go through. For the afternoon shift, we debated with the Harworth officials in front of their men, arguing about pit closures, solidarity and fighting for your job. A lot of the afternoon shift went back. Their officials said they believed what we were saying so we asked them to stand by us.'

But they didn't. Instead they phoned the Nottinghamshire NUM headquarters at Berry Hill in Mansfield to protest. Their news about the picketing caused panic among the officials who were preparing for an Area council meeting. The Yorkshire executive in Barnsley were contacted and they greeted the news in similar fashion.

Frank Cave, the Doncaster Area agent, was despatched to order the pickets home. Dishing out orders didn't work and he was soon begging instead: 'I don't want to take the heat out of this, I want to win this one as much as you do. But the only way we will win is by discipline. What I want to do is to get organised and come back with some discipline in it.'

An older Armthorpe picket described with delight the reaction it provoked: 'The young lads were great. They told him where to go and said they were taking the picketing into their own hands.' Cave went back to Barnsley with his tail between his legs — but the Yorkshire executive then ordered an emergency meeting of Armthorpe miners for Monday evening and sent their vice-president, Sammy Thompson, back to his old pit to speak.

A few days earlier Thompson had been going round urging rank-and-file militants to get organised and active. Now he was desperately trying to rein them in. His position illustrated the classic paradox of the left-wing union official. He had needed the rank-and-file militants' help to ensure that the Yorkshire Area council backed the strike and that it was solid in the Area. But when it came to escalating the strike and winning over the Nottinghamshire miners, Thompson joined the rest of the Yorkshire and Nottinghamshire executives in preferring an arrangement between the officials to the activity of the rank and file.

The pickets were threatening to disrupt an agreement between the two Area executives by which Yorkshire promised to keep the pickets out of Notts until the Area ballot on 16 March. In return the Notts executive would recommend a strike and invite Yorkshire officials to speak at branch meetings.

Three hundred miners in the Armthorpe welfare heard Thompson plead for the pickets to hold off until after the Notts ballot. Outside another 300 miners from Hatfield, Rossington and Edlington waited for Armthorpe's decision. The meeting wasn't impressed by Thompson's call. The young miners in the hall called him a bureaucrat and older militants reminded him of the times when he himself had led unofficial flying pickets in the past, particularly in the 1978 Rescue Brigades strike, when they had been vehemently opposed by Arthur Scargill.

From the floor, one Yorkshire miner explained: 'We can't win with the pits working and we can't expect Ray Chadburn to fight for a strike vote in the ballot. The way we'll stop the pits is the same way as we'll stop the power stations, and that's by mass pickets.' The experience of picketing two shifts at Harworth had proved both the doubt of Notts president Ray Chadburn's claims that he was campaigning for a strike in Nottinghamshire — and that rank-and-file Yorkshire pickets could win Notts miners with their arguments about pit closures.

After the meeting the Armthorpe pickets and those waiting outside went back to Harworth, and began picketing Bevercoates too.

The campaign against the pickets

With the Yorkshire leadership denouncing their own flying pickets, it was not surprising that Notts general secretary Henry Richardson should do the same. He even threatened to withdraw invitations for Yorkshire officials to address Nottinghamshire branch meetings if the pickets stayed! He warned that pickets were 'counter-productive' and 'set the men against the strike' in Friday's ballot.

It never dawned on him that rank-and-file Yorkshire miners might make better ambassadors in Nottinghamshire than full-time officials. Certainly if the Nottinghamshire area council had called on its branches to hold canteen meetings where flying pickets could put their case, the outcome of the vote could have been very different.

Instead, the Notts leaders played straight into the Tories' hands by denouncing miners who dared cross the county boundary. The government's strategy for dealing with the miners depended on keeping the union divided. In this way they hoped a strike ballot would fail and that any Area taking action would quickly become isolated.

The success of the first day's flying pickets in Scotland and Wales stunned the Tories and the Coal Board and made nonsense of the press predictions that the strike would collapse before it could get started. So naturally the press and television responded with a savage attack on the pickets — and what better ammunition to use than miners' leaders in one county denouncing men from another? The campaign to split the union now began.

The Fleet Street tabloids painted a picture of a divided union, with 'thugs' on picket lines kicking men down the pit lane. Their reporting was tantamount to incitement to violence against the strikers and against Arthur Scargill. On Tuesday morning, most papers displayed a photograph of a Harworth miner's wife brandishing a toy gun at the pickets. 'Gunning for Scargill' screamed the **Daily Star** headline, while the picture caption read 'She'd like to get Scargill in her sights'.

Malcolm Pithers in **The Guardian** was more accurate than most in describing Monday night's picket at Harworth: 'Pickets heavily outnumbered police outside the colliery last night and prevented all but a handful of the night shift entering, although there was little sign of physical violence.' In other words, the presence of the mass picket made the Harworth men listen to arguments that their branch officials had never presented before, arguments that persuaded them to turn back from going into work.

On Tuesday the Yorkshire Area council delighted the militants by sanctioning the flying pickets. For Yorkshire president Jack Taylor and the Yorkshire executive it was a desperate attempt to catch up with the rank and file in order to control the situation. For word of the Armthorpe pickets' success at Harworth had spread like wildfire. Small groups from many pits had already sent 'scouting parties' into Nottinghamshire and on Monday night they were saying they would be picketing in the county 'whether the Area sactioned it or not'.

On Tuesday and Wednesday the flying pickets spread out across the coalfield. Each Yorkshire pit had been given a 'target' in Nottinghamshire or Lancashire to picket and they generally met with success.

The Doncaster Area pits moved on from Harworth to Bevercoates with none of the violence the press claimed automatically went with flying pickets. One striker described the scene:

> The police had a cordon with six pickets allowed into the middle. At that time we were allowed to stop the cars and put the case to them. The only thing that caused any aggro there . . . was only a few shouts of 'scabs' at those who were running across the blinking fields to get in. There was no violence whatsoever against any of those men who wanted to work.

The attitude of the branch officials at Bevercoates was important. They stood *with* the Yorkshire pickets urging their members not to cross. By Tuesday night, only one car crossed the picket line.

At Thoresby 500 Yorkshire miners turned back the Tuesday day shift despite a mass police presence. At Cotgrave colliery, 50 pickets turned back the majority of the Tuesday night shift. There were no police present and no trouble. The Wednesday morning shift turned back too with only deputies and apprentices going in. Two police watched the proceedings. At Hucknall, the pickets met similar success and Silverwood miners picketing Creswell Colliery began a steady campaign which had 80 per cent of the miners turning back by Thursday.

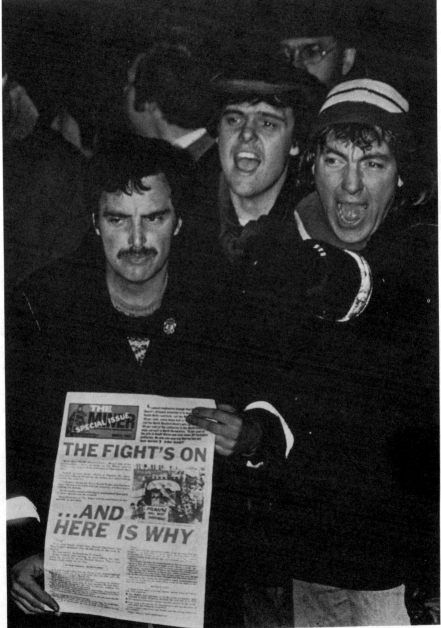

The first Yorkshire pickets at Bevercoates, Nottinghamshire, in March 1984

The Coal Board responded swiftly to the pickets' success. On Tuesday they announced that an injunction was being taken out against the Yorkshire NUM, 'restraining' it from sending pickets to other areas. Meanwhile Ray Chadburn continued his denunciation of the pickets by declaring on television: 'This is not picketing. It's a mass blockade.' He complained about the intimidation of his members and bleated about the need for a ballot.

In the House of Commons, prime minister Margaret Thatcher, bolstered by such comments, told MPs that the 'overwhelming majority of people would support police action in dealing with picket line violence and intimidation.' So would an overwhelming majority of miners, she added. Few could have had in mind the sort of police action she was shortly to unleash.

The Coal Board received their injunction the next day, as flying pickets spread into North Derbyshire and Lancashire as well as Nottinghamshire. Again the Nottinghamshire area council, which was meeting in emergency session, threw trade union principle to the wind. Instead of calling their members out on strike in protest at the use of the Tories' anti-union laws, they instructed their members not to join picket lines — using the court injunction as their excuse!

The Notts pit delegates were supposed to be working for a vote in favour of the strike in the ballot, which was now only two days away, but their main concern seemed to be segregating their members from the Yorkshire pickets.

The national press gave full coverage to the anti-picket hysteria of the Nottinghamshire miners' leaders, the Tories and the Coal Board. But the images they conjured up bore little relation to reality. The **Nottinghamire Evening Post**, however, did a careful survey of the numbers picketing on Wednesday 14 March. The **Post** has a record as an anti-union paper. It is written and printed by non-trade unionists and throughout the miners' strike it championed the cause of those Nottinghamshire miners who refused to respect picket lines. If the **Post**'s report was in any way inaccurate, it could be expected to exaggerate the numbers of pickets in order to highlight the supposed 'intimidation' of Nottinghamshire miners. This is what the **Post** recorded:

Nearly 600 miners from Yorkshire and Scotland swooped on Nottinghamshire in the first full day's picketing at the coalfield's pits — but there were plenty of policemen on hand to deal with them. A team of **Evening Post** feature writers visited all 25 pits within an hour yesterday to see just how much pressure was being put on local miners to discourage them from going to work.

Top of the poll at 'high noon' was Ollerton, which has remained the major trouble spot until it was closed down today following the death of a young miner. Police actually outnumbered the 120 pickets by sending in a squad of 150.

Another 90 pickets were outside the gates of Gedling colliery, where there had been no previous trouble, and the 20 policemen had a relatively peaceful time, although local miners were being stopped and the pickets were making a lot of noise.

Only about half a dozen policemen were keeping a watchful eye on the 60 pickets at Calverton with the same number monitoring the situation at Cotgrave where there were 40 or more Yorkshire miners.

Under the headline: 'WHERE THE PICKETS LINED UP' the paper gave the following figures for midday Wednesday:

Gedling — 90, Calverton — 60, Cotgrave — 40, Babbington — 2, Moorgreen — 0, Pye Hill No 1 — 0, Hucknall — 0, Bestwood — 0, Blidworth — 6, Rufford — 6, Mansfield — 30, Clipstone — 0, Sherwood — 0, Welbeck — 5, Bilsthorpe — 40, Thoresby — 20, Ollerton — 120, Bevercoates — 30, Harworth — 12, Linby — 7, Newstead — 45, Annesley — 12, Bentick — 6, Sutton — 22, Silverhill — 13.[1]

And the Coal Board was forced to admit that these small groups of pickets turned back the afternoon shift at nine Nottinghamshire collieries while, at the remainder, some afternoon shifts were 'undermanned'.[2]

The figures given by the **Evening Post** are significant not simply because they give the lie to the Fleet Street descriptions of 'jackbooted pickets', but because they also show just how few Yorkshire miners were actively involved in the flying picketing. The previous day Jack Taylor had explained the Yorkshire Area council's decision to allow flying pickets, saying: 'The gloves are off now . . . We will step up our campaign in the same organised and disciplined way we have conducted the dispute so far.'[3] What he meant was that the officials would ensure they retained control over their members. As the picketing numbers in Nottinghamshire show, this meant that at many Yorkshire pits, the hundreds who put their names down for picketing at branch meetings the previous week were not contacted or encouraged to take an active part.

Only at Ollerton were events on Wednesday different from those at other pits in the Nottinghamshire coalfield. There, they culminated in the death of David Jones, a Yorkshire picket and the union's first martyr in the 1984 strike.

Throughout that day some 120 Yorkshire pickets stood on the Ollerton pit gates. Both the pickets and the Coal Board understood the significance of the pit. If Bevercoates, Thoresby and Ollerton, the big three profitable pits in the North Nottinghamshire coalfield joined the strike, then traditionally the other pits would follow. The Coal Board had seen the pickets' success at Bevercoates and Thoresby and were determined to prevent the same thing happening at Ollerton.

So too were the police.

Yorkshire miners who went to Ollerton on Wednesday morning expected to picket in the same way as they had done at Harworth, Bevercoates and Thoresby. But they found themselves confronted with police determined to prevent them speaking to the local men. Nevertheless, one miner who picketed all day at Ollerton recalled: 'When the day shift came and saw the pickets were on, instead of going home they stayed at the bottom of the road. By the end, there were only twelve who wanted to work. I was talking to some constables and they were absolutely disgusted that only twelve wanted to work!'

Pickets on the afternoon shift reported that all was quiet after they had spoken to the Ollerton branch officials. Unfortunately though, Jimmy Hood, the branch secretary, asked Ollerton miners to come off the picket lines and not stand with the Yorkshire men — in line with the Notts Area council decision. If local officials had stood with the Yorkshire pickets, the confrontation between police, pickets and Ollerton miners might not have happened and certainly wouldn't have led to the death of David Jones.

No Fleet Street journalist bothered to fully explain events that night, no doubt because it was a Yorkshire picket, not a Nottinghamshire miner who died. If they had done, they would have discovered that the ugly mood in the town that night was the result of the constant press incitement against the pickets, the police attacks on the Yorkshire miners and the indecision of the Ollerton branch officials in telling their members it was 'up to the individual' whether or not to cross the picket line.

Yorkshire miners who had been told that Ollerton wouldn't work the night shift felt cheated by the branch vote that evening to go to work. The majority of Ollerton men didn't cross the picket lines despite their branch vote, and those that did were untouched by the pickets.

All of this was watched by a crowd gathered at the bottom of the pit lane. The **Nottinghamshire Evening Post**, not the most impartial observer of trade union matters, noted: 'Among the crowd gathered outside the pit gates were many local people. Their mood was mixed. Some supported the pickets, others wanted the pickets to go back to their own coalfield. Local wives shouted support to their husbands as they crossed the picket line.'

The **Post** failed to note that local youths, and some Ollerton miners who wanted to work, began the trouble that night from the pub opposite the pit lane. One Ollerton miner described the scene:

> There were women effing and blinding at the Yorkshire pickets to go home. The National Front lads were there with their badges on. Ollerton skinheads were there plus Ollerton blokes wanting to go to work. They started chucking bottles, pint pots, everything. The Yorkshire lads never started any of that you know. It was only that lot coming out of the pub.

Pickets are certain that one of those bricks hit David Jones, a picket from Yorkshire. He collapsed and died as he ran with other Yorkshire miners to protect their cars which sympathetic Ollerton men had told them were being vandalised.

'Davy Jones' death? They're trying to cover it up now,' said a striking Ollerton miner a few days after the tragedy.

Not surprisingly, there were ugly scenes on the Ollerton picket line after word of David Jones' death got around. At 4 a.m. Arthur Scargill appeared to try and defuse the anger.

The police move in

The Yorkshire and Nottinghamshire miners' leaders met in the shadow of David Jones' death on Thursday morning. They quickly agreed a deal whereby the Yorkshire pickets would pull out and Nottinghamshire miners would be called out on strike while they voted in their Area ballot.

When the Nottinghamshire miners' leaders announced the agreement to the press, they didn't take the chance to urge their members to vote for a strike, but denounced the pickets instead. Henry Richardson was asked if the Area strike call meant the flying pickets had won by 'intimidation': 'I suppose in a way they have', he replied, 'but we are thinking about life and limb. One man has already died, and if this carries on other people are going to be injured. We are saying that for the sake of safety we are pulling our membership out.' It was a shameful reply that helped perpetuate the media myth of what was taking place in the coalfield.

In Westminster the success of the pickets and the fighting at Ollerton caused consternation. The **Financial Times** politely described Margaret Thatcher's reaction:

> The prime minister is understood to be angered by the failure of the police to prevent the disturbances. She is believed to have banged the table while making critical remarks about some Chief Constables during a private meeting with some new Tory MPs. She is thought to have said that Chief Constables should learn that their job was to uphold the rule of law, not turn a blind eye to breaches in it.[4]

In parliament, Home Secretary Leon Brittan denounced 'mob rule', and, faced with a 90 per cent shutdown of the British pits, announced that 3,000 police were on hand in Nottinghamshire to deal with further picketing.

It was Friday morning before Fleet Street had its chance to comment on the flying pickets and the death of David Jones. Their editorials nicely coincided with the miners' strike ballot in Nottinghamshire, Lancashire, the Midlands, Derbyshire and Northumberland. **The Sun**, in the best traditions of the yellow press, pinned the blame firmly on the victim: 'Why did he die?' it asked, and answered: 'He was taking part in a mass picket that not only defied the law but aimed to prevent men working by insults, threats and brute force.'

Then, in a shameful sentence that must stick in the throat of anyone who knows the dangers miners face every day in their industry, the paper declared: 'Blood on the coal is a cruel price to pay for political ambition.'

Attorney-General Michael Havers spelled out in the House of Commons the government's interpretation of the law on picketing:

> Police have the power to stop their vehicles on the road and turn them away. Anyone not complying would be committing a criminal offence, obstructing the police in the course of their duty.

The traditional right of pickets to stop cars and explain their case was scrapped. The only right pickets now had was to stand near a workplace — if the police let you through — and wave their arms at those going into work in the hope that someone might stop and come to talk. And even then they risk being charged with obstruction.

Over the weekend, endless streams of police vans poured into Nottinghamshire. Eight thousand police were sent to prevent Yorkshire pickets getting to the Nottinghamshire pits.

As the police went in, the results of the strike vote were announced. In Nottinghamshire 26 per cent of miners had backed a strike, an increase on the 19 per cent in the previous ballot. In Lancashire, the strike vote was lost by 3,765 to 2,596; in the Midlands by about three to one; and in North Derbyshire there was a 16-vote majority against the strike.

The police went to work with a will. Delegates to the Nottinghamshire area council meeting in Mansfield that Sunday found the police had sealed off the road leading to the union's headquarters. NUM officials had to prove their identity before being allowed through. Ray Chadburn complained: 'We have asked the police to leave us alone but they told us it wasn't their decision.' He complained that Nottinghamshire was besieged by police and then typically gave the press a statement opposing the pickets.

The **Yorkshire Post** reported that the Nottinghamshire police were contacting coach operators 'advising' them not to accept bookings from miners going picketing and asking them to report any approaches from the NUM to local police officers! Meanwhile, Kent police blocked the approaches to the Dartford tunnel, east of London, and turned back miners travelling to the Midlands. Miners say they were specifically threatened with arrest if they tried to drive through the tunnel, but the police later claimed that the miners were warned that they 'may' be arrested later for causing a breach of the peace. The roadblocks were in force throughout Sunday 18 March and different police officers gave miners different legal explanations of why they were being stopped.

No doubt lawyers will argue about the technicalities of the case for years to come but the fact was that the police had taken powers no one thought they had, extending the Attorney-General's invitation to turn away pickets' vehicles so that it operated *200 miles* from the pit where that picketing might have occurred. Retrospectively, their actions were upheld by the courts.

In Northumberland, miners from Seafield colliery who'd come down to join picket lines in Ashington found themselves being 'run out of town like the baddies in a cowboy film', according to John

Police seal off Nottinghamshire: a road block near Shirebrook

Neilson, the branch delegate. The whole operation was unprecedented.

The first week of the strike ended with one picket dead, many more injured, the strikers vilified in the press and parliament, their union funds threatened, the largest police operation since the general strike and strike calls defeated in a number of Area ballots. Most commentators were predicting the strike would quickly collapse or that the NUM executive would call a ballot which would go against strike action, despite opinion poll findings to the contrary.

But they reckoned without the miners' sheer determination. Faced with the alternative: fight or surrender to pit closures, the miners stood firm. The more the odds seemed stacked against them, the more determined they became, and their determination was strengthened by the success the pickets found at pits where they *could* talk to other miners.

On Monday morning the police set up road blocks on every road from Yorkshire into Nottinghamshire, but most pickets didn't test them. Instead more than a thousand Yorkshire miners gathered outside their union offices in Barnsley ready to guard them against bailiffs. The Coal Board had brought proceedings against the union for contempt of court in defying the injunction against picketing. This threatened either a massive fine against the Yorkshire NUM, or even the total sequestration of the Area's assets.

But in a surprise move, the Coal Board solicitors told the high court that they wanted to shelve the case. Tory backwoodsmen ranted and raged in the House of Commons and Walter Goldsmith, the director-general of the Institute of Directors, complained bitterly that it 'weakened the authority of the court to see its orders flagrantly ignored.'

But as the **Financial Times** noted: 'Mr Goldsmith is beating at a closed door: the government, not without qualms and arguments, has accepted the view that to press the order would unify the union which it is in its interests to split.'

The government hoped that the massive police operation, legitimised by the Area votes against striking, and the demands of the right wing on the NUM executive for a national ballot would between them do the job.

The government clung to the fiction that they had nothing to do with the police operation. This didn't kid anyone. **The Economist** reported:

> Officially, the police have been keeping the peace on their own initiative. Not in reality. But all government preparations for dealing with the miners' strike have been by word of mouth and informal. The Cabinet Office has taken care to ensure that there are no traceable links with the Coal Board or the police. Even the Prime Minister has been persuaded to restrain her normal eloquence.[5]

The police operation was directed from New Scotland Yard by the National Reporting Centre set up after Saltley. Its aim was made clear by the centre's controller, David Hall, the Chief Constable of Humberside and president of the Association of Chief Police Officers: 'We are determined to ensure that mass picketing is not permitted.' The Home Office was in daily contact with the Reporting Centre.

For the pickets, and even more for the Nottinghamshire miners who supported a strike, the police operation was an exercise in mass intimidation, an attempt to cow them into submission. Despite the police roadblocks some flying pickets did get into Nottinghamshire. At Ollerton five men picketed the day shift on Monday. They were faced by three coach and eight van loads of police! A few miles down the road at Thoresby it was the same. 'We were flooded with police. Every corner, every road in. They were lined up from Edwinstowe [the village where most Thoresby men live] to the pit lane, shoulder to shoulder on each side of the road, like they are in London on rallies.'

And a handful of pickets turned back a quarter of the Notts miners!

At pits such as Thoresby, Bevercoates and Blidworth, where the NUM branch officials had supported the pickets, more than half the workforce respected picket lines. At others, such as Ollerton, where the officials sat on the fence, even **The Guardian** reported that just 100 of the 400-strong day shift went into work past the five-man picket.

As the week went on, the police roadblocks grew increasingly efficient. At one militant Yorkshire pit, an average of 28 of the 30 cars sent out never got through. Those that did were appalled at the police behaviour they found. In one notorious incident at Thoresby, police roped Welsh pickets to a steel fence and smashed the windscreen of Maltby NUM delegate Frank Slater's car. The Chief Constable of Nottinghamshire defended his men's action by saying the police hadn't used a crowbar as pickets alleged, but their truncheons! Later police dealt with a further eight cars from Yorkshire in a similar fashion.

Things were so bad that a delegation of six NUM-sponsored Labour MPs travelled to Nottinghamshire to witness the police behaviour. However, former Northern Ireland minister Roy Mason cleared the visit with Home Secretary Leon Brittan first, promising that the MPs would just 'observe', and not join the pickets.

On Thursday, Notts general secretary Henry Richardson turned again and asked his members not to cross picket lines — while at the same time asking Yorkshire miners to recognise the Nottinghamshire men's right to work. Each twist and turn by the Nottinghamshire leadership merely added to the confusion felt by the majority of Notts miners. But it did now look as if Nottinghamshire was going to stand alone: in clear contrast to the action of the Notts officials, branch officials in Lancashire had joined the flying pickets in closing all but one pit; in North Derbyshire the Area leaders had called on their members to join the pickets; and in the Midlands the left-wing officials had called on their members to respect the picket lines — and then joined the Welsh miners at the pit gates.

The police increased the pressure in Nottinghamshire as the strike appeared to be taking root in other Areas. On Monday 26 April they stopped hundreds of miners in cars on the A1 main road. Not to be thwarted, the miners set off on a seven-mile hike to Ollerton, where they intended to picket. The police allowed them to get within half a mile of their destination before blocking them at Ollerton crossroads. Massively outnumbered, some pickets were arrested and the others were made to wait for hours until transport was arranged to take them back to Yorkshire.

It was straightforward provocation and the next day the pickets struck back. After being turned back at the Nottinghamshire border, they descended on the Coal Board's Doncaster headquarters. After a lively picket they headed for their cars and the motorway, intent on borrowing a tactic successfully used by the French lorry drivers a few months earlier:

'We were making our way down the motorway in a five-mile-an-hour convoy,' a young Frickley miner explained. 'Then the car in front just came to a halt. The driver inside got out and said: "It's snap time." Then everyone got out of their cars for snap time. Cars were stopped all along the motorway for as far as the eye could see!'

But such small victories were rare. Even James Anderton, the god-fearing right-wing Chief Constable of Greater Manchester, complained about police behaviour in the Nottinghamshire mining villages:

'It does appear to the public,' he said, 'that the police have imposed a kind of curfew on the community as a whole, not just on the miners, and also that they have restricted free movement. These features are things we normally only associate with countries behind the iron curtain . . . The police are getting the image of a heavy-handed mob stopping people going about their lawful duties.'[6]

The police had also hit on a new tactic. They began mass arrests, mainly on minor charges such as 'obstructing the highway', then asked the courts to apply strict conditions when granting bail. On 23 March arrested miners were banned from Warwickshire pits until their trial date. A week later, miners were being banned from the Nottinghamshire, Leicestershire, Derbyshire and Staffordshire Areas. And by the first week in April, eight miners from Kent and South Wales were told the whole of Britain except for their own pit village was a no-go area!

The idea behind the bail conditions was to slash the numbers of pickets available to the NUM. They meant that miners could be jailed for breaking bail conditions if they were arrested again, though their original 'crime' might have warranted a £15 fine at most if they hadn't been striking miners. Four miners from Kiverton Park were arrested on a motorway slip road and jailed for two weeks because they'd broken their bail conditions, which were not to picket any Coal Board property. This novel legal twist, extending Coal Board ownership to cover the motorway network so that the police could get their first miners behind bars, was hardly thought worthy of comment on Fleet Street.

But the pickets had to face not only police harassment but a distinct lack of enthusiasm by some of their own officials. Yorkshire Area president Jack Taylor announced on Tuesday 27 March that the £100,000 strike fund had almost gone. 'The strike has already cost us a lot of money and we are looking very carefully at our financial position,' he said. The Area's assets amounted to nearly £8 million at the beginning of the strike, way above the £100,000 strike fund.

The Yorkshire executive were using their control over the purse strings to maintain a far tighter control than had happened in the 1972 strike. A branch committee member at South Kirkby colliery complained bitterly: 'They're blocking extra pickets by rationing the petrol money for cars. Hundreds of lads who want to go picketing cannot because of the squeeze on finance. We are going to have to do our own fund-raising. In fact we need rank-and-file strike committees at every pit. This is the only way to overcome the feeling of being leaderless!' Unfortunately, throughout the strike there were hardly any elected strike committees in Yorkshire.

The campaign for the ballot

While the pickets and the better branch officials were struggling to unite the whole union behind the strike, the right-wing leaders within the union were pulling in the opposite direction. Their intention was to ensure that the national executive meeting on Thursday 12 April would call a national ballot, which they were convinced would vote against the strike.

The key to their campaign was agitation for a ballot from the Notts miners' leaders. Throughout all the twists and turns made by Ray Chadburn and Henry Richardson, their constant theme was for a national ballot. Richardson believed, genuinely but wrongly, that it was the only way to get the Notts miners out on strike. Chadburn, on the other hand, was running with the fox and hunting with the hounds.

A secret meeting of right-wing members of the NUM executive was held in the Brant Inn, at Groby outside Leicester, on Tuesday 27 March. The meeting was organised by Roy Ottey, secretary of the union's Power Group, and Sid Vincent, the Lancashire miners' leader. In his book **The Strike — an insider's story**, Roy Ottey described how he was able to get in touch with Ray Chadburn thanks to the help of Ned Smith, the Coal Board's director of industrial relations! Ottey wrote that Chadburn was enthusiastic about the meeting but couldn't leave London. 'He suggested I got in touch with Nottingham Financial Secretary, Roy Lynk, "Tell him I told him to attend and pledge our two votes".'[7]

The meeting agreed a long statement, which focussed on the call for a national ballot of the union. Only one line talked about the attacks on the miners. There was no mention of pit closures, never mind any recommendation to fight them. Later Tory Energy Secretary Peter Walker congratulated them for holding the meeting.

Sid Vincent rushed back to Lancashire after the meeting and pushed a vote through his executive calling off the week-long strike in the Area. 'I can't hold the members any longer,' he said. But his members had more faith in their union and their strike than he did: two Lancashire pits, Bold and Sutton Manor, voted to continue the strike, and at Parkside colliery, miners voted by a majority of only five to return to work. Picketing by Lancashire and Yorkshire miners prevented his back-sliding having full effect.

In Nottinghamshire, the Area executive agreed to recommend to their Area council that their members should respect picket lines, but only under pressure from Notts miners who were on strike and the decision of the Nottingham train drivers' union branch to black coal trains. Two days later, the Area council overturned the executive recommendation, voting 186 to 72 to continue working and ignore picket lines until the NUM called a national ballot.

The press and television went on endlessly about the need for a ballot. Every journalist and TV reporter asked Arthur Scargill time and time again to call a ballot and to condemn the pickets. To their intense frustration he reminded them repeatedly that the strike was constitutional under the union's Rule 41, and that any decision on a national ballot was in the hands of the executive.

The choice between picketing or a ballot was clear. The Tories, right-wing NUM officials and the press all demanded a ballot. So too did Labour Party leader Neil Kinnock, who was 'working desperately behind the scenes to secure a national ballot on the miners' strike', reported **The Observer**. 'Mr Kinnock . . is having considerable difficulty in keeping his party united behind the "neutralist" stance publicly taken by Labour's leadership. That is the reason why Labour has been so anxious to avoid a full-scale debate in the Commons'.[8]

But the sudden liking for ballots on the part of press and politicians was the utmost hypocrisy. Margaret Thatcher, who told Robin Day on **Panorama** of her concern 'for miners who want to vote and are not being allowed to vote', had never balloted the workers at the GCHQ communications centre in Cheltenham a few months earlier when she stripped them of their trade union rights. Nor had Ian MacGregor asked miners to vote on whether their pits should be closed down. Nor had the right wing on the NUM executive been so partial to ballots when the miners voted in a national ballot to reject the Coal Board's incentive scheme in 1977 — they had immediately overruled the miners' vote.

In reality, all those who screamed for ballots and democracy had a cynical 'take it or leave it' attitude. If the result was in their favour, if for example the majority voted down a minority who were ready to fight against the devastation of their jobs and communities, then they would accept the ballot and crow about democracy. If the ballot went against them, they'd ignore it.

The only reason the Tories and the Coal Board pushed so hard for a ballot was that they knew it would help them beat the miners. The miners were divided, between those whose wages, jobs and conditions were directly under attack and those who felt secure for the time being, between strikers and non-strikers, between active strikers on the picket lines and those sitting passively at home. They believed that after a five-month overtime ban and a four-week strike, with money running short in most miners' homes, with the press and TV hammering home the message that the miners were 'thugs' and couldn't win anyway, a ballot might go against a strike.

But despite the massive campaign, the right wing didn't get their ballot. A majority of the NUM executive were mandated to vote for it until a few days before the executive meeting on Thursday 12 April, and the right wing confidently predicted victory. At the meeting itself, Arthur Scargill listened to the reports from the Area representatives and then ruled from the chair that no vote on a ballot should be taken. He proposed that a special delegate conference of the union should be called. The right wing immediately challenged the ruling, but a vote upholding it was carried by 13 votes to 8. Several executive members who had been mandated to vote for a ballot were saved from breaking their mandate because they were simply able to support the chairman's ruling.

The right wing were routed. The executive then voted 21 to 3 to call the special delegate conference and recommend a change in the NUM's rules to reduce the minimum vote needed to call a strike from 55 per cent to a simple majority.

Those who wanted a ballot screamed about the 'abuse of democracy' but they represented a tiny proportion of the NUM's members. Jack Jones, the Leicestershire president, led the way. He represented fewer than 3,000 miners and had anyway agreed the closure of all the pits in the Leicestershire coalfield! Alongside him stood Ted McKay from North Wales with 1,000 members and Harry Hanlon from Cumberland whose membership was reduced from 600 to 200 in the first month of the strike after a pit closure!

These three together had the same representation on the NUM executive as the Yorkshire Area, though they had less than a tenth of the Yorkshire membership!

The other 'balloteers' were Trevor Bell, who represented the Coal Board's office staff, Sid Vincent, and Roy Lynk — who was to lead the threatened breakaway of the Notts miners from the national union in January 1985. Roy Ottey surpassed himself saying: 'I am determined not to stand by and watch this great union of ours destroyed by civil war.' This devotion and concern for the union surprised some, for since 1972 Ottey had split his workload between the NUM and a seat on the East Midlands Electricity Board. He owed this second job to Nicholas Ridley, the Tory minister who devised the government's plans to break the unions.[9]

The defeat of the call for a ballot was greeted with sheer joy among the thousands of miners lobbying the executive. And it produced yet another about-turn from the Nottinghamshire leaders Ray Chadburn and Henry Richardson. Inside the executive they had begged and pleaded for a ballot. Outside, Chadburn said: 'It's time our members did get off their knees and started to talk about the national union instead of being so parochial. This fight is not about Yorkshire, Scotland, and South Wales only, it's about the preservation of jobs.'

Two days later Henry Richardson spoke at a march in Nottinghamshire to welcome the miners who had marched in protest from Kent after being turned back at the Dartford tunnel by police. He told the crowd: 'It's about time I talked about principles not what I'm told to say. Five to six thousand are not crossing the picket line . . . I appeal to all Notts miners. I know Ray Chadburn supports me, get off your knees and start fighting.' One Ollerton miner turned away sourly saying: 'If he'd said that four or six weeks ago it would have been no bother. The men were more ready to come out then than now.'

The national executive decision had lifted the constitutional shackles with which Scargill had let himself be bound. After the march he addressed the rally, along with Tony Benn. It was a wild emotional affair. It was scorned and sneered at by the Fleet Street journalists who were bundled out of the hall, but for the Notts miners on strike it was the first time they were gathered together, the first time the leaders of the national union had openly backed them. At long last it seemed their isolation would soon be over.

Scargill hammered home the importance of the strike, called on Notts miners to join it and warned: 'In 1926 our union saw a betrayal from the Labour and trade union movement. The lessons, I hope, have been learnt today.' He also nailed the Nottinghamshire leadership firmly to the mast of the strike, telling the audience: 'You shouldn't underestimate the courageous stand and declaration of Chadburn and Richardson.' But that was a bit much for the miners at the rally.

The Nottinghamshire miners' leaders last hope for a ballot was squashed at the special delegate conference on 19 April 1984. Delegates voted to change the rules so that a simple majority would trigger a strike and threw out calls for a ballot. From now on, every miner not working was officially on strike.

The next day the Nottinghamshire miners' delegate conference finally agreed to make the strike official in Notts too. But it was too late. The damage had been done by a month of vacillation.

Driving in the wedge

The government and the Coal Board had failed in their attempt to use the NUM right wing and their call for a ballot as a way of splitting the union. The great majority of miners were now solidly behind the strike. But they had divided one coalfield — and the Coal Board, police and press now stepped up their efforts to widen this division.

Some Notts miners did join the strike once it was official in their

Arthur Scargill on the picket line at Ollerton

Area, but the majority remained at work. The Coal Board now launched a blatant programme of disinformation, claiming that 87 per cent of the Nottinghamshire miners reported for work after the Easter break. This would have meant a higher percentage of miners attending work than at any time since the nationalisation of the pits in 1947! If it was to be believed, absenteeism had been completely eliminated, the sick and injured had been miraculously cured and returned to work and no one was taking holidays. Even then the figures didn't add up.

The Coal Board also claimed output was 80 per cent of normal. In fact they were drawing thousands of tons from coal stocks each week and claimed this was 'normal' output.

Fleet Street dutifully reported the Coal Board stories as gospel truth. They also eagerly helped the NCB and police manufacture another fiction — the wholesale intimidation of working miners by the minority of strikers and the flying pickets. At the end of April, the Coal Board claimed they weren't running a night shift at most collieries in North Nottinghamshire because the miners were scared to leave their homes at night for fear of attack. The real reason was that so many men were striking that they didn't have the manpower to run two full shifts, let alone three.

There was a great deal of tension in the Nottinghamshire mining villages. The coalfield was divided between the two-thirds of miners who continued to work and the one-third who backed the strike. There was friction, there were fights and there was intimidation, but the vast bulk of it was directed at the strikers by the scabs and their army of supporters, the police, whose intervention was often totally arbitrary.

By the end of April, one striker from Ollerton had been arrested three times and had his car wrecked by the police. His third arrest came as he was driving down Ollerton High Street one afternoon. A police transit van suddenly pulled up, officers jumped out, and, he told afterwards, 'punched me, dragged me out of the car and tried to throttle me. They thought they'd broken my arm, but luckily it was only a bad sprain.' His son, who was still at school, was also roughed up by police in full view of scores of witnesses!

By the end of April, Notts strikers could move about their villages only if they produced 'picket cards', a pass proving they were employed at a Notts colliery, at police checkpoints. Under this pass law system, their free movement was totally at the discretion of the police. Even miners who were going into work used to complain that they were being stopped three or four times on the way, while pickets warned each other that it was unwise to walk alone for fear of being attacked.

The experience of one striker, on 27 April, was typical of many:

> I was walking up to the picket line . . . at Ollerton colliery and I was stopped by three policemen. They asked me where I was going and I said 'Ollerton colliery picket line'. They then asked me if I was an official and I said I was — I carried a card . . . which I gave to [a policeman]. He read it and handed it to the biggest one of the three. After he read it I asked for it back . . . The big one tore it up and threw it on the ground and said: 'That's what we think about pickets'. I said they were nowt but a bunch of sods and they weren't stopping me going to the picket line and turned to cross the road.
>
> I was half way across the road when they grabbed me and two of them held me up against the cricket ground fence and one started hitting me round the body. After they finished I was on my knees, winded and feeling a lot of pain. Whilst the police-men were hitting me about half a dozen men were walking to

Ollerton colliery. I shouted for help but they just kept walking.

This overt violence was backed up by police patrols of the mining villages. Housing estates that before never saw a policeman from one month to the next were now constantly patrolled. Their main purpose, according to strikers, was to detect 'outsiders'. Children were asked if they had strangers in the house, and car number plates were constantly checked. Later the government were forced to admit that cars used by miners' pickets were entered on the police national computer register of 'stolen and suspect' vehicles![10]

In short, it was open season on strikers in the Notts coalfield. The government, Coal Board and police meanwhile maintained that it was the minority on the picket line who were intimidating the majority

Village policemen . . .

at work and Fleet Street went along with this lie. Only one Fleet Street journalist, John Pilger, did challenge the 'official' version of events in the Notts pit villages. His excellent report on 'the violence you don't see on TV' was printed in the **Daily Mirror** on 29 August 1984 — three and four months after the incidents he described had occurred!

Raising the tempo

The police violence was the backcloth to a renewed campaign by NUM leaders to bring the Notts miners out and by right wingers to keep the Notts Area scabbing.

Arthur Scargill spoke at the Ollerton Miners' Welfare on 27 April, when he declared 'We've got to raise the tempo of the dispute' and called on every single miner to get on the picket line. He promised a national demonstration 'in the centre of the Notts coalfield . . . not for one day, it could be three days'. Then he led a march down to the Ollerton picket line.

But at an Area delegate conference the previous day, right-wing officials had forced through a motion saying there should be no campaigning for the strike by Area officials! The movers of the resolution were of course campaigning and organising against the strike day in and day out.

On May Day they called a mass rally outside the Notts NUM headquarters in Mansfield to protest at a threat by Henry Richardson and Ray Chadburn to discipline officials who openly encouraged their members to cross picket lines. Three thousand striking Notts miners gathered to defend their offices from 7,000 scabs. The Coal Board had given the scabs an unrestricted rest day so they could join the demonstration.

The size of the scab demonstration was a serious blow to the strike. The Notts coalfield was hopelessly divided. This was obvious to rank-and-file militants, who began to question the leaders' tactics and call for mass pickets. In response to rank-and-file pressure, the Yorkshire Area leaders launched a series of big pickets at individual Nottinghamshire pits.

On 2 May, 3,000 pickets were at Harworth. The next day 3,000 picketed Cotgrave. Then a thousand arrived on the gates at Hucknall. The militants were delighted. They had been calling for mass pickets for weeks. The police couldn't intimidate and knock lumps out of the men on mass pickets as they had done when the flying pickets were spread throughout the country and a few hundred at most stood on a colliery gate.

These mass pickets also provided a meeting ground for young militants from different pits to swap information and discuss the state of the strike. This was vital, given the secret and bureaucratic organisation of much of the strike, and it helped contribute to the pressure on the Area leaders to start the proper picketing of steel.

But these surprise mass pickets were hardly effective. At best they shut down the colliery for a shift, then, once the pickets had gone, work began again. The initial delight the striking Notts miners felt when their pit was chosen for mass picket faded when, next day, they were left isolated again.

The arrival of the 'gypsy pickets' brought with them a new twist in the reporting of the strike. Police estimated the numbers picketing at Harworth on 2 May as 10,000. The **Nottinghamshire Evening Post** raised the figure to 20,000. There had been an increase in the numbers picketing since the NUM special delegate conference but not that number. A realistic figure was 3,000.

The exaggeration was a skillful piece of news management designed to demoralise strikers into believing that mass picketing couldn't work, to sweep aside mounting criticism of the police and to demand reinforcements and a freer hand in dealing with pickets indulging in such 'mass intimidation'.

Throughout the first two weeks of May, the Notts strikers began to organise themselves more effectively. They staged a series of small demonstrations and marches round the pits which encouraged a few more miners to join the strike and they had access to financial help from the Notts Area office for the first time, but everyone in the Area was waiting for the national demonstration Scargill had promised.

When this came it was a march through Mansfield on Monday 14 May. Scargill called for a massive demonstration, not just of miners but of all trade unionists who supported the strike. Its aim was to boost the morale of those Notts miners on strike, to show the police they couldn't turn Nottinghamshire into an island of anti-trade unionism. For many Yorkshire pickets it also held the promise of staying in Nottinghamshire after the rally and joining local picket lines.

The march was a marvellous sight, miners and their families from every coalfield joined by dockers and railway workers and white-collar union banners. At the rally afterwards Arthur Scargill declared to wild applause: 'Thatcher was successful in the Falkland

Islands, but she will lose this battle.'

The day passed off without incident until the police launched a savage attack at the end of the rally, waiting until the majority of demonstrators had dispersed before setting about the remainder. There were 57 arrests and scores of miners injured. Those arrested were charged with 'riot'. The Nottinghamshire Chief Constable Charles McLachlan declared that the riot offence 'carries far greater punishment than the offences we have been charging so far. It's an unlimited fine and unlimited imprisonment.'

Police on the rampage

The riot charges marked a conscious decision to step up the intimidation of miners actively involved in picketing. **The Guardian** reported on 19 May: 'Cabinet sources confirmed yesterday that the government is hoping that police patrols to stop intimidation in the pit villages will lead to more miners breaking the strike.' Nottinghamshire mining villages were now swamped with police and the week that followed the Mansfield march saw a series of extraordinary attacks on Notts strikers and pickets from other Areas.

The most notorious incident occurred in Blidworth when police laid siege to the homes of striking miners who were putting up pickets from Yorkshire Main colliery near Doncaster. The siege lasted a day and a half with the Nottinghamshire strikers being threatened with a new 'criminal' offence — 'harbouring pickets'! The Yorkshire pickets did leave, but only after an NUM solicitor organised a convoy of cars to take them home. The next day police smashed their way through the locked doors of the Blidworth village hall where the strikers had a soup kitchen, terrorising scores of women and children inside. They left without explanation or arrests.

Nottinghamshire strikers were being arrested for shouting 'scab', for obstructing the highway after police pushed them off the pavement, and even for 'trampling winter barley'!

The police activity did demoralise the Nottinghamshire strikers but it wasn't the only attack on the strikers. Two leading scabs, Colin Clarke from Pye Hill and John Liptrot from Sherwood, took out writs against the Notts NUM to get the strike declared unofficial in the Area — and Notts NUM officials immediately withdrew all financial help to the strikers. Ten days later Justice Megarry granted the injunction.

The judgement, however, was not the turning point of the strike in Nottinghamshire. The Mansfield rally had shown that the NUM

The great march: Mansfield, May 1984

would have to win the strike with the majority of Nottinghamshire miners scabbing. The battle for Nottinghamshire was effectively over by the end of May. Ten thousand Nottinghamshire miners had taken some part in the strike but they'd never been organised into the force that could have closed down the coalfield. Instead, the twists and turns of the Area leadership left them passive and isolated in the first few vital weeks.

In the mind of every miner, the Notts NUM members who remained on strike were the bravest and most determined of all the strikers. They were also a sad testimony to what might have been.

For the Tories, their victory in Nottinghamshire was crucial. The coal mined there enabled them to face up to a long strike. The events in Notts also re-established mass scabbing in the British trade union movement for the first time in decades. And that might eventually prove the Tories' greatest long-term gain.

Could it have been different?

The vast majority of Nottinghamshire miners continued to work throughout the strike. Their scabbing first prolonged the strike, then helped the government to get through the winter without power cuts.

From early on, striking miners tried to explain why the Nottinghamshire men continued to work. A favourite answer was to say that the Nottinghamshire miners had always been scabs — since the days of the 'Spencer union' after the 1926 General Strike. This explanation got a new lease of life when the Notts Area threatened to break away from the National Union of Miners in the winter of 1984. But the ghost of Spencer's union can't be blamed for what happened in Nottinghamshire. It doesn't explain why the Notts miners enthusiastically backed the 1972 and 1974 miners' strikes. In fact it only serves to hide what really happened in Nottinghamshire pits before and during the strike.

After a week of flying picketing, a Yorkshire miner summed up the most important problem they faced in Nottinghamshire. 'I've been appalled by the ignorance we've found. Men quite obviously haven't heard the arguments against pit closures at all.'

Nottinghamshire had escaped the pit closures that ravaged other areas, though many miners had transferred into the area during the pit closure programme of the 1960s. And local miners' leaders knew their Area's immunity would not last much longer. At the beginning of 1984, the Notts NUM produced a major document on pit closures and

the threat to jobs in the North and South Nottinghamshire coalfields. It found that 6,000 jobs in the area were immediately threatened, and that one in three faceworkers' jobs would be lost by 1990 as a result of new technology in the remaining pits.

This document was one of the most comprehensive produced by any Area of the union, yet its findings were never presented to the Area's miners. Henry Richardson, the Area secretary, did claim at the start of the strike that this wasn't so. 'We've had a massive expensive campaign,' he said. 'There have been mass meetings at every pit; Heathfield and Scargill have been round the area and leaflets have been put out. It's been very intensive.' A young activist from a South Nottinghamshire colliery put it differently:

> For a long time you get no literature down from the Area telling you what's happening. When it does come, it all comes at once and it's too much to take in. When they put official letters on the union notice board, it's in bureaucratese. Legal talk. You have

to be a solicitor to understand it.

We want plain-speaking truths. It's no good trying to force things into people's minds all at once just before a dispute. Chadburn says he's been campaigning for a year — I've never seen him at a branch meeting. He just sends directives to the branch but that's no good. Only a few people get to know.

Nevertheless, this failure to campaign consistently could have been overcome. The overtime ban was strictly implemented at most Nottinghamshire collieries. Because they had not escaped the crack of the Coal Board whip in the productivity offensive from 1981 onwards, at some pits this fed a militancy over day-to-day issues matched only in the most political Yorkshire pits.

A striking branch official from Thorseby said: 'Thorseby's always been a moderate pit but the very smallest thing, such as a bit of water on the face, could get the men out. And if one face walked out, the others followed. It was one out, everybody out. Usually there's a walkout over water every six months. Last year, we had the pit out, the whole three shifts, for 25p water money for a small team on one face!'

At Cotgrave colliery, a similar militancy prevailed at the start of the overtime ban. One striking miner recalled:

We had a dispute last November [1983]. Sixteen men got £4 short in their bonus. A total of sixty-four quid, and we had five shifts out on strike!

At a meeting the officials said: 'You think you've got a fight on your hands? We've all got a hell of a fight on our hands next year over these pit closures.' The whole hall said 'Yes you're right. We've got to stop the coal now. Don't produce as much, start the overtime ban, cut back on everything. Give them the minimum amount of coal possible.' The overtime ban was doing marvellous. Before the overtime ban production was 26,500 tons a week. We got it down to between 10,000 and 12,000.

There were other signs too. A Calverton miner explained: 'Scargill was down here a fortnight or three weeks before the strike, and was well received. All the people who are scabbing now were standing up at the meeting shouting for more.'

Strikers from other Nottinghamshire pits tell similar if less dramatic stories showing a mood that could have been galvanised into support for the strike. All it needed was a lead.

In the first few days of the strike the flying pickets gave that lead and got results. A Nottinghamshire miner from Geddling colliery explained their impact at his pit: 'Out of 12 lads from South Wales picketing our pit, six had originally voted against strike action. Their pit was picketed out and they joined the flying pickets. That swayed miners behind the strike.'

The tragedy was that the Nottinghamshire Area officials were determined not to let flying pickets talk to their members. And they made sure that Henry Richardson, the left-wing Area secretary, publicly backed their line.

Richardson had been the Broad Left candidate in the election for Notts general secretary the year before and won comfortably. Every militant in the area expected him to use his position to stand up to the right wing. Instead, the right wing controlled him. From the start, he refused to step outside the rule book for fear it would give the right wing the excuse to start a breakaway Notts union, something he was always worried about.

As the miners' strike loomed, the right wing in Notts wanted an Area ballot which they hoped would give legitimacy to their scabbing calls. Richardson went along with it and the right wingers insisted he join Ray Chadburn as public spokesman for the ballot. Militants in Notts believe the Area ballot was a disaster because it gave legitimacy to the scabbing.

But even then, the Nottinghamshire miners could have been won over — if the Area executive had immediately called on their members to respect picket lines and organised those who did into pickets themselves. The police invasion of the county was itself reason enough to do this.

There was support to be tapped: 'At the start of the dispute we had hundreds of men at each branch out on strike,' said one of the striking Bevercoates officials. 'We had half our workforce out on strike at one time.' At Thorseby, a striking official reported: 'We had about 800 on strike for the first six weeks.' Creswell was shut down for several weeks and most pits had at least several hundred on strike.

But, according to a striking Notts NUM executive member, the executive voted 8 to 5 not to instruct members to respect picket lines. 'Richardson and Chadburn weren't there. They were conveniently absent — I think they were seeing a judge . . .' he said.

Even if the executive weren't prepared to make the sort of call being made by the leaders of other areas, Henry Richardson could have done so personally and then have appealed to the Area council for backing. The right wing certainly didn't dominate the Area council meetings in the first weeks of the strike. One delegate explained: 'The Notts Area council all backed the union.' Of the branch officials who were to become prominent scab leaders, 'Colin Clarke was on his own up there. He opened his mouth and showed his colours. The others didn't, not in council meetings, though they did at their own pits by going to work.'

In reality the coalfield was split and incredibly volatile, as a branch meeting in Ollerton near the end of March 1984 showed: 'It was the first time,' explained a striker, 'that Jimmy Hood [the Ollerton branch secretary] spoke his mind — when the men wanted a vote of "no-confidence" in Arthur Scargill and the leadership. There was 500 of them [working miners] and about 200 of us [strikers]. They were all shouting against Scargill. Jimmy Hood stood up and when he'd finished, you know how many voted to no confidence Scargill? Five.'

In most Nottinghamshire pits, those working felt they were scabbing but they also thought it would only last a few weeks until a national ballot either brought them out or ended the strike in Yorkshire. With Chadburn and Richardson twisting and turning daily, most were confused and stayed at work. Meanwhile the only consistent line given to those respecting picket lines was that if they turned back, they weren't to join the picket themselves or set up on their own!

This just compounded the disaster that was unfolding. It meant that the majority of the 7,000 Notts miners who did respect picket lines were not organised for the first two weeks of the strike but left sitting at home. Even some branch officials who enthusiastically backed the strike denied their members an active role. If they had organised unofficially from the start and begun picketing their own, then other Nottinghamshire pits, the police would have found their operations in the county much harder.

But with Henry Richardson convinced that only a national ballot would get Nottinghamshire out, and playing his job as Area secretary absolutely by the book, even the best branch officials lacked confidence. One North Nottinghamshire branch official who had the majority of his members out for almost two months explained: 'The Notts Area decision was that we should go to work if no pickets were there.' And his branch endorsed that position.

This led to ludicrous situations when the police sealed off the county and the majority of flying pickets couldn't get through: 'We were getting maybe 20 or 30 at the bottom of the pit lane picketing. The majority were our own men, unofficial pickets. But if we got *one* from Derbyshire or Yorkshire, that made it an official picket and we all should have turned back.'

If the official picket didn't get through, branch officials went into work even though they were committed to the strike! 'We even had to tell our own lads at the bottom of the lane that they were doing wrong in picketing. Horrible — but that was the decision.'

This state of affairs lasted until the special delegate conference on 19 April. Not surprisingly, men who were turning back at picket lines three or four days a week began to lose heart.

At Calverton, the picture was similar: 'A good percentage of the men wouldn't cross Yorkshire or Derbyshire picket lines. They'd turn back. But when we put our own on, they'd come through. They were making the excuse that the strike was unofficial. The branch secretary used to stand there clapping men as they came through the lines.'

The Coal Board and police certainly knew what was going on and it spurred their efforts to keep the flying pickets out of the county and, if they got through, kick them off the picket line. In one incident at Sherwood colliery police separated Nottinghamshire from Yorkshire pickets and then arrested the Yorkshire men, saying they weren't allowed to picket when local men were doing so. The arrests also made the picket 'unofficial'.

This sort of behaviour led some working miners to join the strike, but without a proper lead it was hard to build on. Furthermore, as the police operation got into full swing and the number of flying pickets getting through diminished, local pickets found it increasingly difficult to talk to working miners. As soon as a picket line was set up it was massively outnumbered by police.

A picket described what it was like: 'They just arrest men for nothing. They don't allow us on the road. We can only wave like penguins with a line of police in front. The police are doing whatever they feel like, everything in their power to make us go to work. If anyone stops to talk, the police are in at the car window telling them to move along or they'll be done for obstruction.'

The story of the early days of the strike in Nottinghamshire is a sorry one, of a tragedy that could have been avoided: if Henry Richardson had given a lead instead of allowing himself to be castrated by the union constitution; if the branch officials and rank-and-file militants who joined the strike had the confidence to organise and act decisively and independently in the first two weeks of the strike; and if the many branch officials who believed it was wrong to cross picket lines had not taken shelter behind the ballot call.

As it was, every delay and every twist and turn by the Area's leaders merely strengthened the hand of the right wing until the majority of Notts miners grew accustomed to scabbing and the hard scabs began to make the political running in the union.

Of course the blame for the events in Nottinghamshire doesn't just lie within the county. The Yorkshire miners' leaders share the responsibility. Jack Taylor knew from 1 March 1984 that his members would be on strike over Cortonwood. He also knew that no single area could take on the Coal Board alone. He had the time and the resources to send teams of Yorkshire miners into other coalfields to leaflet the pits and explain, face to face, what was going on and ask for support. But he didn't, preferring to discuss solidarity with the Area officials instead.

When the flying pickets did go to Nottinghamshire, the Yorkshire leadership were scarcely enthusiastic. Their obsession with keeping control meant that they didn't mobilise the thousands of miners who wanted to go picketing when they were faced with the massive police mobilisation. And they didn't listen to any of the ideas for beating the blockade suggested by the young militants.

Their failure to mobilise all their troops in the first few weeks of the strike was as much to blame for the tragedy in Nottinghamshire as Henry Richardson's vacillations.

Finally, Arthur Scargill didn't do all he could in those crucial first few weeks. He hammered home the message that picket lines were sacred, he rang leading rank-and-file strikers in Nottinghamshire urging them not to lose heart. He also won blacking pledges from the leaders of the transport unions, which were crucial in giving the strike momentum and creating the appearance of support that must have influenced some miners who were wavering.

But for the first month of the strike he was playing strictly by the book, treating the strike as a collection of Area strikes. Too strictly. He was careful not to appeal directly to the Nottinghamshire miners to join the strike until after the special delegate conference in April. And in those crucial weeks he never backed up his statements on the sanctity of picket lines by joining one. If he had, he might have given the militants in Notts the confidence to organise and start their own mass pickets.

4
ORGREAVE AND
THE BATTLE FOR STEEL

MID-APRIL marked the first watershed in the miners' strike. The majority of Nottinghamshire miners were still working, but more than 80 per cent of miners were out on strike. Control of the strike had been formally vested by the conference in the hands of the NUM's national officers with the aim, in Peter Heathfield's words, of 'taking the strike by the scruff of its neck'.

The scale and toughness of the struggle ahead began to sink into ruling-class commentators. The **Financial Times** had already spelled out what was at stake for Thatcher and her cabinet:

> The government regards the miners' dispute as its major industrial test since 1979. It shares the view of Mr Arthur Scargill . . . that the dispute is an all-out challenge to its authority . . . For that reason, and because miners' strikes were instrumental in the downfall of the Heath administration, it cannot lose it. Every tactic pursued by the National Coal Board, by the police and the government itself is viewed in that harsh light: will it bring the government down?[1]

Thatcher established a special inner cabinet of senior ministers to direct the government's strategy. The body, known as MISC 101 and meeting twice a week, consisted of Leon Brittan (Home Office), Nigel Lawson (Treasury), Peter Walker (Energy), Tom King (Employment), Nicholas Ridley (Transport) and Sir Michael Havers (the Attorney-General). Also in attendance were Brigadier Tony Budd and David Goodhall from the government's strike-breaking organisation, the Civil Contingencies Unit, whose role in the strike has been kept very secret.

The Tories had enjoyed one victory so far. **The Times** claimed that the police operation in Nottinghamshire represented a 'shift in the balance of power in outbreaks of violent, or potentially violent industrial disorder' — as significant 'a benchmark in the history of industrial relations' as Saltley had been.[2]

But Thatcher had miscalculated — the campaign to use a national ballot to beat the strike had collapsed dismally. Now she decided to play a waiting game. Hence the care with which the Tories avoided using the 1980 Employment Act, despite the fact that it made mass picketing illegal. The government also did their best to avoid provoking any other group of workers into joining the miners on strike.

What were the choices facing the miners' national strike committee? Could the strike win with Nottinghamshire at least partly working? To do so would require the most determined mass picketing of targets outside the coal industry, designed to affect strategic sectors of the economy as rapidly as possible. These tactics, by showing that the strike was biting, might also persuade the Nottinghamshire scabs that it was worth joining their fellow miners on the picket lines.

In other words, to win victory in 1984 they had to use the methods of 1972. Scargill himself had given the best defence of those methods:

> We took the view that we were in a class war. We were not playing cricket on the village green. Like they did in '26. We were out to defeat Heath and Heath's policies because we were fighting a government. Anyone who thinks otherwise was living in cloud cuckoo land. We had to declare *war* on them and the only way you could declare war was to attack the vulnerable points. They were the points of *energy*: the power stations, the coke depots, the coal depots, the points of supply. And this is what we did.[3]

It was, of course, the flying pickets organised from below which actually carried out this strategy. But official NUM policy in 1972 was also absolutely emphatic in its aim of hitting the economy as hard as possible. Instructions issued to pickets on 12 January 1972 stated: 'The aim of the NUM picket is to prevent the movement of coal and alternative fuels between power stations, coal depots and other coal consumers.' NUM general secretary Lawrence Daly issued detailed guidelines:

2. *Power Stations* — all movement of fuel and stocks at power
stations should be stopped . . .
4. *Steel Works* — coke supplies from coking ovens for steel
works should be stopped.

In 1972 the main picketing battles were fought at the power
stations and coal depots. Two years later in 1974, the steel works, the
main industrial consumers of coal, assumed a greater importance.
Scargill recalled:

> We launched our main attack in Yorkshire on this occasion, at
> the giant Anchor steel works complex in Scunthorpe; because it
> was clear that if we could stop the huge Anchor works we could
> halt British industry . . . The Anchor works closed down in two
> weeks. Production went down to 50 per cent, then 25 per
> cent . . . Historians, when they look at this, will see that the real
> crunch came in the '74 strike with the steel works.[4]

The real crunch came with the steel works in 1984 too. But this
time the story was different. The powerful Area leaders of the NUM
in Yorkshire, Scotland and South Wales chose to allow steel production to continue. And the most serious attempt to use the tactics of
1972 by cutting off the supply of coking coal to Scunthorpe, the mass
pickets at Orgreave in May and June, were to end in defeat for the
miners. How and why did this happen?

The phoney war in steel

Coal consumption in Britain in 1981 was as follows:

Electricity supply industry	87.2 million tonnes
Coke ovens	10.8 million tonnes
Industry	7.0 million tonnes
Domestic coal	8.6 million tonnes
Others	5.0 million tonnes
Total	*118.6 million tonnes*

The Central Electricity Generating Board was far and away the NCB's
biggest customer. But it was clear that even with effective mass
picketing, it would take some time before power cuts were forced on
the CEGB. First, the power stations had massive coal stocks (24.3
million tonnes at the beginning of the strike). Secondly, the strike had
begun in the spring, unlike the 1972 and 1974 disputes, both of which

were fought out in the depths of winter when demand for electricity was high and the closing of a single power station could trigger power cuts.

To win quickly the miners would have to hit directly at industry itself. Steel held the key to this strategy, for not only were the British Steel Corporation's coke ovens the main industrial consumers of coal, but hitting steel would rapidly affect other sectors of the economy, above all the motor and engineering industries. Moreover, steel production was concentrated in four major works, all, naturally enough, near coalfields — Scunthorpe in Yorkshire, Ravenscraig in Scotland, and Port Talbot and Llanwern in South Wales. They were, therefore, well-suited as targets for a co-ordinated campaign of mass picketing.

Indeed, the strike had begun to bite before the end of March. The **Financial Times** reported on 26 March: 'Production at the British Steel Corporation's Scunthorpe works will be cut by half this morning because of a fear of a coal shortage.' The plant had a month's supply of coal (100,000 tonnes) a fortnight earlier, but now stocks were running low. One of Scunthorpe's three blast furnaces was shut down that day.

The paper had more gloomy news for big business the following day: 'Some Midlands foundries may run out of coke this week because of picketing by miners of coke ovens and depots.' It was bad news again on 28 March. Llanwern, the **FT** said, 'may be forced to shut down soon unless it receives fresh supplies.' The implications were plain enough — as steel plants and iron foundries shut down, the motor and engineering industries which depended on them would be forced to cut production.

Tragically, the opportunity created by this situation was thrown away. In the first instance, the miners' leaders relied on agreements with other trade union leaders rather than on mass picketing to halt the movement of coal. The Triple Alliance of coal, steel and rail unions had been created to co-ordinate action in defence of jobs. Militant trade unionists had called its predecessor in the 1920s the 'cripple alliance', and so it was to prove again.

The very composition of the Alliance doomed it to failure. The Iron and Steel Trades Confederation general secretary Bill Sirs was on the right wing of the TUC. He was a firm supporter of the 'new realism'. Indeed, he had practised it at British Steel, acquiescing without a fight in the disappearance of 100,000 jobs in the previous four years. If Sirs wasn't prepared to fight to save steelworkers' jobs, he was hardly likely to exert himself for the miners.

The leaders of the Alliance met on 29 March and pledged to halt the movement of coal. Within 24 hours Sirs had broken ranks. The main thing, he said, was to keep steel production going, even if that meant accepting scab coal. Sirs even had the face to accuse the miners of threatening steelworkers' jobs: his members weren't going to be 'sacrificed on someone else's altar'.

This setback did not cause the miners' leaders to abandon hope of winning the ISTC's co-operation. Instead, their attention focused on the possibility of local alliances. This approach had already been pursued before the strike, especially in Scotland and South Wales. Promising statements were forthcoming from local ISTC leaders. But this locally-based approach had the opposite effect to that intended. Rather than close the steel works down, it led the NUM Area leaderships in Scotland, South Wales and Yorkshire to give 'dispensations' which allowed the supply of coal to the main steel plants.

The dispensations were the result of concerted pressure from BSC management and the steel unions, who argued that if the steel works were deprived of coking coal, their furnaces would fall in. The result would probably be the permanent closure of one of the three steel strip mills, Port Talbot, Ravenscraig or Llanwern.

South Wales pickets applaud as a driver turns back from Port Talbot steelworks

In 1972 and 1974 the instructions from the NUM executive to pickets to cut off all coal to steelworks had been implemented to the letter. The blast furnaces had been shut down, their linings had fallen in, and these had to be rebuilt after the strike. There was, however, nothing inevitable about this. During the 1980 steel strike the furnaces had been 'off wind' for 14 weeks without serious damage being caused.

The threat that one of the three strip mills, probably Ravenscraig, might be closed was a real one. But it had nothing to do with the miners' strike. BSC Chairman Robert Haslam told the House of Commons select committee on industry that he could meet foreseeable demand with two strip mills and still have 10 per cent spare capacity. The possibility of a closure was on the cards anyway — but the government now used this threat to play the Areas off against each other.

The steelworkers were a deeply demoralised group of workers. Their strike had been beaten by the Tories in 1980, and they had seen the workforce more than halved as a result. They had in Bill Sirs a leader who had made a virtue of abject surrender. Now the BSC management tightened the screw. Not only did they hang the threat of closure over the steelworkers' heads. At Scunthorpe they announced that lay-offs would start on 28 May unless coal supplies were guaranteed. BSC boss Bob Haslam accused the miners of trying to persuade the steelworkers to sign a 'suicide pact'.

It was not surprising that the steelworkers should give in to this blackmail. Much more unexpected was that the presidents of the three main left-wing Areas of the miners' union — Jack Taylor of Yorkshire, Mick McGahey of Scotland, and Emlyn Williams of South Wales — should fall in with them. But they did. Williams called the pickets off Llanwern and Port Talbot; McGahey signed an agreement on 6 April under the aegis of the Triple Alliance in Scotland to allow coal into Ravenscraig; and Taylor promised on 10 April to supply Scunthorpe with coal.

The Area leaders justified their actions by arguing that the steelworks were essential to their local economies. McGahey said the Ravenscraig agreement was 'in the interests of Scotland's industrial future'.

Taylor, McGahey and Williams had effectively conceded the argument. To be effective in defending their own jobs the miners had to hit industry. Inevitably this would lead to other workers being laid off. In 1974 Heath had tried to isolate the miners by imposing the three-day week on the whole of industry. But by defending their own conditions then, the miners had made it more difficult for the Tories to attack those of workers in other industries — including steel. The same applied in 1984.

There were many rank-and-file miners who understood this better than their leaders. 'The only way to win the strike is by stopping people working,' said one Scottish miner at the height of the controversy over Ravenscraig. 'First they'll chop us, then they'll chop Ravenscraig,' said another.

The ostensible purpose of the dispensations was to allow enough

coal into the steelworks to keep the blast furnaces stoked — and no more. However, the terms of the agreements concluded were vague enough to allow British Steel to drive a coach and horses through them.

For example, Ravenscraig's normal consumption of coal was 24,000 tonnes of coal a week. Only 6,300 tonnes a week were needed to keep the furnaces going, so the Triple Alliance agreement ought to have led to a sharp fall in the amount of coal going into Ravenscraig. If anything the opposite was true. Although details of the original agreement were not made public, it apparently did not place *any* limit

Fifeshire miners blocking the road after police had stopped them travelling to the BSC Hunterston terminal. Nearly 300 were arrested.

on the tonnage of coal which would be let into the plant. Instead, it merely stated that two trainloads of coal a day would be allowed into the works. As one Scottish miner put it, 'How much is a trainload of coal? It's a bit like asking how long is a piece of string?'

The Ravenscraig works is in Motherwell, near Glasgow. Before the strike it received 14,000 tonnes of imported coal every week through the docks at BSC's own port in Hunterston. The rest of its coal came from Polkemmet colliery. With Polkemmet on strike, all Ravenscraig's coal came through Hunterston. Aryshire miners picketing Hunterston in late April noticed that the train for Ravenscraig had two diesel engines rather than the normal one. They counted the wagons, and there were eight more than usual.

Railway and steel workers sympathetic to the miners estimated that, through tricks of this nature, the two trains were bringing into Ravenscraig 4,000 tonnes of coal a day, far in excess of the 900 needed to keep the furnaces going. One of Ravenscraig's mills achieved record production in April — in other words, McGahey's dispensation was enabling British Steel to maintain or even increase output.

The pattern was similar in Scunthorpe. Miners at Silverwood, Cortonwood and Barrow collieries were asked by Jack Taylor to supply Scunthorpe with 15,700 tonnes of coal a week. This was far in excess of what was needed to keep the furnaces stoked. At the end of April Scunthorpe was producing approximately 24,000 tonnes of steel a week.

The Area dispensations were not to Arthur Scargill's liking. Once the special NUM conference had vested control of the strike in the union's national officers, he intervened. In a speech in Cardiff on 28 April he insisted that no dispensations should be made to allow coal into steelworks.

But Scargill's initiative was blocked by the Area executives. As was to become more and more clear in the course of the strike, the National Union of Mineworkers existed only in name. Power still rested in the hands of the Area unions, and the decisions of the special conference did nothing to alter this. Increasingly Scargill was to come into conflict with his own allies, the left-wing Area officials, over the direction of the strike.

Emlyn Williams, the South Wales NUM president, had warmly applauded Scargill's call for no steel dispensations in Cardiff. He then went on to the Welsh TUC and struck a deal allowing four trainloads of coal into Llanwern steelworks. The plant's stocks of coal had run out at the end of April, posing a direct threat to other parts of industry, since Llanwern produced body panels for Ford, Austin-Rover and Volvo. NUM members at Nantgarw coke works, from which the coal for Llanwern was supposed to come, rejected the deal, but were hammered into line by the Area executive.

A South Wales NUM official told the **Financial Times**: 'We don't want to see Llanwern close, and we are sure enough coke will go through.'[5] One Llanwern steelworker commented:

> Over 4,000 jobs have gone in the last four years since the defeat of the steel strike. There's no guarantee the place will stay open, but one thing is certain: it has even less chance if the miners go down to defeat.

Only in Scotland was there some attempt to reduce the supply of coal to British Steel. On 27 April the miners' and rail unions agreed that only one train of coal would run each day from Hunterston to Ravenscraig.

The BSC management reacted aggressively. On 2 May they announced 'emergency measures'. The coal would be moved by road. Within hours of the announcement convoys of lorries began to make the trip from Hunterston to Ravenscraig. Drivers were paid £50 a trip to scab. The strategy could work only because the steel unions had agreed to handle deliveries by road. The Ravenscraig convenor, Tommy Brennan, declared: 'Our people will use any coal that comes into this plant.'

Over the next few days there were running battles between police and picketing miners outside the steelworks. On 4 May the rail unions decided to halt the daily trainload of coal to Ravenscraig in response to the scab lorry operation. On 7 May 1,000 pickets clashed with the police at Ravenscraig, but the convoy of 58 lorries got in through a back entrance. Fifty-two miners were arrested. The next day mounted police attacked the pickets and 65 miners were arrested.

McGahey told a rally in Glasgow, part of a day of action called in solidarity with the miners by the Scottish TUC: 'I'm calling on the whole of the trade union movement to close Hunterston and Ravenscraig and bring about a solution of this problem.'

The next day Fife miners had a taste of the state of siege in Nottinghamshire. Eight coaches bound for Ravenscraig were stopped by the police on the main Stirling–Glasgow road. The miners reacted to this by sitting down in the middle of the road. Nearly 300 were arrested.

Meanwhile McGahey was busy behind the scenes — not to

mobilise wider solidarity action, but to negotiate a deal with the steel union. On 11 May the Triple Alliance in Scotland announced a new agreement, to allow 18,000 tonnes of coal into Ravenscraig every week, nearly three times more than was needed to keep the furnaces going.

On 17 May an agreement was struck which allowed the supply of coal to Ravenscraig to be resumed. One chance to close the cracks in the steel blockade had been lost.

The dead hand of officialdom

Vacillations by trade union officials, even left-wingers such as Mick McGahey, were nothing new, either in the NUM or generally in the British working-class movement. But from the very start the 1984–5 miners' strike was distinguished especially from its predecessor in 1972 by a very high degree of control exercised by the full-time officials of the various NUM Areas. There was little of the independent rank-and-file organisation so notable in the struggles of the late 1960s and early 1970s.

The precise manner in which the strike was run varied from Area to Area. In South Wales picketing was organised by Area strike committees covering several pits. An official from Tower colliery, where more than half the 600 miners were actively involved in the early weeks of the strike, explained: 'The Welsh NUM executive in Pontypridd tells us the target and the rest is organised by the individual strike committees, who then take it to each lodge. The chain of command is very fast.' Later, as the picketing began to shift from the Midlands pits to secondary targets such as power stations and steelworks, the executive re-established a dominant and deadening hand.

The tremendous rundown of the Scottish pits had left miners scattered widely, many still living where collieries had once been, but were no longer. The organisation of the strike in Scotland was, therefore, geographical, around mining communities rather than on a pit basis.

The smallest unit was the strike centre, typically based on a miners' welfare. The various centres fell under one of the four Area strike committees for Scotland — Ayrshire, Central, Fife and Lothian, and these in turn were subject to the Scottish NUM executive. In Ayrshire, the strike centres were scattered around a 90-mile radius from the two pits, Barony and Killoch. Two centres, at Netherthird and Drongan, co-ordinated the others, having responsibility for eight and five centres respectively, and acting as a channel for funds.

The organisation of the Area strike committees in Scotland varied. While the Ayrshire strike centres were run by committees elected at mass meetings, the Area committee consisted of the NUM agent and the Ayrshire members of the Scottish executive. The Central and Lothian Area committees, however, were composed of delegates from the various strike centres.

This structure made possible a degree of rank-and-file involvement at the strike centres. 'The lodge delegates aren't involved,' said one Ayrshire miner. 'The ordinary men are the ones who run our strike committee.'

Much of the strike centres' activity was, however, devoted to welfare activity — chopping wood, organising soup kitchens, dealing with social security cases. Money and picketing instructions came from the NUM headquarters at Gardiner Street in Edinburgh, via the Area strike committees. The Communist Party and its left Labour allies ran the strike through their control of the Scottish executive and of the Area committees.

Yorkshire, the most important Area out on strike, was organised on rather different lines. No special structure of strike committees was created there, perhaps because of the much denser concentration of miners and pits. Instead the NUM leadership relied on the existing union organisation: the branch committees ran the strike. In practice, the branch officials — the president, secretary, delegate, and treasurer — tended to have a decisive say.

Above the branches were the four Area panels — Doncaster, Barnsley, South Yorkshire and North Yorkshire. But whereas in the strikes of 1969, 1970 and 1972 the panels had acted as a focus for rank-and-file organisation and initiative, in 1984 they acted as channels for instructions from the NUM headquarters in Barnsley which arrived via the NUM agent responsible for the Area.

An Area strike co-ordinating committee was set up, consisting of the three Area officers, Jack Taylor (president), Sammy Thompson (vice-president), and Owen Briscoe (general secretary), along with the president and delegate from each branch. The committee was more an extension of the union bureaucracy than a means of giving control over the strike to the rank and file.

The full-timers did not use this power to encourage the involvement of the mass of the strikers. Rank-and-file activists repeatedly told how strikers would volunteer for picket duty, only to be told they weren't needed. So the history of the strike is one of repeated upsurges of initiative and activity from below, each in turn sat upon by branch and Area officials.

This led to enormous variations in the actual level of picketing, from Area to Area, and from month to month. In Yorkshire, Kent and Durham, for instance, there was a fairly high level of picketing, with about one-sixth of the strikers involved on a more or less regular basis. In Scotland, by contrast, the level of picketing was kept low most of the time, while in Wales an initial flurry of activity was quickly dampened down.

There was plenty of rank-and-file initiative and ingenuity to be tapped, as two examples from Scotland in April show.

In Ayrshire the Coal Board management launched something of an offensive against the strikers over the issue of safety. At Barony colliery they appealed to the miners to go into work to rescue a coalface. The face was at the end of its life, and working would have cost the strikers their social security payments, so they refused.

At the other Ayrshire pit, Killoch, the NCB insisted that all 176 members of the overmen's union, NACODS, should go into work, even through three 14-man shifts were all that was needed to maintain minimum safety cover. The strikers responded with a 350-strong mass picket, which, despite 11 arrests, forced the deputies to operate only minimum cover.

'After these successes there was a huge rise in people's morale,' a member of Netherthird strike committee said. 'Before then we were finding it difficult to get enough people to picket a night. Now the picketing rotas are booked up for three weeks in advance.'

Around this time one miner turned up for picketing duty at Ravenscraig to be told by the miners he was relieving that 17 empty coal lorries had gone in overnight. The drivers had said they were coming in to collect breeze, the decomposed remains left after coal has been burned. A quick telephone call established that breeze, when mixed with powdered coal, makes a combustible substance which can be re-used in power stations. Another phone call brought more pickets to Ravenscraig — and the lorry drivers were persuaded to turn back and dump their loads of breeze.

Small victories of this nature have been used to build up rank-and-file involvement in the strike. But the union officials were not interested in encouraging initiatives from below. On the contrary, they did their best to discourage them. One miner in South Yorkshire described in early April how 'the officials took control of the purse strings' at the beginning of the strike, and used it to keep the pickets in line:

> It was all getting a receipt, sending it to Barnsley, waiting who knows how long for it to come back and being told it might not be paid at all because there's a question-mark over the funds being sequestrated. So lads went out and asked other trade unionists to help us with funds. We started to be able to picket and take initiatives ourselves. When we decided something needed picketing, we went there, without filling in official receipts and forms and whatnot. All of a sudden Barnsley didn't like this and said there was only £2,000 coming into the Area strike fund. Now they've put up a notice saying that any picket going anywhere where he's not been sent by Barnsley will not be legally represented if he gets arrested.

There were also conflicts between the rank and file and the officials in Scotland. Money was an issue there too. The Scottish Area executive sought to centralise financial control by insisting at the beginning of the strike that all donations to the NUM went to Edinburgh. The money was doled out from Gardiner Street in small amounts. Indeed, many of the more active strike centres were in late April dependent on direct donations from other trade unionists for the majority of their funds. For example, one Lothian strike committee, Arniston, had received £1,403 up till 25 April, of which only £600 came from the Area strike committee for pickets' petrol, while the rest came from direct donations.

The other conflict in Scotland was over Ravenscraig. The Triple Alliance agreement caused considerable bitterness among many of the active strikers. 'If you're going to back off, back off, and back off, it's not worth having a strike,' one Lothian miner said. The bitterness was reflected in the support given to an open letter initiated by SWP miners and signed by a number of strike committee members. This called on Mick McGahey 'to come out clearly and publicly with the statement that from NOW ON no coal beyond the minimum required to maintain the furnaces at Ravenscraig will be officially sanctioned.'

The Scottish Area leadership reacted ferociously to the letter. Communist Party members denounced the 'sinister forces' of the SWP at the Lothian joint strike committee. **Socialist Worker** was banned from a number of strike centres in the Lothian and Central Areas. Nevertheless, rank-and-file discontent over the dispensations may have played some part in persuading Mick McGahey to cut down the supply of coal to Ravenscraig at the end of April.

Generally, however, control of the strike was firmly in the hands of the full-time officials. The Yorkshire Area leadership evolved a method, the so-called 'envelope system', which kept the direction of the pickets in the hands of the Barnsley HQ. Each night a sealed letter was sent to every Yorkshire branch telling them where to picket the next day. The system was introduced to prevent the police from learning where the pickets were going in Nottinghamshire, but it put control firmly in the officials' hands. The secrecy made it difficult to campaign openly for mass pickets of strategic targets. Moreover, pickets were often sent to different places each day.

The result was gypsy picketing — the core of activists moving from one place to another. Those miners who were prepared to disobey the instructions would not receive petrol money, and ran the risk of not having the union's legal help if they were arrested. Especially during the battles of Orgreave, the envelope system had disastrous results.

Were the Tories weakening?

Despite the stalemate over steel, the strike had already gone a long way further than the NCB and the government had expected. It had now lasted two months, longer than either of the miners' strikes of 1972 and 1974. Despite vicious press campaigns and policing heavier than any yet seen in an industrial dispute, the Tories had been unable to isolate and crush the militant Areas. Apart from Nottinghamshire, the miners were solid.

There were signs that some on the government side thought it time to back off.

On 23 April Ian MacGregor told the overmen's union NACODS and the coal managers' union that he was prepared to discuss the timescale of the closure programme. There followed some 'shuttle diplomacy' by Labour's energy spokesman, Stan Orme — the Labour leadership were concerned to end the strike because picket-line clashes alienated the floating voters they needed for the next election — and the Coal Board and the miners' executive met on 23 May for the first time since the strike began.

The meeting lasted less than an hour. MacGregor rejected the NUM demand that he call off the closure programme and walked out. But presumably this was for public consumption — for the very next day Jim Cowan, MacGregor's deputy, wrote to the union offering talks on the basis of the 'Plan for Coal'. **The Economist** commented on 26 May:

> The breakdown of Wednesday's talks came after a week of rising expectations that some kind of deal might be patched up. Privately the Coal Board was signalling that it would help construct ladders for Mr Scargill to climb down, without in any way compromising its own plan to close high-cost pits and bring capacity down four per cent in line with demand. It was not to be . . .
>
> Yet the gap between them [the NCB and NUM] . . . appeared very narrow on Wednesday when Mr MacGregor told journalists that he was prepared to be pragmatic about the four million tonnes capacity cut . . . He clearly meant that closures in 1984–5 could now be smaller than the original plan. Partly because of production lost in the past eleven weeks of strikes and nineteen weeks of overtime ban. The board has invited the union to further talks at which, in Mr MacGregor's words, 'the four million tonnes is up for discussion'.[6]

The shift in the Coal Board's stance reflected a change in the government's strategy. As Peter Jenkins emphasised in **The Guardian**, 'every move is their move, every major decision, whether by the police or Mr Ian MacGregor, threads its way back to a member of the cabinet.'[7] Thatcher called Cowan's letter 'a very wise offer'. So why were she and her ministers now prepared to countenance negotiations?

Three factors seem to have been involved. First, there were possible divisions on the Tory side. Peter Jenkins argued that 'peace talk is emanating from what may be called the traditional elements at the National Coal Board. These are the industrial relations specialist managers and the mining engineers.' On the other hand, 'the prime minister and her cabinet are guided by a single paramount consideration: in confrontation with Arthur Scargill and his pickets the elected government must win, win decisively, and be seen to win.'[8]

There was some evidence for this theory, but it does not explain why MacGregor himself adopted a conciliatory approach in May 1984.

A more plausible explanation may be that Thatcher herself was having second thoughts about the strike. As we have already seen, the Tories in all probability did not expect the dispute to escalate into a protracted and intense national confrontation, even if they had made preparations for that eventuality. Already after Scargill's defeat of the NUM right wing in mid-April, some shrewd commentators were sketching out the possibility of a government retreat. Anthony King, an academic advisor to the SDP, wrote:

> Thatcher not only respects power (whether the miners or anyone else's) . . . In the present dispute, Mrs Thatcher has clearly worked out that the NCB has more power than the NUM. Coal stocks are high; the union is divided. The strike will probably not last long. When it peters out, Mr MacGregor will have closed pits and, as a bonus, weakened the union.
>
> But suppose the prime minister has got her sums wrong and the strike becomes economically and politically damaging? . . . then the prime minister will almost certainly signal to the Coal Board that a few pit closures could, after all, be postponed, that there turns out, after all, to be a little slack in the NCB's cash position. [9]

There was, by late May, some evidence that Thatcher had got her sums wrong. The government found itself in the middle of pay negotiations involving power workers, nurses, teachers, water workers, civil servants, railway and postal workers. It therefore faced the danger that other unions might join the miners and open a second front against the Tories.

To this was added the danger that the government's strike-breaking operation might itself provoke other workers to come out on strike. The brief possibility of a Scottish dock strike in mid-May, sparked by ISTC and BSC scabbing at Hunterston, highlighted the risks the Tories were running.

There were also stirrings among Thatcher's opponents on the Tory back benches, the 'wets' led by ex-ministers such as Edward Heath and Francis Pym. Veterans of the strikes of the early 1970s, they were no friends of the miners. But they began to make coded speeches about the strike 'damaging the fabric of society'. They were worried that the government's methods, especially the policing of the strike, might alienate a large and important section of the working class permanently from the state. The British ruling class has always preferred to rule by fraud rather than by force.

There might also be a third, more sinister explanation of the Tory strategy — namely, that Thatcher was playing a double game. In other words, the purpose of the talks might simply have been to string the miners along, softening them up until the government felt confident enough to take the offensive.

On this analysis, Thatcher and MacGregor were the hard cops, ready to rough up the suspect, while the soft cops, the NCB negotiators, offered tea and sympathy. After all, Thatcher had played this game before. In the build-up to the Falklands war, she allowed Francis Pym, then Foreign Secretary, to play the Argentines along with the prospect of negotiations, and then ordered the sinking of the Argentine battleship **General Belgrano**.

In all likelihood, all three factors — internal divisions, a genuine search for compromise, and the velvet glove strategy — were present. Thatcher may well have been uncertain in her own mind about what to do — until the first battle of Orgreave showed that she could, after all, win a decisive victory.

Whatever the truth of these speculations, the talks represented a serious danger to the miners. Had an agreement been made along the lines envisaged in May and June, the closure programme would have been delayed rather than completely abandoned. This would allow MacGregor to resume the attack again whenever the time seemed opportune. It would be very difficult to persuade miners to strike again after all the sacrifices made to achieve an indecisive outcome.

Arthur Scargill seems to have been well aware of this danger. He progressively shifted the focus of the series of talks held between the NUM and the Coal Board to the question of 'uneconomic pits'. It was long-standing policy of the mineworkers' union that pits should be closed only when they had run out of mineable coal reserves. For the government and the NCB, however, the crucial issue was not whether there was any coal left in a pit, but whether it could be extracted profitably. 'Uneconomic' pits, in other words those where the cost of mining coal was too high, should be closed.

The issue was fundamental. Although couched in terms specific to coal mining, it raised a much more general question, that of profitability. Millions of workers in Britain and throughout the world had lost their jobs because it was no longer profitable to employ them. Now the miners were saying that this should stop. It was a challenge to the entire logic of the capitalist economy. If the miners were able to defend 'uneconomic' pits it would be a victory indeed.

The NCB hoped to be able to isolate Scargill within the miners' executive. The right wing were a spent force. But the Board was looking for other elements on the left of the executive who might be more accommodating than Scargill.

All such speculations were, however, rendered idle by the decisive event of the strike — the mass pickets outside Orgreave at the end of May.

Orgreave: the turning point

Pressures from both sides helped to precipitate the battles of Orgreave. The Yorkshire Area's policy of dispensations to the Scunthorpe steelworks was coming under increasing fire. Some of the criticism came from below. At the SWP's initiative an open letter to Arthur Scargill was circulated among Yorkshire miners calling on him to force the Area leaderships in Scotland, Yorkshire, and South Wales to cut off all coal supplies to BSC. Some 250 miners signed the letter. On 22 May several hundred miners took part in an unofficial picket of Scunthorpe which was denounced by the Area strike committee.

It is clear that Scargill himself was pressing Jack Taylor to take some action. A behind-the-scenes conflict between the miners' president and his former close collaborators in the Yorkshire left surfaced publicly during the struggle over Orgreave.

But, as so often during the strike, the initiative that sparked things off came from the other side. The British Steel management at Scunthorpe had insisted on using the coal allowed them by the NUM to continue production, rather than just keep the blast furnaces warm. The quality of coal reaching Scunthorpe had deteriorated dramatically over the previous six weeks as the stocks of prime coking coal in South Yorkshire were used up. The result was a serious deterioration in the two working furnaces, and in the quality of the iron they produced. On 21 May there were two explosions in the Queen Mary's furnace, and a fire.

That same day BSC approached the local ISTC official, Roy Bishop, to demand that they receive 5,000 tonnes of coking coal immediately. Approaches were made to Labour Energy spokesman Stan Orme, and to the Yorkshire NUM. BSC wanted a guaranteed supply of 5,000 tonnes of coking coal a week.

Rather than reject BSC's demands, Jack Taylor promised to raise them at both the Yorkshire and national executive of the NUM. But the Scunthorpe management had observed the successful use of lorry convoys to break the miners' picket lines at Ravenscraig. They decided to organise a similar scab operation, this time to move stocks to Scunthorpe from the Orgreave coking plant near Rotherham.

This decision, like all major moves against the miners, was taken only with Downing Street's approval. **The Observer** reported on 3 June that BSC had 'approached the government early last month for the go-ahead, but it was only two weeks ago that the Cabinet committee looking after the crisis gave British Steel the green light.'

The first scab lorries left Orgreave on Wednesday 23 May. But the Yorkshire NUM leaders were slow to react. Taylor and the Area vice-president, Sammy Thompson, talked to the steel unions in the hope of arriving at a Ravenscraig-style compromise. Meanwhile they continued to send the majority of pickets fruitlessly to Nottingham-shire, dividing the remainder between Orgreave and Scunthorpe.

Nevertheless, the momentum for a mass picket of Orgreave began to build up. Activists in the South Yorkshire pits heard of the scabbing operation around the coke plant and reacted by picketing it unofficially. As one South Yorkshire miner tells:

> They'd started running coke out of Orgreave the previous week. We heard about it from lads who'd inform the South Yorkshire strike centre at Silverwood whenever they saw any coal or coke moving. We went to see what was happening. On the Wednesday pickets who'd returned from Nottingham heard about it and 500 went to Orgreave. The police penned us up against a wall. But some lads got through onto a golf course that runs by the road and bricked lorries as they came off the motorway.

On the Thursday the number picketing rose to about a thousand. Pouring rain deterred militancy on the Friday, but pickets were back in large numbers on the Sunday. Then they were joined by Scargill himself, who called for mass pickets of the coking plant. He repeated the call that evening at a rally for miners from South Kirkby and Frickley collieries. Jack Taylor, who shared the platform with Scargill, studiously avoided mentioning Orgreave. Challenged by activists who said that 15,000 pickets could close the plant, the leader of the biggest NUM Area angrily asked: 'Where do I get 15,000 men from?' There were 50,000 miners in Yorkshire — all of them on strike.

Nevertheless, Taylor was goaded into action. The next day, Monday 28 May, the Yorkshire pickets were sent to Orgreave. There were between two and three thousand of them, heavily outnumbering the police, who seem to have been taken by surprise by the large turn-out. The next day both miners and police were out in force. The result was the greatest violence seen in a British industrial dispute since before the First World War.

The organisation of the picketing at Orgreave that Tuesday gave a glimpse of how the strike could have been won. Every picket in the Yorkshire Area was instructed to be at Orgreave at 7.45 a.m. 'We had a map, instructions where to stand — the best guidance we ever had,' a miner from South Kirkby said afterwards. About five thousand pickets turned up. 'There were people there from South Kirkby we hadn't seen picketing before. It was great.'

The meticulous organisation suggested that Scargill's hand was at work. He took personal charge at the gates of the plant, using a megaphone to direct the pickets as they pushed against the police line. Jack Taylor was also present, but stood at some distance from the picket line, looking on.

The police, this time some five thousand strong, found themselves under serious pressure. The coke works at Orgreave is sited in a hollow through which runs one of the roads between Sheffield and Rotherham. The pickets would assemble on the Sheffield side of the plant, in a housing estate beyond which the roads ran through a railway bridge downhill to the coke works. Between the bridge and

Orgreave: The police horses move in, trapping pickets

the plant the road passes through wheatfields. The police deployed their main force directly in front of the coke works. Mounted police, looking like Civil War cavalry in their riot helmets, were deployed in the field to the right of the road, Alsatian dogs and their handlers to their left. There were more police the other side of the bridge, so that the pickets were surrounded.

Miners as they arrived were forced away from the entrance of the plant, and penned in on a stretch of grass in front of the works on the side of the road. Many pickets simply stood around in this pen. They had spent the previous eleven weeks scattered throughout Nottinghamshire, and had no experience of mass pickets. However, at the end closest to the plant, a minority marshalled by Scargill pushed hard, almost breaking the police line.

The police reacted ferociously. Early in the afternoon, after the lorries had entered the plant, the riot squad, who had been deployed in the main police body in front of the works, were unleashed on the pickets. 'It was like a rugby scrum. The police had their shields up in the air, walloping people with truncheons,' one picket said. A succession of baton charges were made against the pickets — though in one case the police waited until they had passed out of range of a TV camera before drawing their truncheons.

Three of the charges involved mounted as well as foot police. The horsemen went first, followed by foot squads. The mounted police wielded their long riot sticks against the pickets — the first time the sticks had been drawn since anti-Nazi demonstrator Kevin Gately was killed in a mounted police charge in Red Lion Square, London, in June 1974. Two women from the Silverwood miners' support group were among those attacked by mounted police. Police dogs were also used against pickets.

Despite the savagery of the police, and 83 arrests, the miners did not come away from Orgreave that Tuesday disheartened. At last they were using their picketing power against economic targets. Had the picket been sustained and built on, the story of the strike might have been very different. 'Tuesday we were walking on air,' one South Kirkby miner said. Scargill appealed to 'all miners and the whole trade union movement to come here in their thousands.'

But it was not to be. 'Prepare to be disappointed,' a branch official told Silverwood miners that same Tuesday evening. At 3 a.m. the next morning Yorkshire miners received the day's picketing instructions in the sealed envelope from the Area headquarters in Barnsley. They were to go to Nottinghamshire, not Orgreave.

'Sabotage' was one miner's comment.

The decision to divert the pickets to Nottinghamshire was undoubtedly that of Jack Taylor and the Yorkshire Area executive. Scargill himself acknowledged his impotence. When he was asked by flying pickets at Orgreave on Tuesday whether they would be getting help from Scotland and Wales, he replied: 'Each Area has its own autonomy. Unfortunately, I don't have the reins.'

Scargill went to Orgreave that Wednesday morning. Arriving at

Orgreave:
The police
charge

about 7.45 a.m., he found perhaps a hundred pickets there, many of them from outside Yorkshire. Armed with his megaphone, he marshalled about half of them — the rest refused to join in, saying they should wait till more pickets turned up — and led them to where the miners had stood the day before. The senior police officer, Chief Superintendent John Nesbitt, ordered Scargill to move. Scargill refused, and was eventually arrested.

A total of about eight hundred miners eventually went to Or-

greave that day, many after having been turned back by police road blocks in Nottinghamshire. The afternoon saw more fighting, but this time the police had the whip hand.

Some pickets were chased up the road by mounted police and into a brick yard. Riot police pushed them up against a wall and started beating them. Naturally enough the miners defended themselves with whatever came to hand. One of them recalled later:

Ogreave:
Pickets attempt
to break police
lines

A big lad came along and told us to stop bricking. He stood in front of the cops so that if we chucked any more bricks we'd hit him. Suddenly the wall of riot shields opened up and he was dragged in. We could see him on the ground with boots and truncheons going into him.

Orgreave that day saw miners forced by the police violence to abandon the pacifism so deeply rooted in the British labour move-

ment. The scenes — a barricade was built to block the police charges — were more reminiscent of the 1981 inner-city riots than of a picket line. But despite the militancy, the decision to send the pickets to Nottinghamshire had shifted the balance of forces in the state's favour. There were 35 arrests.

The Yorkshire NUM headquarters at Barnsley instructed the Yorkshire pickets to go to Nottinghamshire that Thursday and Friday as well. On Thursday 1,500 miners defied these instructions and went to Orgreave anyway. They pushed at the police lines when the lorry convoys went in and out. But they were directionless. Scargill, once he had been released on bail on Wednesday afternoon, did not return to the picket line that week. To judge by what he said on leaving Barnsley Magistrates' Court, his eyes were now fixed on the talks with the NCB: 'This dispute must be brought to a swift conclusion.' Heathfield too had made his priorities clear on Tuesday evening, declaring: 'I hope we shall be able to lay the foundations of a settlement.'

But it takes two to tango. A settlement would depend on the Tories', as well as the NUM's, willingness to settle. The government and the Coal Board seem to have been drifting towards some sort of compromise. Orgreave transformed the situation. The police had got away with beating up hundreds of miners and arresting Arthur Scargill in the heart of the Yorkshire coalfield, near Sheffield, one of the great centres of the British labour movement.

All the signs are that the Tories scented blood after the first big battle at Orgreave. If they could get away with what they had done there, then they could realistically plan to inflict a decisive defeat on the miners as an example to the rest of the trade union movement. Should power station coal stocks run dangerously low, then the same sort of combination of riot police and scab lorry drivers used at Ravenscraig and Orgreave could be employed to shift the coal stockpiled at the pitheads.

Suddenly the stakes had been sharply raised. On 30 May, the day Scargill was arrested, Thatcher made a speech in Banbury declaring 'the rule of law must prevail over the rule of the mob,' and backing the police riot at Orgreave. Two days later she told an interviewer that she did 'not see an immediate end' to the strike.[10]

On 12 June **The Times** published an interview with Ian MacGregor which torpedoed hopes that the issues might be fudged. 'Uneconomic' pits would have to close, he said, though the surviving miners would be better paid. Ominously he spoke of 'regaining the

Orgreave: Mounted police hunt down pickets

management of the industry', implying an end to consultation with the NUM at all levels.

The interview spelled out what the miners were up against — the logic of world capitalism:

> I think the only thing the government is interested in is seeing this business run properly and by that I mean that its resources are exploited in such a way that it is a positive contribution to our economy rather than a drain. That is all the politics I know of. I am not one of your local characters. I don't vote here — I vote in Florida.

The NUM reacted angrily. Scargill accused MacGregor of being 'intent on butchering this industry'. The miners' leaders were further infuriated to learn that the NCB were thinking of organising their own pithead ballot. The day after the MacGregor interview was published, talks between the NUM and the Coal Board broke up acrimoniously.

The Economist was in no doubt that Downing Street was responsible:

> Why did Mr MacGregor change tactics and speak out? The Coal Board, improbably, denies there was any pressure from the government. Officials say they wanted to disabuse wavering miners who might have thought that concessions were around the corner. But ministers have been growing worried that Mr Scargill was going to get a deal that he could trumpet as a victory. The government wants to be seen to have broken the legendary power of the miners.[11]

The collapse of negotiations cut off the NUM soft left's escape route. It came at a time when the divisions between Scargill and the rest of the left officials were coming into the open. On 7 June, six days before the talks were broken off, thousands of miners had marched through London to lobby parliament. The police attack on the march — 120 arrests were made — brought the war in the coalfields on to the streets of the capital.

Scargill had told the lobby: 'I'd dearly love to see every member of the NUM and every trade unionist down at Orgreave.' Resentment towards him among the Yorkshire officials deepened. A notice was posted up at NUM headquarters in Barnsley: 'All deployment of pickets is done by the Yorkshire Area Strike Organising Committee. Pickets are only to be deployed to targets authorised by them. Any requests for pickets from National Office or other Areas to be referred to the Co-ordinating Committee.' The decision by the union's delegate conference to vest control of the strike in the national officers of the union was a dead letter. Taylor called off the remaining pickets at Orgreave.

Scargill had also clashed with Emlyn Williams, the South Wales NUM president, who attacked his calls for an end to the dispensations to British Steel. 'I run South Wales,' Williams told the media, 'no one else.' On 12 June the South Wales NUM guaranteed Llanwern two dozen trainloads of coal a week.

But the following day, once the government had torpedoed the talks, the Area leaders were forced to shift their ground. Almost overnight they did an about-turn. Meeting on 14 June, the national executive decided to end all dispensations to the steel industry. At the Yorkshire miners' gala in Wakefield that weekend Jack Taylor made a fighting speech. The Coal Board had just been playing a 'game', 'raising the miners up, and then dropping us down again.' In future, there must be 'no secret meetings, no sell-outs and no secret deals.'

This new tough line was soon put to the test, once again at Orgreave. The Yorkshire NUM mobilised 5,000 pickets to the coking plant on Monday 18 June. Again Scargill was there. An orgy of police violence followed.

The police were under heavy pressure, pushed hard by the pickets. One miner described the situation:

> The police reserves kept fanning in to back up the people in front. The police were bunched together 15–20 rows deep. It was very hot and the police were heavily dressed in their riot gear. They were fainting in the ranks, dropping like ninepins. So they started truncheoning us. Before at Orgreave the pickets were let to push. This time two rows back the police were truncheoning pickets. The first three or four rows of pickets got truncheoned. So they started bricking.

Meanwhile about a thousand miners had got into the plant itself from the back. The pump house was attacked and railway waggons full of coal were opened up and immobilised. One of them tells:

> The police sent in squads, there was a little battle. But the police realised they were outnumbered and simply tried to shunt pickets away from the plant. But the majority of the pickets in the plant went on to move against the rear of the main police lines. The police were now sandwiched and under increasing pressure. Any reinforcements they tried to get through were bombarded with bricks and held back.
>
> The main police line was pushed until it was only 200 yards from the main body of pickets. If the main body had charged forward the police line would have been broken and the plant shut. This didn't happen because those with megaphones among the main body of pickets never gave the order.

The incident shows that mass pickets could have beaten the police at Orgreave — especially if the momentum of that day had been built on to get even greater numbers of pickets out the next day. During these offensives by the miners against the police lines, there were very few pickets hurt by the police, or arrests. These came later in the day, as a miner described:

> Then the lorries went out. Normally there was a lull. Lots of people went into the village for a drink. Then when they came back, the police had advanced their line a couple of hundred

yards. People wandered back, and met people like something out of Doomwatch in black masks and overalls.

The riot squads ran amock, flailing with shields and truncheons, and backed up by horsemen. 'They were out to maim,' one miner said, 'not to arrest.' Another miner said:

There weren't many arrests at the time. People got arrested when they went to hospital. One lad was surrounded by horses and beaten to the ground. I tried to talk him to go to hospital. But when we got there we were told not to go in — they were arresting injured miners.

Among those taken to hospital was Arthur Scargill. Tony Clements, Assistant Chief Constable for South Yorkshire, claimed that Scargill had slipped and banged his head on a railway sleeper. A miner from Silverwood described what really happened:

Late on the coppers were pushing us back with cavalry and riot police charges. Some lads were throwing stones. Arthur came down to tell them not to be so stupid and that we need numbers to beat the police. Then he stood on the side of the road, on a small hill, and the riot cops charged again. People legged it. I saw two coppers go up to Arthur. He got a knock with a shield, then I saw batons in the air. I couldn't see any more — I was legging it myself.

This second battle of Orgreave could have been the beginning of a real attempt to win the strike by mass picketing. But the next day the pickets were again sent elsewhere.

There were no more mass pickets of Orgreave after 18 June, but at least mass picketing had been tried there. This could not be said for South Wales or Scotland.

Scargill had persuaded the transport unions to agree to a blockade of power stations and a restriction of BSC's coal supplies on 7 June. The move had the advantage of taking some of the initiative away from the Area unions. On 18 June the Scottish Triple Alliance decided to halt the supply of coal to Ravenscraig — and BSC restarted its road convoys of scab lorries.

In South Wales railwaymen blocked the supply of coal and coke to Llanwern. Then the transport unions threatened to block all supplies of iron ore to BSC to force the steel unions to agree to cut steel production. But talks between the ISTC and the NUM on 29 June ended without agreement — and the TUC steel committee backed ISTC leader Bill Sirs, declaring that 'it would not be practicable to accede to the NUM's request.'

The miners and their allies responded by carrying out their threat to cut off iron ore as well as coal to the steel plants. Railwaymen refused to take their trains across NUM picket lines. BSC mounted an enormous scab operation to move the coal and ore to Ravenscraig and Llanwern by road. By 3 July convoys involving 100 lorries a day were running between Port Talbot and Llanwern.

Kim Howells, a research officer for South Wales NUM who spent much of the strike talking to the media on the union's behalf, argued later that the lorry operation was unbeatable by mass picketing:

Challenging lines of single-minded and well-equipped policemen . . . had already been tried in most spectacular fashion at Orgreave . . . It never succeeded in stopping a single lorry nor a scab and taught us in South Wales a good deal about what to do to win friends and influence people during industrial disputes.[12]

The truth was rather different. The South Wales NUM responded to the lorry convoys to Llanwern by mounting only *token* pickets. **The Times** reported on 23 June: 'The South Wales miners' leaders concluded that they had no need to mobilise their flying

Orgreave: At the end of the day

pickets after their researchers had calculated that the corporation could not possibly maintain supplies to the plant by lorry convoys.'

The researchers calculated wrong. Howells, whose own research department made this brilliant prognosis, admitted six months later: 'By October, the steelmen were receiving over twenty thousand tonnes of coal and coke a week — over twice the amount we'd allowed them before the total "blockade" had been declared.'[13]

The reality was that the South Wales miners' leaders were opposed to mass pickets, and did not use them to enforce the blockade of Llanwern. The same was true of the Scottish NUM, which made no attempt to repeat the mass picketing of Ravenscraig in May.

The lessons of Orgreave

In the wake of the police riot at Orgreave, many people were sympathetic to the argument that the police were now unbeatable. The miners had tried to use the methods of 1972, and had failed. But those who argued thus forgot two things.

First, in 1972 the flying pickets had concentrated their forces on successive targets until the movement of coal and other fuels had been blocked at each site. The way in which the Yorkshire NUM organised pickets in 1984 rendered such an approach impossible. Under the 'envelope system' miners were sent to different targets each day. Taylor and the rest of the Yorkshire Area leadership refused to campaign openly and consistently for a mass picket of Orgreave — even at the Wakefield Gala two days before the second battle of Orgreave on 18 June.

Secondly, the decisive use of flying pickets in 1972 was, of course, at Saltley. But, in Scargill's words, 'the working class closed Saltley,' not the miners. Miners toured Birmingham factories and won an unofficial strike by 100,000 engineering workers, 20,000 of whom joined the miners' picket line at Saltley.

No effort was made at Orgreave to apply this, the most important lesson of Saltley. The first battle of Orgreave was in late May, when most steel and engineering workers in Sheffield and Rotherham were on a week's holiday. But had the Yorkshire miners' leaders campaigned consistently to build the Orgreave picket over a number of days, or even weeks, miners could have been taken round the Sheffield engineering factories to appeal for delegations to join their picket line. Engineering workers who saw the police violence for themselves might then have been willing to mount sympathy action.

Instead, the Yorkshire miners' leaders preferred to rely on spectacular, one-off pickets, and on their connections with full-time officials in other unions. As one Silverwood miner said: 'They wanted to arrange everything between the ISTC and the NUM. They're happy to keep the rank and file passive, keeping all the decisions themselves.'

It remains to explain why it was that the Yorkshire NUM leaders, and their counterparts in other left-wing Areas, behaved so disastrously. They were neither knaves nor fools, but, in the main, dedicated socialists, on the left wing of the Labour Party or in the Communist Party. Many of them had played an active part in the rank-and-file militancy of the late 1960s and early 1970s. What had gone wrong?

Three factors were involved. First, the Yorkshire left in particular had changed. In the early 1970s, they were in opposition to the right-wing Area and national leaderships. They were, in the main, rank-and-file activists, holding office at branch level, if at all. Now they were part of the union bureaucracy.

In power, Jack Taylor and the rest came more and more to identify with the interests of the union machine rather than with the miners they were supposed to represent. Despite the Area's enormous assets (£8 million at the beginning of the strike), they grudged the money needed to sustain effective flying pickets. Their whole strategy had become one of reliance on manoeuvres at the top, treating ordinary miners like a stage army.

Secondly, class collaboration was embedded in the politics of the NUM left. Like the left wing of the trade union bureaucracy generally, they were supporters of the 'alternative economic strategy' — using the power of the state to shore up the British economy. As many of its specific measures showed — notably import controls — the strategy presumed the existence of a common British 'national interest' uniting workers and capitalists against their foreign rivals.

The miners' Area leaders, especially in Scotland and South Wales, had devoted considerable energy to campaigns, often organised with the regional TUCs, to defend their local economies. They had come to see these campaigns as the only effective way of defending their members' jobs. They had lost sight of the fact that Scotland and Wales, not to speak of England, were part of a world economic system controlled by a small minority. The mines and the steelworks belonged, not to those who worked in them, but to the capitalist class.

Class collaboration was deeply rooted in the miners' union itself.

Ever since nationalisation, the NUM had been involved in a ramified system of co-operation with the Coal Board. Even Arthur Scargill, a formidable critic of 'workers' participation' because of its use to co-opt workers' leaders, based his opposition to the closure of high-cost pits on the 1974 Plan for Coal, whose evident aim was to draw the NUM into shared responsibility for running the industry with the Coal Board. The same attitudes were expressed more crudely by other miners' leaders. Jack Taylor, for example, declared: 'Even if he [MacGregor] won this dispute outright, he would lose everything. After all, he can't run a coal industry without the NUM . . . The one thing they can't do is run a successful coal industry on their own.'[14]

There was a third factor. There were two main currents in the NUM left. The first was predominant in Yorkshire, and consisted largely of left-wing members of the Labour Party — Scargill, Heathfield, Taylor and Briscoe, for example. The other was the Communist Party, still, despite its decline, a powerful force in South Wales, Scotland and Kent — though there were important Labour left-wingers in these Areas — Emlyn Williams, for example, and the Scottish NUM general secretary, Eric Clarke.

The Communist Party began, in the early months of the strike, to develop a critique of 'Scargillism' — that is, of reliance on the methods of 1972, above all, of mass picketing. In line with its general rightward or 'Eurocommunist' evolution, the Communist Party argued that the NUM should eschew industrial confrontation, and instead build a 'broad democratic alliance'.

Thus, after the collapse of Mick McGahey's attempt to reduce the flow of coal into Ravenscraig, Peter Carter, the Communist Party's industrial organiser, praised the NUM's 'great and generous concession'. He continued:

But trade union solidarity alone, important though it is, is not enough. A wider public support has to be won to support the miners. It would be dangerous and sectarian to think that a major industrial dispute of this character can be won by industrial muscle alone, even in the face of hostile public opinion . . . Any projection of the strike as a political strike aimed at bringing the government down will be of no help to the miners — quite the reverse.[15]

Carter's alternative was that the miners should concentrate on 'winning wide sympathy . . . building a broad alliance around their

objectives'. George Bolton, Scottish NUM vice-president, spelled out
what this alternative strategy involved a few months later:

> I'm not opposed to mass picketing. The mass pickets are a very
> important weapon in our armoury. What I would argue is that
> you must think very carefully when and how you use it . . . The
> goverment and the board have consistently tried to contain the
> argument to the question of mass pickets, violence and law and
> order; and they have avoided like the plague any discussion of
> what the dispute is all about. Their strategy has been to pin us
> down on the law and order question. That tells you that they
> have a real fear of a mass understanding by the British people of
> what the dispute is all about . . .
>
> A very good example is Ken Livingstone and the GLC.
> He's winning his case because he's finding it possible to talk
> politically in a mass way, and demonstrating in practice that the
> people are backing him and not the Tory government . . . I
> happen to think the question of the culture and the arts is very
> important. We need to try and get the world of entertainment
> identified with us, not least because they get mass audiences.[16]

How a few rock concerts would cow a government which respects
only power, and which had shown itself absolutely determined to
crush the miners, Bolton did not explain. But one thing is crystal
clear: the miners were being led by men unwilling to mobilise their
members' full strength. The only significant exception was Arthur
Scargill himself.

This failure of leadership explains the debacle of Orgreave. The
two battles outside the coke works marked the turning point of the
strike, just as Saltley gates had in 1972. This time, however, the ruling
class won.

5
SOLIDARITY AND BUREAUCRACY

AFTER the Great Miners' Strike ended in March 1985, the Tories were quick to claim that the miners had failed because other workers had refused to support them. Strangely enough, the trade union leaders' explanation of the strike's defeat was exactly the same: their rank-and-file members, they said, had been unwilling to take the solidarity action demanded by the miners.

This was the line taken, for example, by Ron Todd, general secretary-elect of the biggest and traditionally most left-wing union, the Transport and General Workers. He told a solidarity rally towards the end of the strike:

> Don't pretend that we have got an army out there straining at the leash — because we haven't . . . Some of them [rank-and-file trade unionists] put the Tories into power . . . You can't make a backbone out of wishbone.[1]

The reality is somewhat different. Rank-and-file trade unionists displayed considerable solidarity with the miners, sometimes in the form of industrial action, more often in the form of donations of food and money. However, their leaders refused to build on this support, and left the miners to fight on alone.

Rank-and-file solidarity

Throughout the strike there were acts of solidarity which shone through the platitudes, rhetoric and conscience money that were the currency of the trade union leaders.

Pride of place must go to the railway workers of Coalville in Leicestershire. From 3 April 1984 until the end of the strike, they sealed off the working Leicestershire coalfield. The only time the British Rail management got trains out of the Leicestershire pits was when they imported scabs from out of the area to drive the trains and operate signal boxes. Throughout the strike, there were more railway workers backing the NUM in the Leicestershire coalfield than there were miners. They suffered enormous harassment for sticking to trade union principles.

Roy Butlin, secretary of the Coalville NUR branch, told the Mineworkers Defence Committee solidarity conference in December 1984:

> My members at Coalville have not moved any coal by rail in the Leicestershire coalfield for 35 weeks. There were times in the long summer months when we seemed to be the only trade unionists doing anything. We're in the middle of a working coalfield, but we've been holding back half the production from Leicestershire. Virtually every pub and club [in Coalville] has barred us. Of the 19 Labour councillors, 13 are scabs and two are the wives of scabs.

In September 1984, British Rail threatened to close down the Coalville rail depot within a few weeks if the blacking wasn't lifted. On the same evening they issued the ultimatum, British Transport police burst into the homes of seven active supporters of the blacking campaign, looking for 'railway property'. Three men were sacked as a result for 'stealing' a few bars of soap or having a few British Rail cloths.

'The British Rail Board state there's no connection between the arrests and the fact we're not moving coal, even though the police raids were on the same evening as the closure threat!' said Roy Butlin. The Coalville NUR men demanded national action from their union against these victimisations: 'We pleaded with the NUR headquarters in London for some national action in support of the miners and the reply has been: "don't escalate it".'

Unsupported, the Coalville railway men held firm.

Then just before Christmas 1984, British Rail declared one railway worker 'mentally unstable' and removed him from duty. 'It was the dirtiest possible trick,' said Roy Butlin, 'but it gave them a clear line between Bagworth pit and Drakelow power station. We've been patient, waiting for our leaders to do something, but all we've had is assurances that they'd talk to British Rail. I think they are scared of sequestration if it goes further . . . But we want industrial action.'

The signalman was eventually transferred to another box. British Rail was claiming he was 'mentally unstable' and unfit for work, yet they moved him from a goods-only line to a passenger line, just to get him out of the way of the coal trains.

The Coalville men wanted a 24-hour rail strike to warn British Rail against further victimisations and intimidation of those blacking coal. The ASLEF and the NUR executives were forced by rank-and-file pressure to call some action — but limited it to railway workers in the Midland and Eastern regions. 'They are asking the depots that have suffered the most to take a day's strike,' said Roy Butlin. 'The leadership couldn't get away with doing nothing, so they have done the minimum . . .'

It was a spineless response to union members who had given everything to maintain their solidarity with the miners, and other railway workers recognised it by taking unofficial action in support of Coalville.

Police arrest a miner lobbying parliament, June 1984

Of course the Coalville men weren't the only railworkers to deliver real solidarity for the miners. Hardly any coal moved by railway during the strike. Train drivers and guards from the Shirebrook depot, which served eleven North Nottinghamshire pits, and signalmen at Worksop reduced the flow of coal to the Trent Valley power stations from 400,000 tons per week to around 60,000 tons. A Shirebrook NUR official described the pressure they were under to lift the blacking:

> There were threats of sacking, a massive propaganda campaign and British Transport police at the depot — sometimes up to thirty officers in full riot gear. There were even police horses sometimes. The signalmen at Worksop who were blacking coal were visited by management daily and threatened with the sack. They were also taken to the power stations to see the lorry convoys taking in coal and were told that all the jobs would be lost.

Another example of action by railworkers was when ASLEF drivers and NUR guards halted Charing Cross station in London on 7 June after police had stopped an NUM lobby from reaching parliament. The railworkers were angered when police beat up an ASLEF official, John Davies.

All honour to the Coalville railworkers who refused to move coal, but the leadership of the NUR and ASLEF failed to use the resilience of these workers to help the miners effectively. Instead they instructed their members to let head office know when they were sent home from the job for refusing to move coal, so that the union could pay their wages — and ASLEF spent some £250,000 on this, when they should have called all railworkers out in protest. Early in April some railworkers in the North West refused to move coal and were sent home, and the rank and file spontaneously walked out, threatening to bring out signalmen at Warrington, which would have stopped all rail traffic to the North West, including Liverpool and Manchester. The support was there if the rail union leaders had been willing to lead.

The determination of the railworkers who stuck by the miners throughout the strike was remarkable. But the most spectacular acts of solidarity took place in Fleet Street at **The Sun**, which was twice closed when printers blacked the most hysterical and blatant lies it told about the miners.

When editor Kelvin McKenzie proposed to produce a particularly obnoxious front page on 16 May, showing a picture of Scargill with his arm raised under the headline 'Mine Führer', all the chapels (with the significant exception of the journalists) refused to handle the page. The production unions then closed **The Sun** completely for three days after McKenzie refused to print a half-page statement of support to coincide with the South East Regional TUC's Day of Action on 27 June.

At the end of September the paper was closed again after the printers had objected to a headline and editorial calling miners the 'scum of the earth'. An NGA official at the paper explained:

> We were prepared to print it, in its entirety, provided the print unions could add a disclaimer. The management refused, so we asked for equal space for the NUM to reply, or even a paid advert on page two. All they told us was to write a letter, which they would consider for publication — but there was no guarantee.

So the printworkers closed the paper.

The strikes at **The Sun** and blacking by railworkers were the most significant solidarity actions, but far from the only ones. A sizeable minority of trade unionists showed their support for the miners by taking part in regional days of action in solidarity with the NUM in the late spring and summer of 1984.

Many other trade unionists did not feel strong enough to take industrial action, even for a day. But there were other ways in which they could help the miners, above all by collecting food and money for the mining communities. The second month of the strike began to see a growth in miners' support groups, which sprang up in the major urban centres, and spread rapidly throughout the country in the summer.

Much of the impetus behind the miners' support groups came from Labour Party activists. Many constituency Labour Party members were disgusted by Neil Kinnock's fence-sitting. They swung whole-heartedly behind the miners. Their activities were given some legitimacy by a decision at the end of April by the Labour Party's national executive to impose a weekly levy of 50p a head on Labour Party members for the NUM. Typically, the executive did nothing to implement this resolution, leaving it to local activists to give meaning to their words.

Some indication of the scale of the solidarity activity three months into the strike is given by the June issue of the left-wing magazine **London Labour Briefing**. This reported work going on in South London, Greenwich, Redbridge, Newham, Lewisham, Camden, Tower Hamlets, Ealing, Haringey, Hackney, Islington, Croydon and Brent. A national supplement carried reports about the activities of miners' support groups in Birmingham, Exeter, North Staffs, Manchester, Southampton, Cardiff, Brighton, Swansea, Caerphilly and Preston.

The scale of activity was considerable. Tony Benn told a meeting at the Labour Party conference on 29 September that £150,000 had been spent in Chesterfield supporting the miners. 'We have replaced the DHSS,' he said. Chesterfield was, of course, in the heart of the North Derbyshire coalfield, but there were remarkable achievements far from the pits. Dennis Skinner told the same meeting that Tooting Labour Party in South London had raised £20,000. 'That's a challenge,' he said: 'be Tooting!'

The work of the local Labour Parties and the miners' support groups was geographically based. There was, however, an active minority of trade unionists who sought to collect for the miners at work. The Socialist Workers Party organised workplace collections from the very start of the strike. But the work was done by many far beyond the ranks of the organised left.

One of the most imaginative efforts was made, once again, in the heart of Fleet Street's lie machine. In August the NGA and SOGAT printworkers' chapels at the **News of the World** and **The Sun** produced a 'Right to Reply Special'. The sixteen-page paper sought both to reflect the experience of miners and their families, and to explain why printworkers supported their cause. 10,000 were sold, at 50p each, and another 2,000 were given to the NUM free.

The chapels also adopted a pit, Birch Coppice in Staffordshire, and collected £500 a week for the mining community there. John Breen, deputy father of the **News of the World** compositors' chapel, told **Socialist Worker**: 'To be quite honest, I know there are people here who won't send money to the NUM to be used for [pickets'] petrol, but they will give money to miners' wives and kids. That's something they feel they can identify with.'[2]

Twinning — the direct linking of a particular trade union branch or workplace with a pit — began to be widely adopted in the summer and autumn of 1984. Groups of trade unionists began to start regularly visiting the pit villages, creating a network of rank-and-file links between the miners and the rest of the working-class movement.

One early example was again in Fleet Street. Workers at Reuters press agency, who were collecting about £50 a week as well as food and clothing, started to visit Blidworth colliery in Nottinghamshire. As

Doug Shaw of Reuters explained:

Meeting other workers who are giving them support provides a tremendous morale booster for the strikers. Added to that, the visits have stepped up the political level of the people who make the journey. Every time we go we try to take at least two what we call 'neutrals' — people who aren't necessarily socialists and who might have some doubts about the strike. It's these people who are really changed by the experience. When we first went up there they were just stunned by the numbers of police in the village.[3]

These links help to explain why Fleet Street trade unionists collected an estimated £2 million for the miners.

Even in the steel industry, there was considerable support for the NUM. Tommy Cassidy was branch secretary of the Templeborough No. 1 ISTC branch in Rotherham until his union credentials were removed. He told **Socialist Worker** on 1 December 1984: 'I've been charged with "discrediting the union". My only crime is supporting the miners and behaving like a proper trade unionist.'

Workers from Kelloggs in Manchester deliver food and money to a miners' kitchen in Pontefract

Tommy Cassidy had raised £14,000 for the miners from his members by the time he was barred from office. He told local miners that some steelworks were only working a three-day week to prevent electricity cuts — important news for miners who were being told day after day that their strike wasn't biting. And he spoke out for the miners at the ISTC conference. Tommy explained why he'd been able to raise so much money from steelworkers despite the attempts by management, the press, the union officials and Labour leaders to set miner against steelworker.

No steelworker anywhere wants the miners to lose. We all know there's thousands more jobs to go in the industry and if the miners win we've a better chance of success. Of course, we should really be fighting alongside the miners, not hoping that they would go away.

The solidarity movement grew to astonishing proportions. Doreen Massey and Hilary Wainwright tried to summarise its scale early in 1985:

The support from the cities has been massive. On Merseyside there are fourteen support groups, which between them have sent off £1 million (a *million* pounds — from a city itself in desperate poverty), and that's not including workplace collections, and new groups are still being formed. There are normally fifty to sixty miners out in the city centre. From Birmingham support goes to South Wales, and also to other more local coalfields. From London it has gone to Kent, South Wales, Staffordshire and the North East; individual boroughs and support groups have twinning arrangements with pits in many different coalfields. There are people with buckets, collections of food, on high streets everywhere, an anarchy of support groups and what appear to be a number of different attempts to form umbrella organisations.[4]

Support extended far beyond the big cities, natural opponents of Toryism, to 'Thatcherland' — the relatively affluent south and east. The miners' support groups in Cambridge and Milton Keynes, for example, collected respectively around £600 and £800 a week.

Thus, as the strike wore on, a great movement of solidarity gathered round the miners. When it was all over, **The Guardian** estimated that perhaps as much as £60 million was collected. This figure alone gives the lie to the claim that the miners had no support among other workers. A large minority of trade unionists not only sympathised with the miners' cause, but were willing to take some sort of action in their support.

The only question was whether the union leaders were prepared to give some positive direction to this movement.

Official inaction

The trade union leaders publicly reacted to the miners' strike depending on where they fell in the left-right divide within the TUC. The right-wing unions generally spurned the NUM's appeals for help. Bill Sirs, as we have seen, cheerfully encouraged his members to handle scab coal.

The predominantly right-wing power workers' leaders were equally hostile. For example, on 14 April John Lyons, general secretary of the power engineers union (EMA), turned down a request from NUM general secretary Peter Heathfield that the power unions black the movement of coal.

These reactions were predictable enough. The left-led unions were, in formal terms, much more positive. The three rail unions (NUR, ASLEF and TSSA) voted on 29 March along with the Transport and General Workers Union and the seafarers' union (NUS) to block completely the movement of coal. A co-ordinating committee was set up at the TGWU headquarters, Transport House.

The rail unions and the NUS made the most serious efforts to implement this decision. The NUR executive instructed its members to black all coal on 2 April. The seafarers' union issued similar orders the next day. Its members halted coal from being shipped from the Durham and Northumberland pits to the south-eastern power stations until near the end of the strike. The railworkers' efforts had a serious impact. The **Financial Times** reported on 27 February 1985, very late in the strike:

> At present BR is handling about a third of the 600,000 to 700,000 tonnes of coal available per week to be moved. Only 40 coal trains are moving a day out of a possible 300, with 40 to 200 staff suspended daily for refusing to move coal.

The biggest of the left unions, the TGWU, was much less successful. One of the union's most important groups was the lorry drivers, who had in 1979 punched an enormous hole in the Labour government's 'Social Contract'. But TGWU general secretary Moss

Evans admitted afterwards that the miners' strike exposed union organisation in the road haulage industry as 'abysmal'. TGWU members were heavily involved in moving scab coal and iron ore to the steel plants. At the beginning of July, George Wright, the union's South Wales regional secretary, revealed that two-thirds of the scab lorry drivers servicing Llanwern were TGWU members.

Solidarity action by the official trade union machine was at best limited, even on the left. What none of the union leaders were prepared to do was link the miners' strike to issues affecting their own members' direct interests.

Yet early 1984 had seen a stirring among trade unionists far beyond the pits. There were signs of a new mood of militancy among a minority of workers, shown by the considerable support for the national day of action in protest against the ban on unions at GCHQ in Cheltenham. Over a million trade unionists struck, many of them in the engineering and car industries which had been so severely battered by mass redundancies in the previous five years.

There was more to this new mood than anger at Thatcher's arrogance. The British economy experienced in 1983–4 a limited recovery from the depths of the recession. In some industries, workers found that they had greater bargaining power: management, with larger order books, were forced to make concessions in order to keep production going.

BL's Austin Rover car plants at Longbridge and Cowley had experienced one of the toughest management offensives of the 1970s and early 1980s. The improved financial position of Austin Rover now helped to provoke a counter-offensive by the shop floor in early 1984. Cowley experienced a rash of 'downers' — short, sharp, unofficial strikes. In early May Longbridge workers won what one shop steward called 'the first clean factory-wide victory we've had for a long time' when they forced management to abandon plans to reduce manning levels. A month later the plant was closed down again in protest against the sacking of a black driver for punching a racist foreman. Although this strike was defeated, Austin Rover workers were clearly no longer cowed into submission.

There were other disputes of this nature, reflecting workers' greater confidence. British Aerospace's plant at Filton, near Bristol, was paralysed in the summer and early autumn by a ten-week dispute during which two groups of workers occupied parts of the factory. Teachers displayed the first serious wage militancy for ten years or more. Spurred by the effects of the public spending cuts, and an insulting 3 per cent wage offer, they massively supported the programme of selective action decided upon by the NUT conference in April.

The strike figures reflected this new mood. There were 26,564,000 strike-days in 1984, the third highest figure in British history. The miners' strike accounted for the bulk of the working days 'lost' — a mammoth 22,265,000. But the remaining 4,299,000 strike-days are still an increase of more than 26 per cent compared with 1983. Even more impressive is the rise in the number of workers involved in work stoppages outside mining — 1,137,000 in 1984, more than twice the 1983 total of 451,400. The number of strike-days in the crucial metals, engineering and vehicles sector shot up from 1,420,000 in 1983 to 2,024,000, the highest figure in five years.

The situation therefore presented the government with serious dangers once it became clear that the miners' strike was unlikely to collapse quickly. By late April the strike had spilled into the middle of the public sector pay round. Although the Tories had been careful to avoid imposing uniform wage norms in the public sector of the sort which brought Heath and Callaghan down, they ran the risk of provoking a major group of workers to join the miners on strike.

This was especially true of industries where Thatcher had in any case planned to attack. The miners were simply the most important group to be the objects of a concerted government offensive. Crucially, the railworkers were another. In 1981–2, the train drivers had bitterly resisted British Rail's attempts to impose flexible rostering on them. When the rail unions submitted their pay claim in January 1984 BR chairman Bob Reid told them that any wage increase was conditional on their acceptance of major productivity increases — in particular the introduction of one-man trains.

With the miners on strike the situation was transformed. The two manual rail unions, the NUR and ASLEF, were led by left-wing officials. The railways saw the most sustained and significant solidarity action with the miners. Now the rail union leaders, Jimmy Knapp of the NUR and Ray Buckton of ASLEF, reacted to the Rail Board's hard line by calling a ban on overtime and rest-day working from 30 May. Arthur Scargill appealed to the rail unions to come out on strike and open a second front against the Tories.

He had reckoned without the political skill of the government, and the timidity of the left trade union leaders. Thatcher was pursuing a coherent class strategy. Her aim was to beat the miners, and in doing so force the entire trade union movement onto the defensive. Like any good general, she knew that it was essential to concentrate all her forces on one main target, and to avoid fighting on more than one front at the same time.

So the Tories did all they could to isolate the miners. This implied two things in particular. First, the government avoided using the Employment Acts against the NUM in the early months of the strike, resisting pressure from the Tory right wing, and, after Orgreave, from SDP leader David Owen. The reason was simple, as the **Sunday Times** explained: 'A legal action could have caused the escalation the [Coal] Board have so far managed to avoid — and drag in support from mining areas and trade unions which have not given it up to now.'[6]

Secondly, the Tories showed themselves willing to make concessions to other groups of workers in order to keep the miners isolated. Whatever they conceded could, after all, be clawed back in the climate of demoralisation likely to follow a defeat for the NUM. This strategy was essentially a continuation of the 'salami tactics' Thatcher had used against workers since 1979, avoiding, as the Ridley report had advised, confrontations except in circumstances where they could be sure of winning.

The clearest case was that of the rail unions. Government documents leaked to Paul Foot and published in the **Daily Mirror** on 6 June 1984 revealed that pay negotiations between British Rail and the unions were orchestrated from Downing Street. British Rail chairman Bob Reid was first instructed to spin the talks out as long as possible. When the unions retaliated with their threat of an overtime ban, **Daily Mirror** industrial editor Geoffrey Goodman described what happened:

> By early May the Rail Board was prepared to face industrial action . . . Bob Reid warned the unions that he was determined to have greater efficiency and cut costs. He was convinced, at the time, he had government backing.
> *Suddenly the scene changed.*
> A week before the scheduled industrial disruption, the rail union leaders were called in and offered an improved pay deal — 5.2 per cent on basic rates, which, overall, is worth about 7 per cent — and a completely softened line on the productivity clauses of the deal.
> Privately the rail union chiefs confessed that they were 'amazed' at the Rail Board turn-round.

The explanation for the turn-around was to be found in a passage in one of the leaked documents. John Selwyn Gummer, Tory Party chairman and junior Employment Minister, had written to Transport Secretary Nicholas Ridley on 17 April: 'It seems to me to be critical at this juncture to avoid the risk of militants being strengthened in their attempts to block the movement of coal by rail, and to make wider common cause with the miners.'

There was nothing strange about the Tory retreat. What *was* amazing was that the railway workers' leaders should have accepted the improved terms offered them on 23 May. The issue of productivity had only been deferred. Knapp and Buckton threw away an opportunity to take on British Rail at a time when, in conjunction with the miners, they could have forced the Tories onto the defensive.

The **Financial Times** commented on the rail settlement:

> Most importantly for ministers . . . it increases the isolation of groups such as the miners and the teachers who are taking industrial action.[7]

This sorry story was repeated a number of times — the Union of Communications Workers settled in June for 4.9 per cent, the water workers for 4.6 per cent. Generally the government was prepared to lift its wage offers slightly, by half or one per cent, in order to prevent industrial action spreading beyond the coalfields. The trade union leaders were only too ready to accept these miserable offers, and desert the miners, without whom they would not have gained them.

Even Liverpool City Council, led by hard-line Labour left-wingers (including supporters of the **Militant** tendency) fell in with the gadarene rush. The council had refused to implement Tory cuts in local government spending, to set a local budget. Faced with the prospect of imposing government commissioners on Liverpool at the same time as they were mounting an enormous police operation in the coalfields, the Tories retreated.

Environment Secretary Patrick Jenkin cobbled up a deal with Liverpool Council. A combination of creative accounting, a little extra government money, and the council's abandonment of its policy of increasing neither rates nor rents, got the government off the hook.

But, again, confrontation had been only deferred. Jenkin's rate-capping Bill, then on its way through parliament, was the next line of further government attack on Labour councils. Liverpool faced the choice between defying the law or implementing Tory cuts again, in March 1985 a few weeks after the miners' strike ended — so leaving them in a much weaker position than in 1984. Another opportunity had been squandered.

First tragedy, then farce: the dock strikes

Margaret Thatcher was nevertheless pursuing a high-risk strategy. The Tories' various efforts to break miners' picket lines involved the co-operation of other workers — to unload coal and iron ore from freighters, and to transport it to steelworks.

The government was blessed by possessing in the steel industry a particularly craven bunch of trade union leaders and a deeply demoralised workforce. They couldn't always count on such luck. Solidarity action by railworkers forced them to move most coal by road, using scab lorry drivers. There was always the danger that the Tory blacklegging operation might goad a powerful group of workers into action.

This possibility became a reality in July, when scabbing at Immingham provoked a national dock strike. The dockers were in any case in the government's firing line. 1972 had, after all, not only been the miners' year. It had seen the humiliating defeat of the Heath government's attempt to jail five dockers' leaders for defying the Industrial Relations Act.

At the root of both the 1972 and 1984 disputes lay the National Dock Labour Scheme. Introduced in 1947, it had finally put an end to the evil of casual labour in the docks. A register of dock labourers was drawn up; they alone could work in the docks, and were guaranteed fall-back pay when they weren't working. Dock Labour Boards on which unions and managements were equally represented administered the scheme, and agreed on a pre-entry closed shop — only union members could be employed.

On the basis of the scheme the dockers were able to build powerful shop stewards' organisations, and win significant improvements in their wages and conditions. But in the 1960s the spread of containerisation meant that goods could be moved directly from ship to land transport, shifting a large portion of what previously had been dockers' work to inland depots and stores where workers did not possess the strong organisation built by the dockers. Non-registered ports such as Dover and Felixstowe mushroomed.

Registered dockers found their position seriously under threat. Their number shrank from 65,000 to 43,000 between 1967 and 1972. By 1972 more than 14 per cent of the survivors were without work, on the low-paid Temporary Unattached Register.

An unofficial rank-and-file body, the National Port Shop Stewards Committee, took up the challenge. Selected inland container depots were picketed, in defiance of the Industrial Relations Act. After a series of preliminary skirmishes, five militant stewards were imprisoned in July 1972. Rolling unofficial action, spreading from the docks to Fleet Street, transport and engineering, forced the TUC to call a one-day general strike. Suddenly a hitherto unknown figure, the Official Solicitor, appeared and secured the release of the five dockers from Pentonville prison.

The Industrial Relations Act was never the same again. However, the dockers were unable to extend the Scheme to the unregistered ports. A three-week national dock strike called in the summer of 1972 to achieve this goal ended inconclusively after TGWU general secretary Jack Jones cobbled up a deal with Lord Aldington, chairman of the National Association of Port Employers. Its most significant provision was improved terms for dockers accepting voluntary redundancy. By 1984 there were only 13,500 registered dockers left.

The Tories were plainly gunning for the National Dock Labour Scheme. It was precisely the sort of scheme, created by strong workers' organisation, which Thatcher was pledged to destroy. They were also under pressure from port employers to dismantle the Scheme. The **Financial Times** reported on 10 July 1984:

> The issue flared up at the employers' annual luncheon in April. Union leaders were furious at speeches made against the scheme in their presence, though Mr Nicholas Ridley, the Transport Secretary . . . said only that the government was keeping a close eye on the scheme which, he hinted, represented the sort of restrictive practice which was hampering the ports industry. With the mineworkers' strikes just beginning at the time, the government was clearly anxious not to open a second front.

Ridley did say that the ports 'were no longer seen as part of the country's infrastructure, requiring central planning and control. Instead, like any other industry, they should and could compete among themselves.' The message was plain enough.

The Transport and General Workers Union responded to Ridley's speech by threatening an immediate national dock strike if there was any threat to the scheme. It was difficult to know how seriously to take this warning. Two years previously they had put an ultimatum to the government, demanding that the latter extend the scheme to all ports, or face an all-out strike. But the TGWU had conveniently forgotten this challenge a few weeks later, using the Falklands war as a pretext.

Meanwhile scab coal was pouring into the country through non-registered ports such as Wivenhoe in Essex. This not only threatened the miners' strike. It was a dry-run for the sort of black-legging operation which would be needed to smash the Dock Labour Scheme.

The leaders of the TGWU — general secretary Moss Evans, his successor Ron Todd, and national docks officer John Connolly — found themselves in an increasingly difficult position. The TGWU was the biggest union in the country. Since the late 1950s it had been anchor of the broad left in the TUC. Evans' predecessor, Jack Jones, had symbolised the immense power wielded by the trade union bureaucracy in the mid-1970s.

The transport union leaders were worried by the threat to the Dock Labour Scheme. They genuinely wanted to help the miners. They were confronted with the spectacle of their members driving scab coal through miners' picket lines. Yet they were not prepared, until their backs were up against the wall, to take concerted national action against the blacklegging.

The most striking illustration of the TGWU's failure to act was that of iron ore, blacked by the rail, seafarers' and transport unions in June 1984 in an effort to counter the steel unions' scabbing. The iron ore continued to enter Britain through three ports — Port Talbot, Hunterston and Immingham. All three were covered by the Dock Labour Scheme, and employed registered dockers, members of the TGWU. At Port Talbot, for example, these dockers did the trimming and bulldozing on board the iron ore ships essential to removing the ore from the ships' holds.

This was not only a betrayal of the NUM. It also threatened the dockers themselves. This was most clearly illustrated by what happened after Mick McGahey attempted to halt the supply of coal to Ravenscraig in May. The registered dockers at Hunterston agreed to black coal — and British Steel retaliated by using ISTC members and non-union labour to shift the coal. The TGWU threatened a Scottish dock strike.

The crisis was resolved by an agreement on 17 May. Management promised that no one would do the dockers' work. In exchange the TGWU agreed that the ships could continue to be unloaded — without the dockers. They were put on 'alternative work'. The dockers had more or less negotiated themselves out of a job, creating a disastrous precedent.

A similar issue provoked the first dock strike of summer 1984. Train drivers at Immingham refused on 3 July to transport iron ore bound for Scunthorpe steelworks across a miners' picket line. BSC management tried to transfer the ore to lorries. Immingham's registered dockers refused to scab on the train drivers, and walked out. The TGWU leadership, unhappy about the local agreement made at Hunterston, called a national dock strike on 9 July.

Suddenly things didn't look so good for the Tories. They were already under economic pressure. The financial markets were jittery. Share prices experienced in early June their biggest fall since the last miners' strike had brought down the Heath government in March 1974. Various factors were involved — the strike had cut industrial output; high American interest rates were sucking capital from all over the world into the US; the oil price was falling, and so therefore were the North Sea revenues underpinning sterling.

But trouble on the industrial front tipped the balance. On 11 July the Tory Chancellor of the Exchequer, Nigel Lawson, was forced to raise interest rates by 2 per cent to steady the pound on the foreign exchanges.

International capital was beginning to worry about Thatcher. Even before the dock strike, **The Economist**, usually one of Thatcher's staunchest supporters, had launched a fierce attack:

> Mrs Thatcher's second government is stepping out to become Britain's most inept since the war . . . Mrs Thatcher seems to have lost her ability to move . . . without slipping on a banana skin and falling on her face. She looks alarmingly like Mr Harold Wilson in the closing days of his 1966 administration.[8]

Then came the dock strike. Suddenly Thatcher looked like Wilson or Heath, adrift in a sterling crisis and facing widespread industrial militancy. Whitehall dusted off the emergency regulations which the last Tory government had been forced to use five times in the early 1970s. Things like this weren't supposed to happen under the Iron Lady.

The miners' situation was transformed. They had been beaten at Orgreave. But if other trade unionists joined them they could still win. The **Financial Times** reported on 16 July that the oil companies' 'big fear' was that the dock strike would 'escalate', 'bringing the whole of the TGWU into the fight'. That would stop all movement of oil, with catastrophic consequences for the power stations, thanks to the CEGB's policy of replacing coal with oil to beat the strike.

The dock strike put the skids under the talks between the NUM and the Coal Board. Previously it had been MacGregor who had been holding out for victory, now it was Scargill. 'On 9 July the miners' strike looked closer to settlement than at any time since it started', **The Economist** lamented.[9] Then came the dock strike.

The NUM held a special conference on 12 and 13 July. It had probably been called to approve a deal. Instead, it hardened the miners' terms, demanding no pit closures except on grounds of exhaustion, a four-day week, and a £30-a-week pay rise. On 18 July, talks between the miners' union and the NCB ended in stalemate.

The government were in a vulnerable position. The TGWU had called out all its members in the docks — not just 13,500 registered dockers, but also the 19,000 dockers employed in ports outside the Dock Labour Scheme. **The Economist** reported:

> The Confederation of British Industry was playing the effects of the dock strike pretty cool . . . Two facts make that coolness suspect. First, the newer ports on the east coast, which may defy the strike call, handle only about 30 per cent of Britain's non-fuel exports and imports. Second, if the seamen's union successfully blocks container lorries from using Channel ferries at Dover, that would hit six out of every ten tonnes of freight going to the EEC ports which account for a third of Britain's non-oil exports.
>
> The Institute of Directors says it has been showered with telexes from members saying they could not survive a prolonged shutdown.[10]

The strike was initially solid. All 71 registered ports were shut, and the critical roll on/roll off traffic through unregistered ports such as Dover and Felixstowe was halted. The unregistered dockers were the key to winning the strike. Without them the registered dockers could be isolated and beaten.

The trouble was that the unregistered dockers were on strike to defend a scheme of which they were not part. The only way to ensure their solid support was to make the central demand of the strike the extension of the Dock Labour Scheme to all ports.

Dover dockers had spent thirteen weeks out on strike in 1973 demanding that the scheme be applied to them. The strike had been beaten because of the TGWU's refusal to call a national dock strike in

Dover's support.

Legislation passed in 1977 gave the Transport Secretary the power to extend the scheme by statutory order. To use the strike to force Ridley to use this power would have made the issue one of defending the jobs of *all* dockers, not just those in registered ports.

If ever there was a time to launch an offensive strike, to defend the scheme by extending it, it was in July 1984, when the government were already confronted with a miners' strike.

But having called the strike, the transport union leaders did nothing to win it. TGWU deputy general secretary Alec Kitson dropped broad hints that the dock strike was just a shot across the port employers' bows, not a serious battle. Local officials were equally short-sighted. Jimmy Symes, a TGWU full-timer in Liverpool, said: 'It is a great pity this strike has come along now to interrupt our pay negotiations.'

The officials' hand was strengthened by the decline of rank-and-file organisation in the docks since the early 1970s. After the 1983 strike at Tilbury two dockers, Bob Light and Eddie Prevost, had explained:

> Since 1978 the National Port Shop Stewards Committee has achieved virtually nothing . . . The shop stewards' movement has been so depressed that if you're an individual militant shop steward in the docks, without a deep political commitment, you accommodate . . . And the only realistic way you can see of carrying on is to use the official machine.[11]

In 1972 the dock shop stewards had operated independently of, and often against the full-time officials. Now, however, they had become dependent on the TGWU machine. This had serious consequences for the 1984 strike.

Hardly any picketing was organised. This was a particularly gross error in the case of the non-scheme ports. Ports such as Wivenhoe had been deeply involved in the import of scab coal. There was no guarantee that they could be relied on to support the dock strike. Moreover, mass dockers' pickets would have put severe pressure on the state's resources. Policing the miners' strike was strain enough; coping with both miners and dockers might have been too much.

These failures on the part of the dockers' leaders, either to organise mass pickets or to demand the extension of the scheme, doomed the strike. The unregistered ports were clearly the weak link, and it was at Dover that the strike cracked on 19 July. Lorry owner-drivers who were being stopped from using cross-Channel ferries by the strike stormed onto the docks and threatened to burn the port down. The local TGWU officials gave in to this blackmail — while the police, of course, did nothing to prevent this blatant intimidation.

Had the dockers' leaders been willing to involve nearby Kent miners in their picket lines, they could have seen off the lorry drivers. As it was, the strike collapsed. The TGWU national docks officer, John Connolly, rapidly accepted from the port employers a meaningless form of words which he had rejected before the Dover debacle. What had begun as a show of strength ended in a pathetic shambles.

The issue of British Steel's use of registered ports to scab on the miners would not, however, go away. In early August the TGWU leadership persuaded dockers at Hunterston to black the **Ostia**, a ship carrying 95,000 tonnes of coking coal bound for Ravenscraig. But although national union officials such as Ron Todd were vehemently critical of the local agreement earlier struck at Hunterston, their aim was not to halt the flow of coal and iron ore to Ravenscraig completely.

Instead the TGWU leadership offered BSC a quota of 12,500 tonnes of coal a week. In the negotiations which followed, the transport union leaders upped their offer to 18,000 tonnes a week, the amount originally agreed by the Triple Alliance on 11 May. British Steel felt confident enough to reject this quota, proposing instead 22,500 tonnes.

Then after prolonged negotiations involving the West of Scotland and National Dock Labour Boards while the **Ostia** waited offshore, BSC got the go-ahead from Whitehall to berth and unload the ship without an agreement. The TGWU was forced to react. On 31 August the docks delegate conference of the union's Docks and Inland Waterways Group voted by 78 to 12 to call the second national dock strike in six weeks.

Support for the strike was much less solid from the start. A number of ports were now decidedly shaky — dockers at Immingham, for example, who had started the first strike, initially refused to come out. The main non-scheme ports, Dover and Felixstowe, carried on working. Following the pattern in the Notts NUM, scab organisers appeared in the docks mounting back-to-work movements at Tilbury and Hull.

The weakness of the strike was a consequence of the way in which it was led. The TGWU insisted on restricting the issues of the strike to British Steel's breach of established trade union practices in using non-dock labour to unload the **Ostia**. They played down the connection between this dispute and the miners' strike. This was a feeble ploy: every docker knew that BSC used scab labour because the TGWU were blacking coal bound for Ravenscraig.

Again the transport union officials refused to make the extension of the National Dock Labour Scheme the central demand of the strike. They relied instead on appeals to the dockers' loyalty to their union. The dockers' commitment to trade unionism is legendary, but loyalty to workers' organisations is never unconditional. It is sustained only by the organisation's ability to deliver concrete improvements in workers' lives.

Even worse, transport union officials were prepared to make local agreements with the port employers which further undermined dockers' unity. During the strike **Socialist Worker** published details of an amendment to the agreement covering dockers at Felixstowe, the largest non-registered port.[12] This gave the dockers there injury and severance terms similar to those enjoyed by their counterparts in the registered ports. The agreement was signed in August 1984, mid-way between the two dock strikes. The Felixstowe employers' aim was obvious — by concessions to the largest group of workers outside the scheme they hoped to deprive Felixstowe dockers of any incentive to join in a future strike. The scandal was that the TGWU was prepared to fall in with this obvious piece of divide-and-rule.

The very unevenness of the strike made it impossible for militant dockers simply to rely on calls from the full-time officials. Serious mass picketing was mounted. It involved usually only a minority of strikers — 150 at Tilbury, for example, in the first week of the strike. Nonetheless the back-to-work movements were a flop, and dockers at some ports, for example Fleetwood, reversed decisions not to strike.

The activity of a militant minority could not, however, substitute for the lack of any coherent leadership by the TGWU. Without any clear focus, the strike drifted inevitably into haggling between the union leaders and BSC over how much coal should be allowed into Ravenscraig.

The outcome was a victory for British Steel. The final agreement was that Ravenscraig should receive, as its managers had demanded, 22,500 tonnes of coal a week. The steel bosses reserved the right to use non-union labour at Hunterston in certain circumstances.

The dock strike ended on 18 September. As if to hammer home the point, the port employers immediately launched an offensive at Tilbury and Bristol. Tally clerks at Tilbury walked out when confronted with a new set of working practices, including changes in manning levels, operating agreements, and wages. The struggle over the Dock Labour Scheme had only been deferred. Another set of union leaders had backed down at the very point where they had stood the best chance of winning.

Enter the TUC

Despite the debacles in the docks, the summer saw considerable pressure for the labour movement to take action in support of the miners. Orgreave was probably decisive in crystallising this mood. It burned into many minds the image of a state on the rampage, determined to crush the NUM at any price. One photograph, from the second battle of Orgreave, of a mounted policeman charging a woman from the Sheffield Policewatch group, summed it up: the miners weren't just fighting for themselves, they needed everyone's support.

The defeat suffered by the miners at Orgreave thus had a contradictory effect. It pushed the strike onto the defensive, but led many inside and outside the mining communities to think about it in much more general political terms, as a broad class issue.

On 30 June **The Economist** reported an opinion poll which showed that 35 per cent of the British public supported the miners.

But this substantial minority was passive; they did not have the confidence and strength to deliver solidarity action on their own. Ten years of mass redundancies and declining workplace organisation had taken their toll, as in the docks. The support offered — collections of food and money rather than industrial action — reflected this.

But this lack of confidence did not mean those who supported the miners would refuse to take action if they were offered a lead. The general passivity meant that even activists looked towards the official leadership of the labour movement to deliver action. The weakness of workplace organisation generally forced militants to rely much more on the left wing of the trade union bureaucracy and on the Labour Party leadership, than in the early 1970s.

So there were high expectations of the 1984 TUC Congress, to some degree orchestrated by the NUM leadership. Scargill in particular seems, after Orgreave, to have focussed more and more attention on the trade union leaders. This was probably for two reasons. First, the power unions could deliver a decisive blow to the Tories' hopes of getting through the winter without electricity cuts. Secondly, involving the TUC in the strike would mean that, if the miners were defeated, responsibility would be seen to fall on the shoulders of the trade union leaders.

So where did the TUC stand?

This question was posed ever more sharply when on 30 July the first serious legal blow was struck against the miners' union. The South Wales Area was fined £50,000 for refusing to obey an injunction to stop picketing two small road haulage firms involved in the scabbing operation at Port Talbot and Llanwern. When the union refused to pay up, its assets were sequestered two days later.

If one union could be treated like this, they were all under future threat. The TGWU were in an especially embarrassing position, since some of the lorry drivers working for the scab firms were members of the union.

What would the union leaders do?

There was some talk of organising 'massive disruption' — by which was probably meant a national day of action, similar to that of 28 February 1984 in protest against the trade union ban at GCHQ. But the crucial question was: would the transport union leaders now instruct their members not to cross picket lines — and thus avoid situations such as that which led to the South Wales sequestration?

In an interview on BBC radio on 5 August, Ron Todd said: 'What is required from people is not instructions — you cannot have coercion as a substitute for commitment — but a positive, supportive leadership from the whole trade union movement.'

This amounted to an abdication of leadership. The buck was passed to the rank and file, giving the confused, the vacillating, and the straightforwardly hostile a perfect excuse for backsliding. Instructions on their own wouldn't have guaranteed action. But an active campaign by the left-wing trade union leaders to persuade their members of the need for action would have provided a focus for the minority of militants who wanted to help the miners but felt unable to take the initiative themselves.

Despite the left union leaders' hesitations, the TUC met in Brighton on 3 September amid an atmosphere of excitement and anticipation. The previous year's Congress had been dominated by the centre-right of the General Council and their 'new realism' — proposals for close collaboration with government and employers. Scargill had been denounced for his intransigence by Alistair Graham, general secretary of the main civil service union, the CPSA.

This year Scargill was cheered to the echo when he addressed the Congress, and Graham was forced off the General Council as a result of the Broad Left's capture of the CPSA executive. A General Council statement supporting the miners was overwhelmingly passed. The trade union right was openly split, with David Basnett of GMBATU and Gavin Laird of the AUEW clashing with Eric Hammond and John Lyons, leaders respectively of the electricians' and power engineers' unions and the only noteworthy opponents of the statement.

This realignment of forces, bringing the TUC centre-right and the left together and isolating the far right, was not simply a consequence of the miners' strike. The 'new realism' had been scuppered by the NGA dispute at Warrington and the ban on unions at GCHQ in Cheltenham earlier in the year. It had assumed that if the trade union leaders abandoned defiance of the government and turned to co-operation then Thatcher would reciprocate. Her contemptuous dismissal of the TUC delegation who went to 10 Downing Street to plead the cause of the GCHQ unions made it clear that she would not.

Trade union leaders such as Len Murray, David Basnett, and Moss Evans did not want confrontation with the government. Their role was essentially that of negotiators, seekers of compromise. They looked back wistfully to the trade union bureaucracy's heyday in the 1950s, 1960s and 1970s, when they had enjoyed ready access to 10 Downing Street.

But the willingness of the ruling class to admit the TUC to the corridors of power then was a reflection of the strength of organised labour. This power had, of course, been at its height in the early 1970s when trade union resistance brought down the Heath government. But workers' strength had been eroded in the decade after Heath's fall.

Thatcher felt she no longer needed the TUC's active co-operation. Not that she aimed to destroy organised labour. There was still a place for the trade union bureaucracy in the Tory dispensation, though a much reduced one, politically subordinated to capital, and denied much of the elaborate structures of consultation with government and big business typical of the post-war era.

The Trade Union Act of 1984 was part of this strategy. It required the use of secret ballots for strikes, union elections, the political levy for the Labour Party, and closed shops. Failure to comply with the provisions of the Act would make the unions liable to court action. The aim was to make the structure of industrial relations much more formal, increasing the power of the union bureaucracy over its members and thus preventing unofficial strikes. At the same time, the new law sought to push the union leaders rightwards, and to undermine their links with the Labour Party.

This was a recipe for the Americanisation of the trade unions.

Hardly any of even the right-wing union leaders were prepared to embrace such a prospect with any enthusiasm. The main exception was the electricians' union, which concluded no-strike agreements with several multinational firms. But such business unionism was unpalatable to TUC heavyweights who had once enjoyed access to Whitehall.

The miners' strike posed these union leaders with a dilemma. They had no time for what David Basnett was later to denounce as 'Scargillism' — meeting Thatcher's class-war Toryism with labour's own class-war methods. On the other hand, a defeat for the miners would gravely weaken the trade union movement, and further undermine its leaders' bargaining power. 'We don't want Arthur to win, but we can't let the miners lose,' one TUC leader told the press.

So the General Council came off the fence. In May Len Murray had denounced regional TUCs who held days of action in support of the miners — for example, in Yorkshire and Humberside and in Wales. Now he told the TUC:

> We now stand shoulder to shoulder with them [the miners]. Our purpose is to bring the concentrated power of this movement to bear on the NCB and the government, to get the Board back to the negotiating table and in a frame of mind to make an agreement. This is the paramount objective. The whole of Congress must be aware of the serious consequences for all if the movement fails to give the NUM the proper support it needs and if the NUM is defeated in this dispute.

David Basnett of the GMBATU delivered the same message. He was the key figure in the re-alignment of the General Council. Moreover, as the leader of the main manual union in the power industry, he would have a decisive say in any decision concerning solidarity action with the miners.

At the NUM's request Basnett took part in the negotiations between the miners' leaders and representatives of the TUC General Council the week before the Congress. The result was a statement from the General Council which asked two chief things of affiliated unions — first 'not moving coal or coke, or oil substitutes for coal or coke, across NUM official picket lines, or using such materials taken across such picket lines'; second, 'not moving oil which is substituted for coal'.

There was a price to be paid by the NUM in exchange. Up to this point the miners' leaders had firmly kept the TUC at arm's length, refusing to involve them in negotiations. Now they had to let the General Council into the direction of the strike. The statement approved by Congress included the following clause: 'The NUM acknowledge that the practical implementation of these points will need detailed discussion with the General Council and agreement with unions who would be directly involved.'

The TUC leaders spelt out the implications. They had not been won to 'Scargillism' — they applauded Neil Kinnock's 'fraternal address' in which he once again denounced the pickets. Their aim was to get the strike settled as quickly as possible. Len Murray — before the miners' strike ended he was Lord Murray — said:

> To date, at the wish of the NUM, the General Council have not been involved although many unions have. Now we are involved to the hilt . . . The purpose of the procedures set out in the statement is to devise arrangements to make the dispute more effective and to make mass picketing unnecessary.

David Basnett was even more explicit. Speaking after talks between the miners' leaders and the Coal Board had been announced, he said:

> We are involved. We have applied pressure on the NCB and the government and we have succeeded. That was the purpose of the TUC statement. It wasn't and couldn't be a blueprint for spreading strike action in the coal-using industry — even if that was desirable and deliverable.

The TUC leaders were horrified when the talks seemed to fall through later in the week because of MacGregor's obduracy. Their pacific intentions were made clear in other debates. The General Council were able to beat off left-wing attempts to withdraw permanently from the National Economic Development Council, a forum involving government, unions and employers. They were prepared to put pressure on the Tories, but only with the aim of winning readmission to the corridors of power. 'I am a negotiator, let me negotiate,' Basnett successfully pleaded.

The pattern was the same throughout the week. The centre-right retained control of the General Council. Although the NGA won a vote of censure on the General Council for their handling of the Warrington dispute, the more important portion of their resolution — automatic support for any union in conflict with the Tory laws — was defeated.

Thus although the TUC had formally pledged itself to achieving a miners' victory, it was plain that the General Council had no serious intention of implementing this policy. No wonder that **The Economist** concluded after the TUC that the miners' defeat was inevitable:

> Mr Scargill's defeat will come from within the union movement . . . On Monday, the Trades Union Congress took the first shambling step, six months too late, towards this defeat when its moderate executive gathered the miners into the bear-hug of 'total support' — support which it has neither the capacity nor the intention to deliver . . . The TUC may be an ironic weapon for Mrs Thatcher to wave in the face of union militants. But at present it is the best she has.[13]

The miners and the Labour left

The 1984 labour Party conference later that month was also very different from its predecessor of a year before. This had met in the wake of Labour's disastrous defeat in the June 1983 general election. The objective of the new leadership under Neil Kinnock was to avoid defeat next time.

Kinnock's strategy was straightforward. The Labour share of the vote had declined catastrophically from its all-time high of 51 per cent to a mere 27.6 per cent in 1983, barely two points ahead of the SDP/Liberal Alliance. This reflected a massive exodus of working-class voters — only 39 per cent of all trade unionists voted Labour in 1983. Since the electorate had moved to the right, so too must the Labour Party.

From Kinnock's point of view the miners' strike was a disaster. It set up a road block across Labour's path rightwards and allowed the Tories to attach to Kinnock precisely the sort of class-struggle politics which he was trying to drop. At the same time, a mere refusal to back the miners would bring down on Kinnock the wrath of the Labour left. So he sought to balance between the two sides in the dispute, calling for a ballot and supporting the strike; even-handedly denouncing both police and pickets; pressing the NUM into negotiations and attacking Thatcher for her intransigence.

At the same time, the miners' strike revitalised the demoralised Labour left. Labour Party activists did much of the work of the miners' support groups. Many who had begun to think that the Greenham peace women were a more plausible force for change than the industrial working class now found themselves enthusiastically working around a major strike. Confidence which had drained away in June 1983, leaving the pessimistic belief that 'Thatcherism' was unstoppable, was restored. Many heard the miners chant 'We will win' and believed it.

This new mood inevitably reflected itself within the Labour Party. The strike dominated the conference.

'The miners have totally transformed the atmosphere of the conference,' said Tony Benn at the fringe meeting held by the Campaign Group of Labour MPs on 29 September. Dennis Skinner said at the same meeting: 'Confidence is oozing out of the Labour Party everywhere up and down the country . . . We've got them on the run, and it's a nice feeling.' He also attacked Kinnock, to massive applause:

Arthur Scargill and Neil Kinnock meet at Durham in July

'Stop talking about violence unless you want to talk about police violence. Get on the picket line and see it for yourself.' The meeting showed where it stood by donating £1,000 to the NUM, and giving Peter Heathfield a standing ovation.

The mood was much the same when the conference itself discussed the strike, on 1 October. Scargill was greeted with adulation and the NUM's resolution calling for support overwhelmingly passed. Kinnock had to sit by while speaker after speaker condemned police violence and refused to criticise the miners. He had to listen while Tony Benn, summing up for the Labour Party national executive, told conference that the party was 100 per cent behind the NUM, and that if the miners were beaten, Labour's chances of winning the next election would be gone.

In the subsequent debate on the police, the conference ignored the executive's recommendation, and passed two resolutions, one moved by a striking Notts miner, the other by supporters of the **Militant** tendency. These called on a future Labour government to disband the riot squads, exclude the police from any industrial disputes, and give local authorities control over their local police forces.

In the final debate of the day, Kinnock saw his attempt to prevent left-wing constituency parties from removing right-wing Labour MPs, by giving the final say in the reselection of sitting MPs to a ballot of all party members, go down to ignominious defeat. No wonder that Ken Livingstone told the **Labour Herald** rally that evening: 'Today has been one of the best days I can remember at a Labour Party conference. The working-class movement is beginning to rebuild its confidence.'

The next day the same delegates who had given Arthur Scargill a standing ovation rose to applaud Neil Kinnock. His parliamentary report was a clever speech. Much of it was an attack on the evils of Thatcherism. But, carefully inserted for the television microphones and the Fleet Street journalists, were the signals of Kinnock's 'statesmanship': 'I condemn violence — yes — of the stone throwers and the battering ram carriers, and of the cavalry charges, the truncheon groups and the shield bangers. I condemn all violence without fear or favour. That's what makes me different from Thatcher — I don't have double standards.'

He went on to argue that trade unions and local councils must respect even Tory laws: 'We cannot sharpen legality as our main weapon for the future and simultaneously scorn legality if it doesn't suit us at the present time.'

For those willing to listen there were plenty of signs that the words in the resolution passed by the TUC Congress and the Labour Party conference would not be put into effect. David Basnett warned during the Labour conference debate on the miners against 'over-politicising' the dispute: 'The ballot box will get rid of Thatcher, negotiations round a table will settle the strike.' He said to Scargill: 'Arthur, you should tell your members: "Do not let them provoke you into violence." '

The Tories had no such scruples. Scargill was served on the conference floor itself with a summons alleging contempt of court for defying a court ruling that the strike was illegal in Yorkshire. Moss Evans considered moving an emergency resolution defying the law but was dissuaded on the grounds that it would make the Labour Party guilty of contempt of court. The Labour and trade union leaders had no serious intention of fulfilling their activists' hopes.

The NACODS disaster

Both the high risks the Tories were running and the cowardice of the trade union leaders were soon graphically illustrated. The Tories' attempts to engineer a 'surge back to work' in August nearly provoked the total shutdown of the mining industry, which the NUM had been unable to achieve since March.

On 15 August the Coal Board unilaterally ripped up an agreement they had with the pit deputies and overmen's union, NACODS, which guaranteed their pay if they turned back at NUM picket lines. Ned Smith, then Coal Board industrial relations chief, sent out a directive to the Board's area directors: 'When mineworkers are going through pickets then in the board's view there can be no good reason why officials should not go as well.'

NACODS members are legally responsible for safety underground. If they don't work, no-one can go down the pits. Within a month, NACODS members at 14 Yorkshire pits had joined NUM members at the picket lines as the Coal Board stopped the wages of 3,000 men for 'not making sufficient effort to get into work'.

This incredible blunder by the Coal Board came just as leading Tories were talking more and more openly about smashing the miners' union. **The Observer** reported on 23 September: 'The prime minister's associates are talking in terms of a straight victory. "Now is the time to hit Scargill hard," one colleague said.'

Now ministers watched with horror as the NACODS executive

called a strike ballot, strongly and unanimously recommended a strike against both the new guidelines on picket lines and against pit closures, and then won the support of 82.5 per cent of their members. If NACODS came out nationally, even the Nottinghamshire scab pits would be forced to stop working.

Shocked Fleet Street commentators tried to explain why a union that had never been on strike before should suddenly appear so militant. They tried to draw comfort by saying the vote was merely to give their union leaders a better bargaining hand in negotiations and not really a vote for action. That certainly was how NACODS general secretary Peter McNestry and the other union officials used their astonishing ballot result, but it wasn't sufficient explanation of the vote.

All NACODS members were angered at the way the Coal Board ripped up the agreement which, in effect, gave the deputies all the benefits the miners might win through a strike but with none of the pain of losing money. On top of this there was real fear about MacGregor's plans for the industry. These affected NACODS members as directly as NUM members and in April some 54 per cent of NACODS members had voted to join the NUM on strike over pit closures. The vote had been just short of the necessary majority for an actual strike.

In addition, many NACODS members were getting worried about the resentment and settling of scores they would have to face after the strike for having a 'paid holiday' while the men they had to supervise, and their families, suffered increasing hardship and privation. No one in the mining communities of Yorkshire, Durham, Kent and South Wales expected the scabs to face their former workmates once the strike was over. They would either take redundancy or a transfer to Nottinghamshire. But transfers were not open to NACODS members who crossed miners' picket lines and provoked the police rampage through their villages that inevitably followed.

Finally, all NACODS members were once in the NUM and many had been ordinary miners in 1972 and 1974. Many too had brothers, sons or other relatives on the picket line and they knew that a NACODS strike would force the government to negotiate seriously and abandon its plans to grind the NUM into the ground.

But from the start, the hope of NUM members on the picket lines, that the deputies were coming to their aid, was tempered by the knowledge that the deputies had 'always ridden on the backs of the miners' and never fought themselves. The caution was justified, for no sooner was the ballot result announced than NACODS president Ken Sampey declared that any strike would be postponed for a week. 'Negotiations with the board from now on are from a position of strength,' he said.[14]

Three weeks of stop-start talks followed between NACODS, the NUM, the Coal Board and the arbitration service ACAS. On 9 October the threatened NACODS strike was again delayed to allow for more talks. The events that followed were quite extraordinary.

Coal Board chairman Ian MacGregor picked a fight with NACODS over the new picket line 'guidelines'. Then, in the middle of further negotiations, he went onto the BBC television **Newsnight** programme and announced that NACODS had in fact *agreed* the new guidelines — when they plainly had not. To round off a performance borrowed straight from a 'Carry On' film, he then hinted that the Coal Board could run the industry without the pit deputies anyway!

A row followed between MacGregor and Ned Smith which led to Smith departing on 'indefinite leave' caused by a 'bad back'. The **Sunday Times** commented:

> The performance of the Coal Board's 72 year old chairman is causing particular dismay among the several key cabinet ministers; even the prime minister is disappointed with his recent actions. There is a disturbing ring of truth in McNestry's account in the **Daily Mail** of his dealings with MacGregor: 'We tried and tried but he just kept saying "Nope". Then when ACAS decided to end the talks, he said: "Good, now we can all go home".'
>
> Despite all the speculation there are no plans to remove MacGregor. 'We cannot ditch the general in the middle of battle' one cabinet minister told the **Sunday Times**.[15]

After this performance, with very little to show for their efforts, NACODS gave seven days' notice of a strike. Peter McNestry declared: 'We haven't looked for this confrontation. We have done our best to avoid it but it's been forced upon us.'[16]

Four days later the talks were on again. The government, Coal Board and NACODS all desperately wanted a settlement. They quickly thrashed one out. Even the TUC urged NACODS to delay settlement so they could put more pressure on the government to settle with the miners, but with less than 24 hours to go before the first ever deputies' strike, the union leaders called it off.

The NACODS deal marked a shift in tone but not substance by the Coal Board. They agreed to amend the existing Colliery Review

Procedure by creating an independent appeals body to which pit closures and other issues could be referred. The five pits named for closure on 6 March would, the agreement read, 'remain open to be considered in common with all other pits, under the modified colliery review procedure'. The Coal Board also promised to reconsider its proposals to cut capacity 'as a result of the dispute and the changes in need of the market arising also from the circumstances of the dispute.'

The **Financial Times** declared on 25 October: 'The board has effectively given NACODS everything it had asked for.' But the NUM rejected the settlement out of hand, and quite rightly. The offer on the five pits was worse than a promise extracted during earlier negotiations that the pits would be kept open subject only to mining engineers' reports on their safety and exhaustion. But most important of all, there was no guarantee that the Coal Board would alter its plans for the industry one iota. Once the review procedure was exhausted the Coal Board would continue to close pits just as it had done before the strike.

As the NACODS strike was called off, the High Court ordered the sequestration of all the NUM's assets. Again, the miners' union had been left to fight on alone.

Why the lights didn't go out

The decisive betrayal, however, was the TUC's failure to implement the guidelines it had agreed in early September to stop scab coal and oil entering the power stations. In February 1985, Ned Smith, just retired as the NCB's industrial relations director, said it was this that guaranteed the miners' defeat.

In the long run the power stations were bound to be decisive. Power cuts had marked the Tories' defeat in the 1972 and 1974 strikes. The Thatcher government was desperate to avoid them this time. Coal stocks in the power stations were at a record level of 24.3 million tonnes at the start of the strike in March 1984. Nevertheless, **The Economist** calculated on 21 April that the stocks would last for 24 weeks: on this estimate, power cuts would be inevitable in the autumn.

In the end, there were no serious power cuts. This was partly the result of government preparations, and partly because the scabbing in the Nottinghamshire pits meant that coal was kept flowing into the Trent Valley power stations. But even with all these cards up their sleeve, the trumps which the CEGB and government needed to survive were the trade union leaders.

Pickets at Eggborough power station in the summer

First, the trade unions in the power industry settled their 1984 pay claim with indecent haste so there would be no prospect of a power stations dispute while the miners were on strike. On 11 April 1984, officials from the electricians' union, GMBATU, TGWU and the engineers' union met the Central Electricity Generating Board (CEGB) for a first negotiating session. Within hours, they had signed and sealed a 13-month agreement for a 5.2 per cent wage increase.

It was remarkable. No one was consulted, not union executives and certainly not union officials in the power industry. While other trade unions managed to squeeze a little bit extra from their employers in 1984, on the backs of the miners' strike, the unions representing manual workers in the power stations grabbed the first offer on the table. Thus they effectively signalled to the employers that they would co-operate fully in the struggle against the miners.

As miners' pickets appeared at the power station gates and miners' leaders wrote to the power industry unions for support, that is just what the power unions did.

Power workers allowed the CEGB radically to change their working patterns in order to make coal stocks last. Their union leaders either openly encouraged this, or turned a blind eye to it.

In normal times, 80 per cent of electricity is generated by

coal-fired stations, 14 per cent by nuclear power stations, and the rest — a mere 6 per cent — by oil-fired stations. During the miners' strike, coal-generated electricity was reduced to 40 per cent of the total, while oil rose to account for 40 per cent and nuclear power to 20 per cent.[17] The **Financial Times** reported:

> The CEGB — with government support — decided on 28 March to maximise its oil burn at any cost and within weeks it was all systems go at the Isle of Grain and Littlebrook power stations, long ago regarded as white elephants. Also hard at work were Fawley and Pembroke in the South West, for years regarded as too costly to run for more than six hours a day. North of the border, the South of Scotland Electricity Board switched on its own oil-burning white elephant at Inverkip to export power to England.[18]

As the oil-fired stations came on stream, coal stations were taken off. First Didcot near Oxford and Aberthaw in South Wales were shut down, then nearly 90 per cent of the main coal-fired generating capacity in the North of England was taken out of action to conserve coal stocks until winter.[19]

The unions allowed an extraordinary situation to develop where their members in coal-fired power stations in the solid areas of the strike were blacking coal, while other union members were in effect scabbing by doing massive overtime to get the CEGB through to winter. Some unions, notably ASLEF, the NUR and the seafarers' union, did organise blacking of coal. The Transport and General Workers Union, on the other hand, did very little.

At the beginning of the strike Moss Evans declared that not one ton of coal would be allowed to be moved from the open-cast mines, where TGWU members were producing the coal. However, from early November, 150,000 tons of coal were moved every week from the open-cast mines without the TGWU leadership ever condemning this or calling on their members to stop work.

On 7 June Arthur Scargill and Mick McGahey addressed a meeting of TGWU national, regional and executive officials. Afterwards TGWU general secretary Moss Evans asked his members not to cross picket lines and to black the movement of coal and oil for power stations. **The Guardian** reported: 'Mr Moss Evans . . . said the union could not order its members to comply but the order was "something tantamount to an instruction".'[20]

Throughout the strike, the solidarity action by railway workers and seafarers was undermined by lorry drivers while, despite the TGWU's 'something tantamount to an instruction', the union did little to stop the convoys. Of course it wouldn't have been an easy task, but it was never seriously undertaken.

The Scottish firm of Yull and Dodds were threatened with blacking for running convoys into Ravenscraig, but the threat swiftly evaporated. Similarly the TGWU threatened to remove the union cards of drivers running scab coal into Llanwern — not for scabbing, but because they were behind with their union dues, a problem that was quickly 'sorted out'.

But the real betrayal of the miners came after the TUC Congress in September.

Three weeks after the TUC vote, the GMBATU, the union with the largest membership in the power stations, produced proposals which the **Financial Times** said 'could, if implemented by its members, result in power cuts by mid-November'. The proposals were for the power station workers to refuse scab coal, whether it be imported, from open cast or from working pits. It also called on power station workers not to accept more than the usual amount of oil. The **FT** explained that GMBATU 'believes it can win acceptance among its own and TGWU members who also handle fuel — since they rely on the concept of "working normally' rather than taking specific disruptive action.'[21]

Furthermore, the unions which agreed to take action, GMBATU, TGWU, AUEW and the building workers' union UCATT, were sure that the electricians' union and the Engineers and Managers Association, who had spurned the miners' calls, would not do work that had been blacked.

After a series of power station meetings in early October, union officials confidently predicted power cuts within the month, but there was one crucial weakness. Neither the transport workers' nor the GMBATU leaders actually instructed their members to operate the blacking. Instead they 'advised' their members to abide by the TUC guidelines. Union officials claimed: 'It is better to win support than to order it' — a statement that would be more credible if there had been a serious campaign round the power stations.

The real reason for the lack of an instruction was fear of the courts, as a steward from the coal-fired Longannet power station in Scotland explained: 'They say they won't issue instructions because they might not get support. That might be partly true. But if anything, what they fear is actually getting the support and then being bank-rupted by the courts.'[22]

No meetings were organised by the TGWU and GMBATU between shop stewards in the power stations and miners' represen-tatives. The first meeting between Arthur Scargill and shop stewards in the power stations in the Yorkshire Area did not take place until the strike had been going for ten and a half months — on 16 January 1985.

This half-hearted attempt to stop the power stations proved disastrous both for those militants inside the power stations who *were* fighting to get the TUC guidelines implemented, and for the miners whose leaders believed that TGWU and GMBATU officials were winning the battle inside the power stations.

Coal stocks at the power stations fell from 24 million tons to 14.5 million tons between March and November 1984, despite the use of oil-fired power stations and without the 'TUC guidelines'. In November, using detailed CEGB figures, **Socialist Worker** estimated that stocks would be down to nine million tons by Christmas 1984, 6.5 million tons at the end of January 1984 and 3.5 million tons at the end of February 1984, by which time there would either be power cuts, or the government would have to try a massive operation to bring pithead stocks to the power stations, with the likelihood of confronta-tion and mass picketing such as that seen at Orgreave.

But we were wrong. The **Financial Times** reported:

On Christmas eve, Mr Peter Walker . . . received a surprise present from Sir Walter Marshall, Chairman of the Central Electricity Generating Board. It was a confidential disclosure that although the worst of the winter might lie ahead, so much coal was reaching power stations that he could start planning to reduce the amount of coal being used during the miners' strike.[23]

Coal deliveries to power stations had risen from 500,000 tons a week in the summer to 750,000 a week by November and December.

There was another, less well-documented innovation by the CEGB to break the miners' strike. During the summer, when the big coal stations were taken off stream, some of the coal-burners were converted to use oil — something which had first been proposed in the Ridley Report back in 1978. Very few power union members blacked the enormous amounts of extra oil that were being burnt. In some stations, union officials even encouraged their members to accept the extra oil, saying they were normal deliveries!

The final card in the management's hands was the massive

Police hold back South Wales pickets as fuel oil tankers go into Didcot power station in October 1984

publicity throughout the autumn of the miners' 'drift back to work'. The CEGB used this to apply the pressure to power station workers who lived outside the solidly striking coalfields to get them to lift their blacking on coal. This eventually happened at Didcot and in Lancashire at the small Bold power station.

At the same time the CEGB was careful not to provoke power workers in the core areas of the miners' strike. They never ran scab coal into the Yorkshire power stations, for example. And the coal stocks moved from Yorkshire pits towards the end of the strike were not needed in the power stations. Those operations were simply to demoralise the miners and make them feel their battle was lost.

The scale and complexity of the scabbing operation were vast. A **Channel 4 News** report on 7 March 1985, after the strike was over, revealed that the power stations were burning 600,000 tonnes of oil a week during the winter. This involved the CEGB buying heavily on the world oil markets — their requirements were equivalent to *one third* of OPEC's total fuel oil production. At $190 a tonne the weekly oil bill amounted to about £106.5 million. However, the report concluded, 'if the TUC guidelines had carried more weight', the government's enormous and costly operation would have been 'irrelevant'.

There *was* support to be tapped. Workers at Didcot power station made a brave attempt to black coal. Oil tanker drivers blacked oil going into some power stations, and suffered as a result. Shell drivers lost a contract to take heavy fuel oil into Eggborough power station because they respected miners' picket lines. Esso and Petrofina both lost contracts to supply the Yorkshire power stations. Even in Nottingham TGWU drivers respected picket lines. In East London Texaco drivers walked out after their work was given to scabs.

These instances of solidarity action by rank-and-file workers are signs of what could be achieved if the trade union leaders had been prepared to campaign systematically in support of the miners. Their failure to do so doomed the strike to defeat. The leaders of the most powerful left-wing union, the giant TGWU, carry a particularly heavy responsibility.

6
COMMUNITIES UNDER SIEGE

THE MINERS' DEFEAT at Orgreave and their desertion by the TUC forced the strike increasingly onto the the defensive. The Coal Board began aggressively to encourage scabbing. This led to police invasions of a succession of mining villages to get the scabs into work. The miners were forced to concentrate on picketing their own pits. The courts were now brought into play against the NUM.

The scale of the Tory offensive evoked a heroic response. Whole mining communities rose up in revolt with women often playing a leading role.

After Orgreave Thatcher and MacGregor believed they could not only break the strike through a massive surge 'back to work' but break Arthur Scargill too. They hoped to copy the success of the scabs' organisation in Nottinghamshire nationally, in order to lead men back to work and break the grip of the left on the national union.

After Orgreave, Ian MacGregor's first line of attack in June was to propose a Coal Board ballot of the miners. MacGregor and Thatcher believed the strike was being held together by a minority of 'hooligan pickets' at each pit who intimidated the majority who wanted to go to work.

But MacGregor's advisors agreed that it was better to *assert* that a majority would go back if it weren't for wholesale intimidation, than to put it to the test. The ballot was scrapped and replaced by the first of MacGregor's letters to each miner's home, backed up by weekend speeches from Thatcher and Energy Secretary Peter Walker. The impact was minimal. The Coal Board claimed 300 back in North Derbyshire and 30 back at Bilston Glen in Scotland. They were straws in the wind, but nothing more.

Police invade the Yorkshire villages

As the government and Coal Board went onto the offensive, so too did the police. They slowly transferred their operations from Nottinghamshire to Yorkshire, and on 9 July the first pitched battles between police and Yorkshire mining communities occurred at Rossington, near Doncaster, and Fitzwilliam, near Pontefract.

At Rossington, pickets felled trees across the pit lane and stretched barbed wire round the pit yard when they heard that two scabs would be brought into the pit. Eventually, 250 police cleared the road and brought in colliery managers, members of an area manage-

A dose of their own medicine: a picket turns a hose on police at Rossington

ment team and, the pickets believe, two scabs.

Word that scabs were back at the pit spread quickly and by midday a large crowd had gathered. They re-occupied the pit yard, held the management hostage, destroyed the colliery's personal records (to make it harder for management to victimise individuals for absenteeism or other disciplinary charges) and rebuilt the barricades.

The police, outnumbered and unsure what to do, agreed with Rossington branch officials to call in the Yorkshire Area miners' leaders to disperse the crowd. Jack Taylor, Sammy Thompson, Owen Briscoe and Frank Cave all appeared, calling for calm and for the pickets to go home. 'We must be organised and disciplined,' they

said. 'We are the generals. If you don't take our leadership the fight will be lost. What you are doing is illegal. You'll be charged with unlawful assembly and riotous behaviour.' But no one paid any attention.

At tea-time the crowd began to disperse, but quickly returned as police reinforcements arrived in the village. Again, the police asked Jack Taylor and the Rossington branch officials if they could bring out the management 'hostages'. Jack Taylor eagerly agreed, and even told a radio interviewer: 'I'll walk with them. I'll drive the vans. I'll do anything to get them out except carry them on my back!' But the pickets weren't interested.

After much argument, the Rossington officials led two police vans through into the pit yard to transport the management to safety. The police were in such a panic that they left without the assistant colliery manager, who'd become entangled on barbed wire. He was eventually rescued an hour later. As the police drove down the pit lane, pickets bombarded their vans with bricks.

The press of course described the events in Rossington as a riot. But it was, in reality, the whole community coming out to defend their pit and their strike from a few individuals who were threatening to destroy their months of sacrifice. One miner explained why the community reacted so strongly: 'Doncaster is a militant area. The Coal Board is desperate to get a scab back here. It would be a very dangerous situation if you got a pit scabbing. That's why we've got to stop them.'

The community beat the police in Rossington but in Fitzwilliam that night, things were different. The police weren't surprised by the overwhelming response of the local community, but the other way round.

A night of fighting began when police, without a warrant, went to the home of Brendan Conway and tried to arrest him for 'vandalism'. The local community believe the police's real reason was that the Conways were active in the local Labour Party Young Socialists branch. Mick Conway, Brendan's brother, described what happened:

Brendan wouldn't let them in without a warrant, so they left to get one. Within half an hour about 200 people, miners, non-miners, women and children blocked the street off so the police couldn't get in. After waiting for an hour the crowd moved to Hemsworth police station to protest.

Frank Clark of the Yorkshire NUM went in and was given

Rossington: The colliery manager leaves the pit

an assurance by Inspector Rufton that there would be no further harassment. He told the crowd that he had negotiated an agreement and that Brendan could go with a solicitor to the police station. Frank said it was a good deal and that everyone should go home. But afterwards the police started driving up and down the street shouting: 'Brendan we're coming for you — we're going to get you.'

Mick and Brendan went to the nearby Fitzwilliam Hotel. Just before closing time, squads of West Yorkshire police descended on the pub.

In the trial that followed the Fitzwilliam events, Lord Gifford, who defended those arrested, described what happened next:

It is undisputable that 50 police officers charged into the area, on the double, with no warning, synchronised, in a pincer movement. They entered private property without the invitation or consent of the landlord. How could this be justified? The prosecution said it was reasonable action in view of a breach of the peace that occurred. In fact it was a police riot. A punitive expedition by a newly-arrived chief inspector determined to stamp his authority on the community.[1]

Not surprisingly, a battle developed outside the pub. 'Even people who would never have dreamt of having a go were fighting back because they were so terrified,' said Mick Conway. Peter Hurst, who was savagely beaten, explained: 'We thought they were fetching the Notts laws up here. Everyone gathered round to make sure they couldn't do it.'

In the street fighting that followed, police handcuffed Brendan Conway and another prisoner back-to-back round a lamp post and used them as a shield against miners who'd been throwing stones.

The police attack on Fitzwilliam was a vicious attempt to cow the local mining community. The trial of the nine arrested that night was similar. The police carefully drew up the charges to avoid a jury trial. Peter Hurst was jailed for six months for breach of the peace and assault. Six others, mainly miners, received three- or four-month jail sentences suspended for two years. Two were acquitted. The usual sentences for such offences are a fine or a conditional discharge.

The police prosecuting counsel ensured the trial was political, asking all the defendants and witnesses: 'Are you a member of a political organisation? Are you a member of the NUM? Do you go picketing? Were you at Orgreave?' The police frankly admitted beating those they arrested but justified it saying they were under attack. Yet the police doctor had to treat six of the nine defendants — and only one policeman!

Three police officers claimed that one of the defendants, Peter Doody, had been lying on his back kicking and throwing stones, so they hit him seven times on the arms and chest with their truncheons. Yet the front of Peter's body was unmarked, while photographs showed 15 truncheon weals on his back! Peter also suffered a displaced fracture of the shoulder.

The battles of Rossington and Fitzwilliam were a foretaste of things to come when the 'back to work' drive got into full swing in the autumn. They showed how the mining communities could be mobilised, but they also showed how the Yorkshire NUM leaders preferred to calm the disturbances in the pit villages rather than use them as a catalyst for mass pickets and demonstrations where they could have a direct effect on the strike.

If the Yorkshire NUM had called for mining communities to take to the streets whenever such an incident occurred, the police could not have controlled the situation, but they were never put to that sort of test.

The offensive in the courts

The increased police pressure in the mining villages was matched by mounting legal pressure on the union. On Tuesday 10 July, Mr Justice Megarry declared that proposed changes to the miners' union rules, to allow the union to discipline scab officials, were illegal. The next day a miners' special delegate conference passed the rule changes anyway.

When Megarry repeated his ruling a week later, he didn't fine the NUM. The dockers had joined the miners on strike and the government feared that a heavy fine against the NUM at that point might have brought yet more workers out in support.

By the end of July the docks strike was over. At once the courts started getting heavy. On 30 July the South Wales NUM was fined £50,000 for contempt of court. Then its funds were seized. The case had been brought by two Gloucestershire haulage contractors who wanted the union to stop picketing their lorries carrying scab coal to the Llanwern steelworks.

Arthur Scargill answered the ruling: 'It has not penetrated the minds of this government or the judiciary that you cannot sequester an idea or imprison a belief. I call on the British trade union movement to now honour the undertakings made at the TUC Special Congress at Wembley in 1981 and give total physical support to the NUM.' Scargill was to repeat this with increasing urgency as the legal attacks on the NUM unfolded during the summer and autumn of 1984. The TUC remained deaf.

The Tories and the Coal Board were also trying to rally support. Ministers launched an unprecedented propaganda attack on the miners while the scabs, with help from businessmen and 'advice' from the Tories and the Coal Board, tried to build a national organisation to confront the NUM. On 20 July 30 scabs from around the country met in London to discuss how to create a back to work drive.

Shortly afterwards the mysterious 'Silver Birch' emerged. Apparently franchised by **The Mail on Sunday**, he travelled the striking coalfields rallying the scabs. Silver Birch was marketed by the press as an ordinary miner championing the cause of the 'silent majority'. In reality, Silver Birch — a blacksmith from Bevercoates colliery named Chris Butcher — made no secret of who provided the money for his campaign: 'It's from wealthy business people who want the strike to finish,' he said.[2]

Butcher constantly attacked picket line 'intimidation' and 'violence'. The Tories, Coal Board and the scab leaders knew it was the best issue on which to isolate the miners from the rest of the trade union movement. They also began to believe their own propaganda about the strike being held together only by threats and thuggery.

The Times carried on 3 August a hysterical article headed 'Hit Scargill, help miners', by David Hart. It eulogised the scabs:

> The Nottinghamshire men are fighting a battle not just for themselves, but for their country. They are in the front line and they are quite aware of it. 'Scargill is trying to destroy the democratic rights of working-class people,' said one Nottingham delegate. 'If we fail, the country will have to look out,' said another.
>
> The grass roots no longer belongs to Scargill and his likes . . . The battle has been joined. If it is to be won speedily, all who love freedom and believe in democracy should do what they can to help the working miners financially or in any other way.

David Hart wasn't just an hysterical right-wing columnist. In 1983, The Times had described him as a 'special advisor to the Prime Minister', and during August 1984 he attended a series of meetings that were to lead to the establishment of the National Working Miners' Committee. One member of that committee who later resigned in disgust said Hart was 'the money-man'.[3]

Hart involved Tim Bell, a director of Saatchi and Saatchi, and another 'close advisor' to the prime minister. Bell designed one of the Working Miners Committee brochures while Hart arranged newspaper advertisements for them. As the miners' strike wore on the press openly described both men as MacGregor's closest advisors, but in August all this was secret.

Meanwhile Butcher had got in touch with Robert Taylor and Ken Foulstone from Manton colliery in Yorkshire, and declared that 80 per cent of Yorkshire miners wanted to go back to work.[4] In May Taylor and Foulstone had tried to get a return to work at Manton but were shouted down by 1,200 men in a union meeting.

Three months later they tried a different line of attack. Butcher had put them in touch with his lawyers in Newark. They now announced they were taking legal action against the Yorkshire NUM. It was the start of a legal process that would ultimately lead to the sequestration of the miners' funds. The Financial Times noted: 'Anti-strike miners' apparent switch of tactics to the courts comes as the National Coal Board efforts to stimulate a return to work appear once more to be failing.'[5]

The press focused on Taylor and Foulstone's demand for a

national ballot: their legal action sought to ban the taking or counting of any vote at an NUM conference. At Area level they sought to restrain Yorkshire NUM officials from telling members not to cross picket lines and their writ asked the court to order the Area executive not to implement any resolution of the Area council or to instruct or mandate any delegate to any conference until fresh elections had been called.

It was the most comprehensive legal attack on a trade union for decades, and Taylor and Foulstone's solicitors, the Newark firm of Hodgkinson and Tallents, set out to get maximum publicity for their clients. As Michael Crick wrote: 'It so happened that a partner in Hodgkinson and Tallents was Chairman of the Grantham Conservative Association, whose MP is Douglas Hogg, the husband of Sarah Hogg, Economics Editor of **The Times**.' Mrs Hogg kindly offered 'advice on how to handle the media coverage', supplying contacts such as the home telephone number of Sir Alastair Burnet, the ITN newsreader.[6]

Meanwhile, the **Financial Times** was reporting how businessmen had donated £30,000 to the scabs in three weeks. 'Sir Hector Laing, chairman of United Biscuits, is believed to be among the businessmen.'

Over the weekend of 10–11 August, the National Working Miners Committee held its first informal meetings. On Saturday nine scab miners met with David Hart at the Castle Donnington Guest House near the East Midlands airport. On Sunday they met again, this time at Longlands Farm, Knightwick, near Worcester, the constituency of Peter Walker. The farm was owned by Captain Edward Evans, a supporter of the right-wing christian organisation Moral Rearmament.

This time they were joined by Graham Turner, a **Sunday Telegraph** feature writer who that morning had an exclusive interview with Ian MacGregor printed on the paper's front page. MacGregor confidently predicted a mass return to work and declared: 'I think Arthur Scargill's biggest problem is going to be the centre of his battle-line in Yorkshire. That's the place which is going to crack the quickest.' He must have known exactly what Hart was up to.

The occupations begin

A handful of scabs went into Yorkshire pits in the week beginning 20 August and provoked the second round of fighting in the pit villages. The first scab back at Silverwood in South Yorkshire brought the biggest turnout at a branch meeting since the start of the strike. They voted not to return to work until the scab was sacked, and the next day there was a pitched battle between police and pickets at the pit.

The first scabs went into Armthorpe near Doncaster on 21 August, surrounded by a massive police escort. The Armthorpe miners were the first to picket Nottinghamshire. Now three of them were breaking the strike. The village was stunned, not just by the scabs but by the Manchester police who accompanied them. The police seemed intent on provoking a battle. They amused themselves by taunting the pickets, waving wage packets and five-pound notes at them.

They got their battle the next morning when pickets occupied pit yards and built barricades at Bentley, Yorkshire Main and Armthorpe — all within a few miles of each other. The Bentley and Yorkshire Main incidents were quickly over but the battle of Armthorpe lasted all day.

Early in the morning, hundreds of pickets barricaded the pit with a mobile crane and large concrete blocks to prevent the scabs getting in. The police kept out of the village until 8.30 a.m. when suddenly 50 transit vans roared up to the pit gate and discharged riot police who immediately set about the pickets. Hundreds more police fanned out in the woods round the Armthorpe pit to catch pickets running away. The whole operation looked cleverly planned and coldly executed.

The village was sealed off for the next 12 hours. For a while it was even impossible to phone in or out. The police ran riot. They chased pickets down streets, through gardens and into houses. One Armthorpe miner described the scene:

> Everywhere round the pit, within half a mile of the pit, if the pigs chased you, people called 'come into our house'. Not just miners but ordinary working people. It totally changed the attitude of people who are not miners. That day there were six to seven hundred from Armthorpe outside their houses, at the end of their gardens, shouting 'Pigs', 'Bastards', 'Nazi storm-troopers'.

For the whole day, pickets hid under beds, in attics and even in coal bunkers to avoid the police. Even there they weren't safe as police came bursting into homes smashing windows, doors and furniture. The scenes could have come straight from Northern Ireland.

Police blockade outside Cortonwood colliery

The police claimed that the occupation of Armthorpe pit and the subsequent battles in the village were the work of 'sinister paramilitary' squads. In fact they were sparked by the determination of the police to get their scabs into work at all costs. And the determination of the community to resist.

Two days later, Easington in County Durham got the same treatment. Like Armthorpe, Easington prided itself on being a militant pit, and like Armthorpe the Coal Board tried desperately to get someone back at work. They found their man in Paul Wilkinson, a miner who'd recently been transferred to the pit. For four days, the police tried to get Wilkinson to work, but gave up when confronted by 1,000 pickets.

Ben Hardy, the Easington lodge delegate, explained what happened next: 'The Tory MP for Newcastle Central, Piers Marchant, made a scathing attack on the Chief Constable of County Durham saying he didn't have the guts to get the man in. We knew there was something floating about on the Friday because we'd heard the previous day that there was police contingents coming up from Northampton, Cleveland and Sussex.'

Sure enough, the police got Wilkinson into the pit on Friday morning. They took him through a back entrance — breaking an agreement between the colliery manager and the NUM lodge.

The lodge officials tried to keep calm on the picket lines while

Pickets vent their anger as three scabs leave Allerton Bywater pit in West Yorkshire

they demanded that management send Wilkinson home. Ben Hardy continued: 'Then the police arrived in riot gear and they were deployed in the yard. We'd talked about an hour to no avail, so the lads took things into their own hands and had a rampage. It didn't last more than three or four minutes.' Cars were overturned, windows broken and fire extinguishers turned on police to drive them away from one miner they seemed intent on kicking to death.

Billy Stobbs, chairman of the Easington NUM and a member of the national executive, declared: 'I've lived in Easington all my life and never thought in my wildest dreams that I would see police baton-charging workers fighting for their jobs . . .'[7]

The fighting in the village was over quickly, but the police stayed for days. Riot police marched about the village, shields on their arms and batons drawn. Easington miners claim that up to 3,000 police occupied their village. 'For the first few days people couldn't go anywhere,' said Ben Hardy.

A rank-and-file miner continued: 'They stopped the service buses going in and out of the village and searched people.' Easington was cut off from the rest of Britain for days while the police occupied it like a conquering army.

Heather Woods, who helped run the Easington soup kitchens, described the impact the police made: 'My kids now call the police "pigs". I didn't teach them. They've seen what has happened and they've learned it for themselves. I used to see it on the telly, kids in Northern Ireland treating police like this and thought the parents must be to blame. But now, you see you don't need to indoctrinate them. The police do it for them.'

The Coal Board expected every miner they got back to work would act like a magnet drawing others around them. But the arrival of the first scabs had precisely the opposite effect. It brought miners who'd done nothing throughout the strike rushing to the picket line. A single scab brought a whole community onto the streets.

In Scotland the Coal Board now claimed 100 men were working at Bilston Glen colliery. Yet a month before, they had claimed 120. The union estimated that only 37 NUM men were scabbing.

At Castlehill the Coal Board claimed two miners were back, but they turned out to be nurses sent back to work by the union! In Durham the Coal Board claimed a major breakthrough at Monkwearmouth colliery where 14 scabs crossed the picket lines. But they were all office workers or supervisors belonging to COSA, and as the scabs went into Wearmouth, 17 deputies who normally provided safety cover walked out.

On Fleet Street, only the **Financial Times** maintained a sense of perspective: 'Every area has at least one working miner — just' ran a headline, while underneath the text noted mournfully that the scabs who'd returned to work in Durham, South Yorkshire, South Wales and Kent represented just 0.15 per cent of the strikers![9]

A meeting of Socialist Workers Party supporters in the NUM held in early September discussed how to deal with the new defensive stage of the strike. The suggestions were simple — contact every striker and try to get them involved.

A Silverwood miner explained how they had organised after the first scab went into their pit:

> We went round knocking on people's doors trying to get them out picketing. The response was good, people would come out. They felt they had to fight. We began to suss out some of the problems. There are people who are basically scared, and for every miner who says he's scared there are ten that think it. We're scared, but we're used to it. Many sit at home watching police violence on TV and it terrifies them. We've got to understand that when we get people out picketing.

A miner from a Barnsley Area pit where there were no scabs tried to get a similar operation going with activists whose bail conditions barred them from the picket line.

> We pulled a few of the lads who'd been arrested together and we started going round knocking on doors and had some success in getting people out. Then we put resolutions to the branch. It said we should get a list of everyone's name and address who had been arrested and can't go out picketing and form them into recruiting teams. We should also get a list of everyone who's been passive then the recruiting teams could visit them.

But the branch committee refused to accept the resolution, then blocked the idea at the next branch meeting even though a majority there wanted to discuss it. It was, they said, 'an invasion of privacy'.

The importance of stopping the scabs before they emerged was emphasised by another Yorkshire miner:

> Even in a pit where there are no scabs you can still go round talking to people because that way you are neutralising any potential scabs. The people who are stuck at home watching TV and reading their papers have their heads filled with all sorts of rubbish. When we go and start arguing with them we are putting them off any ideas of going back to work. You also start to hear about anyone who's weakening, who's thinking of going back to work, and you can start arguing with them before it reaches the stage where they will scab.

A miner from the Longannet complex in Scotland warned of another problem: 'The Scottish Area coordinating committee see leafletting as an end in itself, as part of a community campaign, rather than a way to step up mass picketing. We've got to be clear that mass picketing is the only way to win this strike,' he stressed.

His point was emphasised by a miner from the Lothian region who talked about the scabbing at Bilston Glen. 'In a week of mass pickets we got the number of scabs down from seventeen to five. But then the officials made a deal with the police that there would only be six pickets and six police on the gates.' Once the mass picket was lifted, more scabs were going in every day.

These ideas of how to consolidate the strike should have come from the area leaders of the NUM, but they didn't.

In Yorkshire, for example, the Area leaders offered no new tactics for the defensive period of the strike. Instead Jack Taylor repeatedly assured his members that if they stood firm, 'General Winter' would win the strike for them. Many miners accepted this

A miner is arrested at Easington after police invaded the village in the last weeks of the strike

recipe for passivity, particularly as the back-to-work movement seemed stalled and the TUC Congress promised massive support.

The police against the pit villages

Any lingering doubts about the Tories' intentions should have been swept away when on 11 September Home Secretary Leon Brittan made his infamous 'jackboot pickets' speech. Brittan told a delighted audience at a Tory rally in Worksop:

> Those tempted to try their hand at violence and crime in future might care to reflect that arson, assault causing grievous bodily harm and criminal damage with intent to endanger life are offences which carry life sentences as a maximum.

The Economist magazine explained that Brittan's speech wasn't simply playing to the gallery. 'The government's worst nightmare is that a tired Mr MacGregor might agree some compromise dreamed up by his industrial relations staff. Mr Leon Brittan did his best to avert a settlement.'

Anyone who had had any contact with the policing of the strike knew only too well that the 'jackboots' were worn by the police — so too were the helmets, gauntlets, shields and other riot gear. Brittan's

Ian Wright of Hammersmith miners' support group after the police charge at Maltby

speech was also a signal to the courts and police to intensify their attacks on the miners and the mining communities.

Throughout the strike the courts were one of the Tories' major weapons. By 4 September nearly 6,500 miners had been arrested, most on relatively minor charges such as breach of the peace or obstruction. But more than 400 faced charges which carried possible life sentences.

The rising tide of arrests and police violence was designed to remove militants from the picket line and frighten off miners who were tempted to join pickets for the first time. In the face of this, the South Yorkshire Council police committee tried to restore some control over the local police. They threatened to cut the mounted police and dog units, using the excuse that they could not afford to keep them because of the cost of policing the strike.

The next morning the police horses were unleashed for the first time since Orgreave on a mass picket at Kiveton Park. Their use was unnecessary but was milked by the police for all the publicity they could get. This was the first event in a fortnight of vicious police tactics and cynical news manipulation designed to shake off criticism while at the same time maintaining the image of wholesale 'intimidation' by the striking miners.

The Kiveton Park picket was followed by one at Maltby on Friday 21 September where the police claimed they were subjected to a four-hour barrage of bricks, bottles, air-gun pellets and catapult-launched ball bearings from 5,000 miners. 'It was orchestrated without a doubt,' claimed Superintendent Eric Vallance. 'It was a very well planned picket and escalated at an alarming rate.'[10]

In fact, 2,000 pickets faced police with horses and dogs from the South and West Yorkshire constabularies. There were no air rifles on the picket line. The police did face sporadic brick throwing, but only after they had baton-charged the pickets.

The following Monday, there was another confrontation at Maltby where, the **Daily Express** claimed: 'Pickets opened fire with deadly new weapons', as '500 brave policemen faced 5,000 raging pickets.'[11] Ted Millward, the Maltby branch treasurer, told a different story of just 1,000 pickets confronted by a massive police presence. 'We couldn't get near the pit gate,' he said. 'They shoved us right away to the perimeter of the village . . . There was some stones thrown, but very little.'[12]

The police waited until most of the pickets had dispersed, then a squad of boiler-suited officers emerged from the woods to launch a savage attack on those remaining. 'I was involved at Orgreave but I've never seen anything like this. And a lot of the public who were on their way back to work saw it all,' Ted Millward explained.

Ian Wright, a member of the Hammersmith miners' support committee on a visit to South Yorkshire, was repeatedly truncheoned about the head as he lay on the ground. As miners tried to comfort him, the police screamed: 'Let the bastard die.'[13]

Labour MP Kevin Baron was attacked as he walked to his car: 'The police were bludgeoning people to the ground. When I went back later there was still a pool of blood on the pavement. I have never seen anything so brutal in my life.'[14]

Bob Mounsey, a 50-year-old miner who used to be the Maltby NUM branch delegate, was also a victim. He described his experiences:

I'd just walked back to the Maltby bus stop to let my wife know I was OK. She'd seen the aggro earlier. As I walked back past the Lumbley Arms, about 35 to 40 police came out behind me.

I dodged two, one who struck at my head with his yard-stick and another who tried to knee me between the legs. Then I was hit on the hip. It paralysed my leg. As I stumbled another hit me on the leg and head. A group of them kicked me on the floor.

I wasn't knocked out. I just lay there dazed. An old chap came across to see if I was OK. I tried to get up but he told me to stay down because the police were still hanging about. The police had no intention of arresting anyone. It was just a commando raid to dish out some hammer.

Bob's injuries included bruises across his kidneys, down his left leg from the hip to the knee, on both shoulders and he had a lump on the back of his head.[15]

Maltby NUM officials knew exactly why the police had been so savage. 'They have adopted the tactic of terrifying or injuring our lads,' said Ted Millward, while Ron Buck, the Maltby branch secretary, explained why the size and behaviour of the pickets had been so distorted: 'It gives the police justification for their turnout and behaviour.'

The next day members of the South Yorkshire police committee met Home Secretary Leon Brittan. He offered to review the government's contribution to the policing costs in the self-proclaimed 'socialist republic'. With that the police committee reprieved the horses.

The police attacks on the mining communities increased during October. Perhaps the most notorious was at Grimethorpe where police with riot shields attacked men, women and children picking coal on the colliery tip. As word of the attacks got round the village, the miners replied by first picketing and then attacking lorries which had dispensations to take coal from the pit. For two days there was

Picking coal at South Kirkby

guerrilla warfare in Grimethorpe between miners determined to get revenge and the police who were equally determined to beat the community into submission.

The heat was eventually taken out of the confrontation when the South Yorkshire police committee called a public meeting where local residents could complain about the police.

'I've been assaulted, kicked, punched and handcuffed,' said Norman Whittaker, the town mayor. Miner's wife Elaine Crawford told the meeting: 'I was going home about 11.30, when a police van came screaming round the corner with no lights on. The bobbies pounced on a young boy and kicked hell out of him. We were shouting and screaming at them to stop. You know what they called me?' she asked. "Get home you prostitute, you whore." '

George Moores, the chairman of the police committee, was moved to liken some of the picket line police to 'Nazi stormtroopers'. At the end of the meeting, Frank Gutsell, the Assistant Chief Constable of South Yorkshire, got up and said: 'I apologise, apologise unreservedly' for some of the police behaviour.

It was a unique statement by a senior policeman during the miners' strike and it was widely reported. But the stories told by the people of Grimethorpe were quickly forgotten by Fleet Street.

Women — the backbone of the strike

'If someone had said to me before this began that I'd be picketing, organising and addressing meetings, I'd never have believed them.' Those words came from the lips of thousands of women from the mining communities during the 12-month strike.

From the very start of the strike the women of the mining communities have refused to play the role that the press usually ascribes to the wives and girlfriends of strikers. As usual, the press attempted to play on the minds of striking miners by using women to undermine the dispute. They either presented women as the victims of the irresponsible action of the NUM, or in Nottinghamshire, as strident campaigners against the strike.

In direct answer to the press and TV, women's action groups sprang up in many pit villages in the first few weeks of the strike. They quickly got involved in all aspects of the strike, until they became the driving force behind much of the organisation which held the strike together on a day-to-day basis.

First and foremost, these groups generally set up and maintained the food kitchens which were as much a feature of the strike as the picketing. Often the Women's Action groups were set up independently of the union, but the union could not have survived without them. Isabell, who helped start the women's action group for the wives and girlfriends of miners at Yorkshire Main colliery near Doncaster, explained how they began:

It started because I couldn't stand the TV making out that the wives weren't behind their men. I was so angry and frustrated for a week that in the end Brian [Isabell's husband] took me round the wives of some other militants in the pit. Ten of us sat up half the night talking about what to do and five of us decided to go and picket Thorseby in Nottinghamshire that night. Brian made *my* snap for a change! And he made us a banner. We called ourselves an action group because everyone says they support the miners but we want to be active.

As we walked up to Thorseby the pickets were moaning: 'Oh god not the women again'. They'd had the local wives nagging them, but when they found out we were from Yorkshire this fantastic cheer went up. It was brilliant. I knew we'd done the right thing. Men from Kent and South Wales were there. They'd been sleeping in Nottingham [Sherwood] forest to keep

Preparing Christmas dinner at Cadeby miners' kitchen

away from the police. They were bedraggled and hungry.

One young lad from South Wales — he can't have been more than 18 — he had been sleeping rough. He came up and the way he said: 'Have you got a cup of tea for me please?', it just filled me up. I just thought if he had that much faith in what he was doing to go through that, I'd got to do something too.

Involvement in the strike produced commitment to it. At Yorkshire Main, Isabell and her friend set out to organise the other women in the community. Their first efforts were both painstakingly slow, and a sign of the determination that made the women so crucial to the strike. 'We all sat down and wrote out leaflets by hand and distributed them through the doors. We made some posters too. We didn't get a great response, but 15 women came to a meeting and we decided to set up the kitchen.'

They were convinced from the start that they were in for a long bitter strike: 'Some said they'd raise money, some said they'd speak at meetings to raise money and some just said they'd cook the meals but nearly all of us want to keep up the picketing too,' said Isabell. Then the hard work of finding premises, scrounging equipment and raising the necessary funds began. The same scene was unfolding in all the coalfields.

Sometimes, the women's determination to hang onto their independent organisation and be more than cooks for the pickets led to confrontations with NUM officials over picketing and the running of the kitchens. Lorraine Bowler of the Barnsley Women's Action Group summed it up when she spoke after a women's march through Barnsley in support of the miners: 'At the beginning of the strike women in the Barnsley group wanted to go picketing and we were told that it was a bad enough job organising the men.' But, said Lorraine, the women don't need organising. They can do it themselves.

Indeed, the kitchens often became centres of strike organisation. Bentley Women's Action Group ran one of the most successful kitchens. They were twinned with Camden council workers in London and the regular donations sent to Bentley allowed them to feed 500 miners and their families every day. With less than half the active pickets attending union meetings, the kitchen became an important place for the pickets to meet and discuss. As one striker said: 'Coming here you learn more about the strike than you do at most union meetings. This is the place we get most of our information about what's going on.'

The kitchens increased in importance as a meeting place during the Coal Board's back-to-work campaigns. A miner from Westoe explained how the kitchen stopped men drifting back to work. 'We used to go down to the kitchen when the weekly food parcels were being given out. There were new faces for the meals and the parcels and we used to talk to them and get them more involved in the strike and the picketing. We would also use the opportunity to sort out hardship problems. One time a bloke was going back to work because his electricity was going to be cut off and he had a young kid. We found out about it, sorted it out and he stayed on strike.'

The best organised women's support groups did more than simply feed the communities and go picketing. A member of the Pontefract Women's support group explained:

We realised that a support group meant supporting the miners in every aspect. The first thing that came up was the electricity and gas putting pressure on people. The NUM weren't taking it far enough. They just gave out a letter to people threatened with disconnection which asked the gas and electricity board workers not to do it.

The women's support group told the gas and electricity boards, and the unions, that they'd form a picket line round any

A women's action group picket at Yorkshire Main — after the Area agreed to limit pickets to six

house threatened with disconnection. The electricity board back off when they see the support group because we're an organised body.

The women's support groups round the Pontefract area campaigned to force the local authority to increase the clothing grant to striking miners' children. Under-fives were getting nothing and school age children just £25 paid in quarterly instalments.

As the government's determination to starve the miners into submission became obvious, the sheer size of the organisation needed to maintain the mining communities grew enormously. The women's action groups rose to the task. At Maerdy in South Wales, for example, the women's support group committee met every week to arrange the distribution of food parcels. At a single meeting in early October they also planned how to approach shop stewards in sweet and toy factories for Xmas, planned a bonfire party, a jumble sale, a sponsored marathon, and the next week's fund raising.

Like many women's support groups, for many months they raised much of the money they needed by collecting in their own communities. But Jean Bromage explained, 'Our community has been run down so much, everyone is in the same boat — you can only take off your own for so long.' So they were forced to take part in the delegation work done in every major city and town in Britain. Many trade unionists found that women put the miners' case better than their men.

One London fireman told how 'it was the way the women explained what it meant for their families if the pits shut down that really got to people. By the time the delegation of women left one London fire station we had filled a van with food and toys we had collected.'

The effect on the women of the mining communities was electric. Jean Bromage explained: 'We send women to Oxford and Birmingham where our lads are picketing and we do the meetings. The first meeting I ever did was in a college in Oxford. I'd never spoken in my life — I was shaking like a leaf. I still get the shakes but I do it. Thatcher has had the shock of her life during this strike. She never thought women could react like this. Before the strike I knew nothing about unions. I didn't want to know.'

The Bold miners' wives support group in Lancashire prepared themselves a little better. Lorraine Johnson, secretary of the group, had experience of public speaking — she'd called the numbers at the Old Folk's Bingo in the miners' welfare before the strike! She was quickly addressing mass meetings and organising a training scheme for other women to build up their confidence.

In many ways, the women's action groups, the food kitchens, the delegations and fund-raising trips, the logging teams who got wood to keep the striking communities warm, the struggle to keep the strike alive during the autumn and winter of 1984 were the most inspiring parts of the strike. They showed the depths of skill, talent, humour, guts and sheer organising ability that had lain untapped in the mining communities. They also hinted at what might have happened in the strike if these qualities had been channelled by the union from the start.

The organisation and participation of women in the miners' strike was unique in recent British history. Without it, the miners would have been beaten long before the eventual return to work.

Of course, women workers have always taken part in industrial battles. The Barking hospital strikers began their strike alongside the miners in March 1984 and were still out when the miners went back to work, while the past ten years have seen a string of major women's strikes from the Fords sewing machinists, Trico, Grunwick, through to Chix and Lee Jeans. What makes the women's involvement in the miners' strike unique is both its sheer scale, and that it involved women outside the workforce in a prolonged war of attrition.

The involvement of women in the Great Miners' Strike has broken down the idea that only those whose jobs are threatened can fight a strike. The women of the mining communities have proved that working-class women are as capable of fighting and leading a strike as their men. And in so doing, they have transformed their lives and their expectations. Things have changed on the union side too: there will be no pictures of semi-nude women in the **Yorkshire Miner** again, or in other miners' publications, as was the policy a few years before the strike. The relations between women and men have been radically improved.

As Anne O'Donnel, from Bentley, said: 'There's no way I would return to the kitchen sink now. I'm not going back to how things were before. Both me and my husband were fairly unpolitical before the strike but now we've both changed!'

Back to the courts

At the end of September, Mr Justice Nichols ruled in the High Court that the strikes in the Yorkshire and North Derbyshire Areas were unlawful. 'The NUM's action will not be lawful unless and until it does hold a national ballot which shows a majority in favour of the strike action,' he declared.

Robert Taylor and Ken Foulstone, the Manton scabs who brought the case against the Yorkshire Area, were granted injunctions preventing the Yorkshire Area from calling the strike or pickets 'official' or disciplining scabs. Arthur Scargill replied on television:

I am going to say this, and quite clearly: that any miner in this union and any official in this union who urges or crosses a picket line in defiance of our union's instructions runs the risk of being disciplined under our rules. And there is no high court judge going to take away the democratic right to deal with internal affairs. We are an independent democratic union.

David Potts, the Manton branch secretary, was particularly upset. 'They talk about democracy. They're only interested as long as it goes their way,' he said. The Manton branch met a few days before the injunction was granted and 750 miners had voted overwhelmingly to continue the strike and condemn the legal action against the union.

Despite their High Court triumph, Taylor and Foulstone could find only two other Manton men to cross the picket line with them. In the rest of Yorkshire, only one other 'new face' turned up for work.

The High Court gave Arthur Scargill five days to 'consider' his contempt. Scargill repeated: 'If the choice is to spend a term in Pentonville or any other prison or to live by the imprisonment of my mind for betraying my class, the choice is that I stand by my class and my union!'[16]

On Wednesday 10 October Scargill was fined £1,000 and the NUM £200,000.

Even the **Daily Mirror** called for the fine to be paid. 'Mr Arthur Scargill and the miners' executive have broken the law and must face the consequences. It is not a Tory law. It is an English law. It does not mean submitting to a Tory government but to parliamentary government.'[17]

This 'law' was in fact a legal action paid for by businessmen, brought by two men who professed to represent the silent minority of the NUM, but could only get two others at their own pit to join them in crossing the picket line.

This wasn't the end of the legal onslaught. Taylor and Foulstone's lawyers served yet more legal orders on the miners' leaders. This time they sought to make all the members of the NUM executive, and the coordinating committee that ran the strike, personally liable for contempt if the court order was broken again.

Thirteen days later the NUM's assets were seized. And on 1 November, the two men's lawyers announced that they were beginning legal action to make each of the 25 members of the NUM executive personally liable to pay the full £200,000 fine. More legal actions followed. They became a constant threat to the NUM leaders and a constant distraction from the fight to maintain the strike and prevent the drift back to work.

Government on the offensive

The miners' union, shorn of its funds, now faced a mounting attack from the government. Energy Secretary Peter Walker told the House of Commons on Monday 29 October that the government would give no more ground. The agreement between the Coal Board and the deputies union NACODS was their final offer.

The TUC tried desperately to get the NACODS deal accepted by the NUM, but the miners' negotiating team of Scargill, Heathfield and McGahey wouldn't budge. However, the right wing on the miners' executive were interested. They showed their hand for the first time since April, demanded a national ballot on the NACODS terms, and were defeated by only 11 votes to 9.

Scargill called a national delegate conference to counteract the pressure he faced from the executive and he called on the TUC and Labour Party to deliver the 'total support' they had promised.

We believe the time has come to involve as much as possible in a public way, the wider trade union and Labour movement in a dispute which the Tories see clearly as the fight on the part of the establishment against an individual union. We are asking the trade union movement to respond accordingly and give the same sort of support to the NUM.

The NUM also called a series of rallies for the strikers and, as a symbol of the support they had earlier pledged, asked TUC leaders and Neil Kinnock to take part. But the more the miners needed help, the more thay were spurned by those they asked. Neil Kinnock refused to attend, claiming his diary was 'too full'. Willis did speak, and used the platform to denounce the miners' pickets.

Now the Coal Board announced a £650 bonus — or bribe — for men returning to work. The campaign to break the strike had begun in earnest and it was prosecuted most ruthlessly in North Derbyshire.

Focus on North Derbyshire

The **Financial Times** described the Coal Board's operation:

From the start of the strike, the management has armed itself with names, addresses and telephone numbers of workers and plotted their residence and likely attitude on large maps. The plan, which is being copied in Yorkshire and Durham, was to concentrate on workers living outside the immediate areas of the pit villages. The management also drew up lists of men believed to be strongly hostile to the strike, or even those who had worked a lot of overtime and might therefore be finding things particularly difficult. The management began telephoning and visiting those likely to return.

The scabs of the 'Working Miners Committee' rushed to the management's aid. At Shirebrook, Roland Taylor explained: 'I've thought things through with management at my own pit. They suggested we use the phones to call people up — they gave us lists and lent us vans. Shirebrook has been a well oiled machine.'[18]

While the Coal Board were giving the scabs money to harass strikers and their families at home, Taylor's colleagues on the Working Miners Committee were securing injunctions preventing the miners' union spending money to hold the strike together!

The North Derbyshire officials, meanwhile, were complacent, claiming that the strike in the Area was '90 per cent solid'. Area president Gordon Butler said that in the face of the Coal Board offensive 'to change tactics would be seen . . . as the act of desperate people.'

But the back-to-work pressure began to have an effect on miners in North Derbyshire, many of whom had not been drawn into activity in the nine months of the strike so far. Within a week a series of mass meetings were called in miners' welfares.

Peter Elliot, branch secretary at Warsop and an area executive member, spoke to 300 miners at North Wingfield. He described how some North Derbyshire miners had rejoined the strike after going into work to be told by the colliery manager 'I'm the union now' and ordered to sign a promise not to strike again. He pulled no punches: 'The Coal Board are out to destroy the union,' he said. 'Imagine life in the pit without it.' And this was the argument that won the previously-divided audience.

The next day local MP Dennis Skinner needed all his oratorical powers to carry a meeting in Plessley miners' welfare where hundreds of men had expected a vote to go back.

At both meetings, the questions from the floor hammered home the failure of the movement to back the miners. 'Where's the TUC?' 'What's Kinnock playing at?' 'How the hell do we get the money to carry on?'

The union carried the day but it had been left desperately late: 'We failed to keep the membership in touch,' admitted Alan Gascoyne, the Shirebrook branch secretary. 'We dished out **The Miner** and leaflets but it wasn't enough. We never got down to the nitty gritty, going into the welfares and telling people the facts, what's really going on.'

There was one other crucial weakness in North Derbyshire. The level of welfare facilities for the strikers was woefully inadequate, far worse than was available in most Yorkshire pit villages. Few North Derbyshire pits had kitchens for the strikers and their families. Instead the women's support groups struggled to make up food parcels — the contents generally inadequate to feed a family for a day.

Few pits were 'twinned' with trade union branches or miners support groups in the major cities, instead funds were raised and food distributed centrally from Chesterfield.

But this only provided a pit such as Shirebrook with 90 food parcels a week when they needed 600! In such areas it was real tribute to the miners that so many took the meagre food parcel and not the Coal Board bribe.

The 'carrot', the chance of a wage packet, was backed up by force. In the early months of the strike pit villages like Shirebrook were subject to Nottinghamshire-style policing when the Coal Board expected the strike to crumble.

As the scabbing at Shirebrook increased in October and November, the police came back, in force. They swamped the village first at shift changing times, then constantly. Arrests on the picket line soared as the police tried to break the spirit of the militants.

The police had another string to their bow too. The back to work movement picked up steam as many of the North Derbyshire miners who had been arrested early on in the strike were appearing in court. They often found the police adding extra charges while the stipendiary magistrates — who are paid full-timers rather than the usual part-time local dignitaries — handed down savage sentences.

A higher proportion of Derbyshire miners were jailed or sacked than in many other areas. Some were offered their jobs back — providing they crossed the picket lines. And after Christmas, in an even more disgusting bribe, men who had been sacked were told that sons or nephews who had been offered jobs with the Coal Board, but hadn't started because of the strike, would not be employed unless they returned to work themselves.

This was the systematic intimidation of strikers that was going on during the 'back-to-work' drive, the real intimidation in the mining villages that was never reported by the papers or TV. And it was enough to crack some, but not the majority of miners in North Derbyshire.

Back to confrontation

If North Derbyshire got the worst of the Coal Board's back-to-work drive, other areas felt the pressure too — but still the Area leaders didn't spell out what needed to be done to defend the strike.

Instead they seemed transfixed by a series of blows that rained down on the union. The sequestrators traced £2.8 million of the miners' funds to Ireland, and the High Court ordered the North Derbyshire NUM not to spend any money on the strike.

To make matters worse, the NUM became even more isolated in its defiance of the Tory anti-union laws when Austin Rover won an injunction against nine unions declaring a wages strike at their plants was illegal. One by one the unions withdrew official backing until the strike eventually collapsed.

In the first week of their back-to-work bribe in November, the Coal Board claimed 2,100 men back at work for the first time. As a percentage of those striking it was pitiful — 3.5 per cent of the Scottish miners, 0.4 per cent of the Yorkshire miners, 0.2 per cent of the Northumberland and Durham miners and 0.1 per cent in South Wales. But the increase in scabbing did have a real impact on the spirit of the strikers, their supporters and those other groups of workers who had taken solidarity action.

The numbers going back to work increased during the second week of the Coal Board offer and led to confrontations between pickets and police in South Yorkshire. Where serious fighting did take place, it was generally provoked by the police. Dinnington saw the heaviest fighting, and the description given by Ken Moulds, the branch delegate, differed markedly from that written by the Fleet Street journalists, who got no closer to the action than the police press conference.

'We set up a picket line about midnight. Soon after six vans of riot police arrived. They poured out with their shields and everything. People were getting hurt straight away.' Ken described how the pickets at first ran away but then counter-attacked when they saw the police were attacking one of their comrades sprawled on the ground.

From then on the police escalated it all the day, charging pickets, shouting out war cries, beating their shields. The pickets replied by throwing things and the police quite openly threw them back although they are protected by riot shields and our lads aren't. A lot of lads were hit like that.

Six of our lads needed hospital treatment, one was detained with head injuries, another was discharged but taken back. His skull was broken. They chased the pickets 600 yards from the pit. It was then that the pickets put a barricade across the road to stop themselves being driven back further.

After this the men had gone through a barrier, any police were fair game and some went to attack the police station. We've just got beyond the stage where you stand back and let the police truncheon you.[19]

In the next month, this scene was repeated in scores of pit villages, where, as soon as the Coal Board got one scab at a pit the police would invade the community in a bid to establish control of the area. Local people then had the choice, either to allow a single scab with his massive police escort to go to work unchallenged, or to fight back.

TUC general secretary Norman Willis did manage to condemn 'scenes of unprovoked police aggression' when he spoke at a miners' rally in Aberavon on 13 November. But the miners bore the brunt of his notorious 'violence is not the way' speech and responded by dangling a noose in front of him to go with the placards that read 'Where's Ramsey McKinnock?'

'Any miner who resorts to violence damages the miners' case far more than they weaken their opponents' resolve,' Willis declared. 'Violence creates more violence,' he said — and he wasn't referring to how the violence of the police was forcing miners to retaliate. 'Such acts if they are done by miners are alien to our common trade union tradition, however, not just because they were counter-productive but because they are wrong.'

Having satisfied Fleet Street, Willis continued with some cringing apologetics for the TUC's failure to deliver the solidarity they had promised. 'The TUC is not an army and I am not a field marshal. When I see hardship, when I see sacrifice, I wish I could guarantee you all the support you need. But I don't kid trade unionists and I'll never mislead the miners.'

It was an extraordinary statement. In the two months since the TUC Congress pledged its total support to the miners, the TUC General Council had not issued one leaflet, printed one poster or even called a single rally or march in support of the miners.

Indeed, throughout November and December, the more the miners needed support, the more craven the TUC and Labour leaders became.

Neil Kinnock in inimitable style accused the miners' leaders of wanting a 'glorious defeat'; while on 15 November Roy Hattersley called on the NUM leaders to ballot their members on the strike. The GMBATU cut off its daily £1,000 payment to the NUM.

But on a trip to Russia towards the end of November, Neil Kinnock surpassed himself. Russian press reports of starving miners being beaten by the police were exaggerated, he said: 'I told them that while people were enduring very great hardship there was no hunger, and that the reports of deprivation on that scale were somewhat misleading.'[20]

The July issue of the Coal Board paper **Coal News** had claimed 57,000 miners were working. The August edition put the figure at 'more than 60,000'. Yet in the week beginning 12 November, the Coal Board estimated 53,000 at work.

Perhaps the most spectacular fiddle, though, came in **The Sun**. Early editions of the 20 November issue reported 47,631 miners at work but an infuriated editor changed this total to 62,631 in later editions, saying the true figure 'would aid Scargill'![21]

The drift back to work petered out at the end of November when the Coal Board's Christmas bribe ended. The Coal Board were certainly more successful than they'd been in the summer, but they had hardly advanced at all in the core areas of the strike. The strikers included 98 per cent of Yorkshire miners, 99 per cent of South Wales miners, 90 per cent of North East miners, and 66 per cent of North Derbyshire miners.

They had won a majority back to work at only a handful of pits. These included Bersham in North Wales, Shirebrook in North Derbyshire, Whittle in Northumberland and Shireoaks in South Yorkshire. However, they had broken the taboo of scabbing at most pits in the core areas of the strike.

As individual scabs appeared at more and more pits, the miners' leaders dropped mass picketing and ordered men to picket their own colliery. Very quickly, this led to the emergence of flying police instead of flying pickets. Squads of police would shift from pit to pit, sweeping pickets aside as they brought scabs into work and then moved on to the next pit. The frustration and resentment this caused led some pickets to believe that individual acts of violence could substitute for the mass picketing that was now being blocked. The media naturally picked on these acts to try to isolate the pickets.

These acts were an attempt to overcome the lack of clear leadership from their Area officials, and the way the police not only battered them on the picket lines but also comprehensively outmanoeuvred them to get the scabs into work. The most notorious incident came on Friday 30 November when David Wilkie, a taxi driver, was killed when two concrete posts smashed through his windscreen as he was taking a pair of scabs into Merthyr Vale colliery in Aberfan. He was the first person to die in the strike who was not on the side of the pickets — several NUM members had died before this.

The press were, naturally, hysterical. None bothered to find out what had provoked the miners to the attack. If they had talked to local miners they would have found out how the police had swamped Merthyr Vale and Aberfan village to get the scabs into work.

Bill King, the branch secretary, explained how pickets were outnumbered three-to-one by police; how people were stopped going to work and even stopped from going to school so the scabs could get into work undisturbed. As in Yorkshire, a common complaint of the pickets was that police were waving £5 and £10 notes at them. Even the local vicar had been on the picket line and complained about the 'community being provoked by police methods'.

The police had only allowed one mass picket at Merthyr Vale, and that only consisted of a few hundred. It occurred earlier in the week in which David Wilkie was killed and during it, the scabs' taxi ran down three policemen!

After this incident, the police sealed off both ends of the valley leading to Merthyr Vale to keep pickets away. Men wanting to picket their own pit couldn't get through the roadblocks. The more determined found alternative routes. 'Boys were walking over the mountains to get to the picket. Sometimes they have to walk ten or fifteen

The shame of a scab

miles to picket their own pit,' explained a Merthyr Vale miner.

For a day or two, scrambling over the mountains in the pitch dark of the early morning was a challenge, but in the cold and rain of the November nights, a few miners decided there must be an easier and more effective way to scare the scabs than to struggle for hours to get to a picket line where you'd then be dwarfed by the giant police presence.

'It was the police who spread the pickets out, and that's why the incident happened — out of frustration,' explained another miner.

Of course the pickets were shocked by the killing of David Wilkie, but, as one miner said: 'They knew the risks — the driver was kitted up with a police riot helmet — and they were all well paid for it. The money they've spent on bringing these scabs into work could have opened up new reserves at this pit and secured all our jobs.'

Local anger was deep-rooted because, before the strike began, the union had repeatedly fought to save the jobs of the two Merthyr Vale scabs who were in the taxi. Union officials say they'd four times prevented the sacking of one and had to threaten a strike to save the job of the other, after he was given his cards for absenteeism!

Their determination to continue the strike was deeper-rooted still. It is eighteen years since 100 children and 40 adults died when the colliery spoil heap swept away houses and the school in Aberfan. A middle-aged miner summed up the way local people felt: 'They've taken away our children and now they're trying to take away our livelihood.'

The death of David Wilkie occurred on the day Neil Kinnock had finally arranged to speak at a miners' support rally. It gave him the perfect weapon to beat the NUM for the conduct of the strike.

The place he finally chose to 'put the case' was Stoke on Trent, in the heart of the Staffordshire coalfield where a majority of miners were working. There, Kinnock told the miners: 'The violence has got to stop and stop now. For, as the violence endangers others, so you deface this miners' cause and you disgust the trade union movement.'

Arthur Scargill, who sat stony-faced throughout Kinnock's performance, was also forced to condemn violence 'which occurred away from the picket line'.

There *is* a good argument against individual acts of violence and the 'hit squads' that sprang up in some mining communities, but it had nothing to do with the hypocrisy of Neil Kinnock and the TUC leaders. It is best illustrated by the events around Fryston colliery, where Michael Fletcher was attacked by striking miners after he returned to work in November.

Fletcher's return to work brought with it the usual invasion by police, the usual baton-charge on the picket line, and the usual crop of injuries among the strikers. One man, 48-year-old Charles Maxwell, was detained in hospital for a week after the beating he received from the police.

If that weren't provocation enough, Fletcher lived opposite the food kitchen, and had been taking striker's food parcels until days before he returned to work. Furthermore, since he began working at Fryston in 1978, the Coal Board had tried to sack him three times — only for the union to save his job.

It was not surprising then that a group of frustrated strikers attacked Fletcher in his home a few days after he returned to work.

Of course the press seized on it. The scab became a star. TV cameras crowded round his hospital bed as Ian MacGregor rushed north to make a presentation to him. Just down the corridor lay Charles Maxwell. No one bothered to interview him. He'd only been hospitalised by the police.

Like the media and the Coal Board, the police seized their chance and began a wholesale round-up of militants at the pit. Fifty activists were arrested. The press and TV talked gravely of 'criminal conspiracies'. Roy Wright, the branch secretary, was charged with 'causing grievous bodily harm on the basis of inciting, aiding or abetting'. After four weeks remanded in Armley jail and another seven in exile, away from the mining areas, Roy's case finally came to court, and the police announced they had no evidence against him!

It was one of the starkest illustrations in the whole strike of how the police have used arrests, charges and bail conditions to neutralise the militants and demoralise the rest of the strikers.

The arrests in Fryston after the attack on Fletcher had just the purpose the police intended. They removed one of the best officials in the North Yorkshire area from the action and the best militants in the branch from the picket line. As a result the atmosphere on the Fryston picket line was more demoralised and depressed by the mass arrests than the return of the first scab to the pit.

This was a story repeated time and again in the core areas of the strike, of how the police would use an attack on a scab to round up young militants and try and force a confession from them. One North Yorkshire miner explained how militants began to fear the 'knock on the door' that was the first step to the police cells. He described how arrested miners were held for 72 hours without access to solicitors or their families, and how the police tried to fit them up.

They told people that if they didn't plead guilty to something, they would be charged with smashing up the pit office. Anyone found guilty of that would automatically be sacked by the Coal Board. Once they agree to plead guilty, then they find they have bail conditions slapped on them which in a number of cases have amounted to house arrest. [22]

And this illustrates the real argument against 'hit squads' and attacks on individual scabs. It is nothing to do with upholding the rule of law, nor is it that violence is 'alien to the British trade union movement' as Kinnock said.

After a year on strike, after 10,000 often arbitrary arrests, after the ludicrous charges and bail conditions imposed on miners, after the lives lost on the picket line, after the thousands of terrible injuries inflicted by the police and their invasion of the mining villages, after a year of privation and media abuse, the miners had every right to take any action they saw fit to defend their strike.

The only argument against attacks on individual scabs was that they were not a way to win the strike. They were not a substitute for mass picketing involving whole communities, which characterised the beginning of the back to work movement. And they weren't a substitute for real solidarity, which the trade union leaders who eagerly denounced the miners' violence promised but never delivered.

'I am the NUM'

The final assault on the NUM in 1984 came when the courts handed the union over, lock, stock and barrel, to a Tory lawyer.

The High Court replaced the elected officials of the miners' union with a 'Receiver' on 31 November. This followed contempt proceedings against the union (for not paying its £200,000 fine) brought by sixteen of the scabs so carefully cultivated by MacGregor and Thatcher's aides back in August. The court's chosen custodian of the union was Herbert Brewer, chairman of the Nottinghamshire and Derbyshire branch of Mrs Thatcher's favourite business pressure group, the Institute of Directors, and a former Conservative party official!

Brewer rushed off to Luxemburg, where the bulk of the union's money had been traced, and tried to repatriate the NUM's funds. While knocking on the door of the bank where the money was deposited, he even declared: 'I am the NUM!' — something no elected official of the union had ever done.

It was an extraordinary situation. The union was under orders not to call the strike official, not to spend money on supporting its members and not to do anything to counter the Coal Board's back-to-work pressure. In addition, the NUM were told they had to 'purge their contempt' before they could recover their funds. And that meant abandoning the strike!

Scargill spelt out what was at stake. The Receiver's appointment, he said, posed 'the most fundamental threat to every trade union in the country' and put at 'immediate risk the very existence of the NUM.'[23]

There were dangerous signs of weakening resolve when the NUM executive met in emergency session on Sunday 2 December. The meeting agreed by 11 votes to 6, with the Yorkshire Area abstaining, to cooperate with the Receiver by bringing the union's funds back to Britain. Fortunately this was overturned at an emergency delegate conference of the union the next day. Jack Collins from Kent knew how shocked the militants were by the executive's decision and what a disaster it would be to bring the money back: 'The executive misread the mood . . . We have to send a clear message to the lads on the picket lines that there is no compromise, no surrender.'

The delegates called on the TUC now to organise industrial action in support of the miners and after the conference, Arthur Scargill appealed once more for solidarity:

> The trade union movement has a choice. It can either be in contempt of the law or in contempt of its members. If it ever loses the support of its members and they hold it in contempt then the trade union movement is lost. This most serious threat by the High Court to smash the NUM is but a prelude to the smashing of the entire trade union and Labour movement. I only hope that trade unionists recognise that they must stand up and fight.

But the call fell on deaf ears. No sooner had the NUM asked for industrial action than the TUC replied that it was out of the question, as was any action in support of the NUM that might leave the TUC itself liable for contempt proceedings. That meant they would offer the NUM neither funds, buildings or even a phone to operate from if the Receiver took over their Sheffield headquarters!

It was the most abject surrender by the TUC leaders. But they went further. Not content with washing their hands of the miners in their hour of greatest need, they insisted they'd worked their fingers to the bone trying to drum up solidarity. According to the **Financial Times**, Arthur Scargill was told: 'Union leaders had made genuine and sustained attempts to drum up industrial support and that their failure was not due to lack of will or lack of effort.'[24]

For the rest of December, Kinnock and Norman Willis limited themselves to begging the government to return to talks. But the lower Kinnock and Willis stooped, the more the Tories put the boot into the miners. Each time they sued for peace instead of campaigning for solidarity, the rhetoric from Tory ministers got stronger.

As Christmas approached, miners' supporters from every town and city flooded into the coalfields, bringing with them hundreds of thousands of pounds to give the miners a decent Christmas. They laid on kids' parties, turkeys, food parcels, presents. It was one of the most overwhelming displays of support ever seen in an industrial dispute.

It put new heart into many mining communities. Their very real nightmares of a cold, hungry and isolated Christmas were swept aside by the tidal wave of gifts and solidarity. Many mining families talked about this Christmas on strike as their best ever

The contrast between this tribute to the courage of the miners and their families and the words of the official leaders of the trade union and labour movement had never been starker.

Christmas picketing at Rossington

7
THE UNNECESSARY DEFEAT

AGAINST all the odds the striking miners and their families held firm into the New Year. Deserted though they had been by the TUC, the mining communities fought on, sustained by the vast solidarity network which had grown up around them. They had been out for ten months, nearly three months longer than the 1926 lockout. It was an astounding achievement.

Then in mid-January the strike began to crumble. The number of miners breaking the strike began to rise. Coal Board hopes of a post-Christmas 'surge back to work' were disappointed, but 5,170 miners crossed picket lines according to the NCB in the first full working fortnight of 1985.

Then the trickle threatened to become a flood on Monday 21 January. The strike was crumbling fast in the Northumberland coalfield and 593 went back in one day in Yorkshire, the heart of the strike. The **Financial Times** called it 'a very black Monday' for the NUM.

What had happened so to weaken the strikers' resolve? Two elements were involved. One was the NCB's domino strategy. They concentrated their efforts on particularly vulnerable areas, then used successes there to widen the cracks in the strike elsewhere. This strategy of undermining the strike piecemeal, Area by Area, had a number of advantages.

Psychologically it was difficult for strikers to hold on once a majority of the miners in their Area had gone back. Also banks and building societies had had little incentive to foreclose on miners' families in an area where the strike was solid — the effect would simply be to bring down property prices. Once most miners were back at work it was much easier to put pressure on those still out to join them or lose their homes.

The NCB had already pursued this strategy back in the late summer and early winter, devoting attention to pits closest to Nottinghamshire — the North Derbyshire coalfield and Manton and Shireoaks in South Yorkshire. Now they drove deeper into the Yorkshire coalfield, concentrating their efforts on the pits nearest to where scabbing had already taken off — Kiveton Park and Dinnington — and on pits in the traditionally less militant North Yorkshire panel. They also aimed first at the more isolated miners, living not in close-knit mining communities, but scattered across the Leeds and Sheffield conurbations.

The strategy paid off on Black Monday — 21 January. At three pits — Kiveton Park in South Yorkshire, Kellingley in North Yorkshire, and Killoch in Ayrshire — miners went back in organised groups of respectively 150, 70, and 135, according to the Coal Board. By the end of the week the management at Kiveton Park was claiming that 432 out of 735 miners were scabbing. The surge in scabbing took place even though Arthur Scargill had spoken at Kellingley and Jack Taylor at Kiveton Park the previous weekend.

The NCB's inroads were made possible by a growing sense of directionlessness among the strikers, even in the most militant pits. A miner from Silverwood in South Yorkshire put it like this:

> Before Christmas, people who were loyal to the union had something to look to. There were supporters bringing stuff down. We didn't feel so isolated. Now people are actually seeing the possibility of defeat . . . People are asking what's happening; they hear stories, and they're not getting answers from the officials. Even people who are active in the strike are discontented.

The fact that there were no significant power cuts was an important element in the demoralisation. When Peter Walker claimed early in the New Year that there would be no power cuts, Peter Heathfield agreed with him, to the despair of many strikers. Activists hoped that the first national executive of the New Year would put forward a new initiative to deal with this situation, but the NUM leadership as a whole pretended there was no problem. The Yorkshire leaders continued to wind down the picketing, and none of the other Area leaders criticised them — though for the first time Arthur

Scargill addressed a meeting of Yorkshire power stewards. As a Silverwood miner said:

> The strikers have been told all along: 'Don't bother with your own activity, General Winter will do it for you.' Now General Winter is here, and it's not been done for them. They can see their backs are against the wall and they're saying: 'If we can't get out of this one way, why don't we get round the table for a compromise?'

Neither the Yorkshire Area nor branch officials did anything to counter this. On the contrary, they blocked efforts to involve more miners in picketing. One Yorkshire miner told **Socialist Worker**:

> Since Christmas all the militants have had the stuffing knocked out of them by the official committee. It's taken all the picket transport off. We had 60 or 70 really good militants from one village, but there was only one van left to take them to the picket line. And then our treasurer says: 'Don't fetch them anyway, we haven't got much money.'

The effect of do-nothing officials was most evident in North Yorkshire. Here the key pit was Kellingley, the biggest pit in Europe, with 2,300 miners. If Kellingley cracked, it would undermine the heartland of the strike. As one Kellingley miner said:

> I'll tell you what breaks people in this pit. The union delegate here is a bloke called Howard Wadsworth. He stood up a few weeks ago and said: 'We've lost.' Then he sent out these little letters asking you what you felt about the strike and the union. He did it without the union's backing.
>
> There must have been 250 blokes went back because of that. He admitted it at a meeting: 'It's my fault. I take responsibility.' But the union have taken no action against him. There's a lot of feeling against him in the rank and file.

Another North Yorkshire pit, Fryston near Castleford, stayed solid, with only 20 scabs out of 1,100 miners at the end of February. The branch president, Roy Wright, who had been kept away from the strike by jail and then bail conditions for three months, returned to Fryston mid-February:

> When I came back, I was shocked at how the strike had turned the other way in North Yorkshire. Some of the lads who've gone

back have been on picket lines. They've given up through bad leadership.

From day one of the strike I've got up at one, two, three in the morning to go everywhere in England with my pickets. But what's running this strike down is that other branch officials have gone home to bed after paying out the lads to go picketing.

They're out for a free ride on the union. They got union positions, then they get on the council — they get on this and on to that. They don't want to know about the men who put them in power.

This failure of leadership by the branch officials could have been countered by a clear initiative from the Area executive. But in Yorkshire Jack Taylor and the rest of the leadership let things drift until the end of January, when they organised mass pickets at Cortonwood and Houghton Main. But these were solid pits in the heartland of the strike, much less in need of a boost than the more exposed collieries where the NCB offensive was at its fiercest. The neglect of these pits increased the scabbing there, as one Kellingley striker explained:

When there was mass picketing, it was good for the morale. You're in the majority and you feel you're all behind the strike in a mass picket. But when only a few of you stand there, you see the scabs all going in, nothing happens, you go home, pick up the paper and read lies, watch the telly. No wonder people are losing faith.

The officials' failure did not mean that nothing could be done. Where the militants organised independently the strike held solid. One example was Silverwood, where in mid-February only 27 out of a workforce of over 1,200 were scabbing. This success was all the more remarkable because many Silverwood miners lived in Sheffield or Rotherham rather than in pit villages. One Silverwood miner told **Socialist Worker**:

In some pits men who haven't been involved in the strike who then find themselves in very serious financial difficulty, are too embarrassed to come and ask the union for help. They think that because they haven't been active and the first time they've been down is to ask for help, that the union will just laugh at them. It's those miners that the NCB hope to break.

What we've done is to go round and explain to people that,

A greeting for the scabs at Silverwood

no matter what, if they've got a problem, contact us and see us. I can tell you it's worked. One kid I saw had no gas on and had got three kids. He'd got gas central heating. Just imagine, in this weather, no heating, no hot water, and three kids. He couldn't do any cooking because he had a gas cooker. After I saw him, I contacted the branch treasurer, who got onto Sheffield NALGO. Within two days we had his gas back on. Now this same bloke was up at 4.30 this morning out picketing with us.

At Easington, where there were pickets of 500 or more even in January, the militants scored a notable success when they organised the whole village to jeer at a scab who tried to walk into work instead of taking the NCB bus. His massive police escort — the village had been under virtual military occupation since the summer — were out-numbered and unable to make mass arrests. The next day there were nine fewer scabs, and the man who had been the focus of the village's wrath was on the picket line.

These examples pointed to a strategy which could counter the Coal Board's back-to-work drives — a strategy of building the involvement of every striker, of visiting the doubters, of returning to the mass pickets, above all of overcoming the divide between the active minority of pickets and the majority of passive strikers. It was a strategy that appealed to many activists — as was shown by the success of a series of meetings organised by the Socialist Workers Party, by the wide sale of the **Socialist Worker** pamphlet 'How to turn the tide', and by the impact of leaflets produced by an informal group of Yorkshire miners who were independent of the SWP. But it was a strategy that the Area leaderships and many branch committees rejected. Amazingly, even as the scale of the scabbing grew, some branch officials were refusing to allow pickets to visit miners at home.

Consequently, the return to work was extremely uneven. The **Financial Times** acknowledged on 6 February that 'substantial pockets' were still 'nearly 100 per cent solid', including the entire South Wales and Kent Areas:

> In Scotland . . . there is a particularly sharp 'north/south' divide, with pits in the south showing on average a 50 per cent attendance, and the northern pits — in Fife — . . . very few . . .
>
> In Yorkshire, with 6,272 men back from around 50,000 miners the pits are split . . . In the Barnsley pits of Dearne Valley, Kinsley Drift, Darfield Main, Grimethorpe and Royston Drift at most eight miners are back at each pit, going down to as few as two. In the whole of the Doncaster area, only 404 men have returned to 10 pits, with Frickley, Goldthorpe and Hickleton being among the most solid.
>
> In the North East the traditionally moderate Northumberland field has shown a return to work of some 50 per cent: in Durham, however, a group of pits have bucked an otherwise rapid return to work trend. These are Easington, with 61 back out of 2,169 men; Murton, with 110 back out of 1,502; and Eppleton, with 180 back out of 864.

The strike had been weakened, but not broken. It would take a section of allegedly left-wing officials to do that.

The union split?

There was a second major threat to the miners' strike in January 1985 — the possibility of a breakaway scab union. A number of branch officials had played a crucial role in organising the strikebreaking in Nottinghamshire from the very start. Area elections held in July 1984 swept supporters of the strike from branch office in Nottinghamshire. The scabs now controlled the branch committees. They included 27 of the 31 delegates to the Notts Area council, and every member of the Area executive except Ray Chadburn and Henry Richardson.

The scabs waited until December, when it was clear the TUC would do nothing to defend the miners' union against the courts. The Notts Area council met on 20 December, and voted to change their rule book to give them autonomy from the NUM.

The scab delegates voted to delete the area's rule 30: 'In all matters in which the rules of the [Area] union and those of the national union conflict, the rules of the national union shall apply, and in all cases of doubt or dispute the matter shall be decided by the National Executive Committee of the national union.'

This decision exposed the truth behind the scab leaders' declarations of loyalty to the national union. The essence of the decision to form the NUM in 1944 had been to create a genuinely *national* union in the coalfields for the first time, in which the miners' delegate conference was the 'supreme authority and government' of the union. Now the scab organisers were committing themselves to a reversion back to the days before 1944, of a federation of autonomous county unions.

The NUM national executive voted to summon a special delegate conference on 30 January. They would recommend that the scabs be expelled unless the Notts Area council withdrew the rule change.

They also approved further amendments to the NUM's own rule-book. Changes to rule 12, which determines the composition of the national executive, had been demanded by the 1983 NUM conference, to end the scandal whereby, for example, three small right-wing Areas — Cumberland, Leicestershire, and North Wales — had between them a tenth of Yorkshire's members and the same number of seats on the national executive. The nub of the proposals was to reduce the number of Areas from 18 to 12. To all intents and purposes, Lancashire would absorb Cumberland and North Wales, and Midlands swallow up Leicestershire, South Derbyshire and Power Group.

The proposed change was basically democratic. It aimed to make the executive genuinely representative of the union's membership. But, coming with the threat to expel the Notts scabs, the executive decision helped to galvanise support for a breakaway union. A Notts delegate conference voted on 16 January to sack Henry Richardson as Area general secretary because of his support for the strike.

Roy Lynk was appointed to act in his place, and announced that he was preparing to form a new national miners' union if the NUM conference carried out its threat of expulsion. Two other scab Areas, both threatened with extinction by the proposals, South Derbyshire and Leicestershire, voted to support rule changes which made them, like Notts, autonomous.

The prospect of a breakaway union presented a serious danger to the NUM. The miners' leaders offered a deal to those involved. Scargill met the South Derbyshire leaders on 22 January, and the national executive meeting the next day voted to defer indefinitely the special conference. The organisational changes which had so angered South Derbyshire and Leicestershire were shelved.

The scab organisers too had good reasons for avoiding a show-down with the NUM. There was evidence that many working Notts miners did not want a breakaway. Up to a third had early on supported the strike, and many more might have done so had they not been so badly misled by Chadburn and Richardson. Scabbing on the rest of the NUM had been legitimised by appeal to the national union's rule book which the scab leaders now wanted to tear up.

So opposition to a split built up. At Ollerton a branch meeting voted 117 to 94 against a split, only to have their decision ruled out of order by the chair. Colin Clarke, Pye Hill branch secretary, who had proposed the rule change giving Notts autonomy, suffered the humili-ation of his own branch voting two to one to discuss a proposal to invite Scargill to address them. The arch-democrats controlling the branch committee reacted by walking out of the meeting.

Also, despite all their public enthusiasm for ballots, the Notts Area officials never considered holding an Area ballot on the rule change that was to separate them from the national union.

Arthur Scargill's endgame

The **Financial Times** pronounced on 26 January:

> The mineworkers' strike, as a living entity with some sap left in it, is over. The final moves are of vital, perhaps paramount, importance: but they *are* the end game.

Despite this judgement, the strike was to last for another month or more. Perhaps the miners didn't read the **FT**. The strike lasted so long, despite the hammer blows it suffered in January, because there was still much to play for.

If the NUM was faced with defeat, there was more than one sort of defeat. One was devastation — unconditional surrender by the leadership, and the disintegration of the union as a fighting organisation. The other was a defeat in which the miners held together, preserving their organisation and fighting spirit. One would allow the Coal Board to rule the pits with a rod of iron, the other would allow the miners to rebuild their strength and fight again.

The Tories knew this perfectly well, which is why for the next month they held out against any fudged settlement of the strike which would allow the miners to claim anything remotely like victory. But avoiding devastating defeat meant that the miners themselves had to hang on and avoid ending the strike on just any terms.

The Tories weren't invulnerable. The early weeks of 1985 saw turmoil on the world's financial markets, as the dollar soared and the pound sterling sunk lower and lower. The costs of the strike had been enormous. A document leaked to Channel Four News revealed that the CEGB would lose over £2 billion because of the switch from coal to oil. Estimates of the total costs by the time the strike ended varied, but £4 billion seemed like a minimum — far more than Thatcher had spent to reconquer the Falkland Islands.

The NUM's hand was strengthened by the solidity of the core areas of the strike — South Wales, Kent, and parts of the Yorkshire, Scottish, and Durham coalfields. If the militant areas held firm, the Tories might find themselves forced by economic pressures and the prospect of the strike lasting through much of 1985 to concede terms which would at least leave the issue of pit closures open and stop victimisations.

There followed a poker game between the government and the NUM leaders, in which each side played on the other's nerves, in the hope of causing them to crack. Arthur Scargill came into his own. Back in July he had won the grudging admiration of the **Financial Times** labour editor, John Lloyd, who had written: 'In his willpower, tactical intelligence and lack of inhibition he surpasses all his colleagues in the leadership.' Now Scargill devised stratagem after stratagem to keep the strike going.

It was a brilliant performance. Scargill was fighting for his political life, as well as for the future of the NUM. He had the backing of the other two national officers, Peter Heathfield and Mick McGahey. But their hard line was only possible because of the courage and determination of the communities in the core areas of the strike.

Scargill toured the North East. For the first time he no longer talked of victory at his rallies. Instead he appealed to miners not to return to work, but to stay out until a 'sensibly negotiated solution' had been reached, warning that scabbing would lead to a position 'where management control your lives to a life-and-death situation'. When the miners returned at the end of the strike, he said, they would 'walk back together in the knowledge that you fought not only as hard as anyone could, but more besides.'

Peter Heathfield met the NCB industrial relations director, Ned Smith, on Monday 21 January. Smith was one of the old school of Coal Board officials, highly critical of MacGregor's abrasive style. Clashes with the NCB chairman had led to Smith's early retirement, due on 3 February. Here was his chance to pull off a final coup, and settle the strike.

Heathfield and Smith went a long way towards drafting an agreement. The closure programme would be withdrawn until stocks were rebuilt. Both sides would reserve their respective rights — the NCB's to manage the industry, the NUM to defend miners' interests. The miners' union would continue to oppose closures of 'uneconomic' pits.

Smith had exceeded his brief. Heathfield left the meeting and read a report in the **Evening Standard** that the talks were a flop. The story was the result of a briefing from Downing Street, but the same line came from NCB headquarters.

Three days later Ian MacGregor moved to torpedo the settlement, after consulting Energy Secretary Peter Walker. While the miners' leaders were meeting in Sheffield, the Coal Board issued a statement demanding 'a written indication that the union is prepared to help resolve the problem of uneconomic capacity' and that the NUM 'co-operates with the essential tasks of loss-making pits.' It was a call for unconditional surrender.

Thatcher moved quickly to back MacGregor up, first during Question Time in the House of Commons that afternoon, and later on television, where she reaffirmed the NCB demand for the miners' surrender: 'Let's get it written down. I want it dead straight, honest and no fudging.'

The **Observer** reported on 27 January:

Throughout these shifting debates, it has been clear that Downing Street and the Coal Board have been closely in touch. The shadowy figure of David Hart, usually described as an 'adviser' to Mrs Thatcher, but whose role is played down in public, was much in evidence, acting as a go-between for Downing Street and MacGregor . . .

The **Financial Times** (26 January 1985) discerned

two main currents within government and the NCB. One, favoured by the Board's senior, consensual-minded officials, their Energy Department counterparts and at least at times, Mr Peter Walker, the Energy Secretary, and Mr David Hunt, his Coal Minister, is that a negotiated settlement should result in a clear statement of the Coal Board's right to manage and close loss-making pits, but not what could be seen as a public humiliation.

Mr MacGregor and the Prime Minister, together with their advisors (some of whom are common to both) have a different aim. That is to ensure that the end of the dispute makes it wholly clear that 'Scargillism', which they define as a mixture of industrial coercion allied to revolutionary ambitions, must be seen to fail, and fail utterly.

The flurry of publicity surrounding these brief talks nevertheless managed to slow down the return to work. The Coal Board's figures for Monday 28 January and Tuesday 29 January were 915 and 182 respectively, sharply down compared to a week before. The effect was, however, only temporary.

Meanwhile a campaign was beginning to form, among NUM officials, for a return to work without a settlement. The idea surfaced publicly in the **Financial Times** on Saturday 2 February, but had been circulating around the NUM headquarters at the beginning of that week. Scargill dismissed the proposal as a 'complete fantasy'. However, it had support in South Wales, where the Area's research officer, Kim Howells, was one of the first to raise the idea publicly.

The proposal was put on the agenda for the NUM executive. Jack Taylor said it should be discussed 'very seriously'. Scargill, it seemed, was being boxed in.

Once again Houdini escaped from the trap. Scargill produced, like a rabbit from a hat, the leaders of the deputies union, NACODS. Scargill had been quick to point out that the NCB's demand that the miners' union accept the principle of the closure of 'uneconomic' pits meant that the Board's agreement with NACODS in October wasn't worth the paper it was written on. On the other hand, Peter Walker had told a radio interviewer on 30 January that if the NUM accepted the NACODS agreement 'there would be an immediate end to the dispute'.

Scargill moved quickly to exploit this contradiction, and at the same time to head off pressure within the miners' leadership for either surrender or a return to work without an agreement. The NUM executive meeting turned into a joint session of the two union's executives. They issued a statement calling on the Board 'immediately [to] resume full negotiations without pre-conditions.'

Scargill had won another round in his poker game with Thatcher. The return to work figures the following week were half the previous week's figures. But he had bought only a little more time. The NACODS executive refused to include a threat of industrial action in their joint statement with the miners' leaders. They asked only for talks.

The Tories increased the pressure. Thatcher told the Young Conservatives that the miners' leaders had 'brought Luddism back to Britain'. She backed up the Coal Board's demand for unconditional surrender:

> If the NUM accept that economic factors must be taken into account in deciding the future of pits, if they accept the right of the Board to take the final decision after all the procedures have been completed — then a settlement is ready and waiting.

If the miners accepted all that, what need would there be for negotiations?

On cue, the courts moved into action. Mr Justice Scott granted scabs an injunction banning mass picketing at five South Wales and eleven Yorkshire pits. Writing the Tory picketing guidelines into law, he ruled that there could be no more than six pickets at any one colliery. On 18 February Mr Justice Staughton granted the ship-owners Stephenson Clarke an injunction ordering the crews of three ships to end their eleven-month ban on moving coal from the North-East to the Thames power stations. The judge granted an order even though the seafarers had overwhelmingly voted in a ballot to continue the blacking. So much for the judiciary's enthusiasm for ballots.

The NUS leader, Jim Slater, went to see the crews the following day, and told them he was withdrawing any advice or instructions he had given them to black coal. Only two months earlier he had told a rally in Blyth on 12 December that, 'rather than back down from supporting the miners' he would 'do a term of imprisonment.'

Slater wasn't the only left trade union leader now to be getting cold feet. British Rail decided at the beginning of the year to move against workers at Coalville depot, who had stopped coal moving from the scab Leicestershire coalfield since 3 April 1984. Three railworkers were sacked. The Coalville men demanded action from the NUR leadership, which responded by calling a one-day strike on 17 January in the Midlands and Eastern regions, rather than bringing the entire weight of the national union behind them.

The extent of the solidarity that could be tapped was shown on 17 January — not only were the affected regions solid, but unofficial action halted many Southern Region lines. Still, it was plain enough that the railworkers' leaders wanted out, despite their public protestations of solidarity.

The growing isolation of the miners from the rest of the trade union movement was to be underlined during the next, and as it proved, final stage of negotiations. Norman Willis, the TUC general secretary, now moved into the limelight. Willis got in touch with Ian MacGregor. After half a dozen meetings a document, drafted by the Coal Board but modified by the TUC, emerged on 13 February. Willis presented the draft to the NUM and NACODS executives meeting at Congress House on Friday 15 February.

The draft incorporated the NCB's basic demands: an 'economically sound industry' was in 'the interests of the membership of the NUM'; 'uneconomic' pits would have to be closed. The miners' executive responded by proposing a four-paragraph statement deleting all references to 'economics', which was swiftly rejected by the Board in its turn.

There followed a weekend of executive meetings. Scargill wanted to stand firm against the Coal Board document. But according to the **Financial Times** on 19 February, 'the majority of executive members, led by Mr Emlyn Williams . . . and Mr Jack Taylor . . . told Mr Arthur Scargill . . . that he could no longer get support for his policy of rejecting the NCB's document . . . out of hand.' Taylor and Williams 'warned Mr Scargill that if no new initiative could be got off the ground in 48 hours, they would consider leading their men back to work,' the paper had said the previous day. Williams had come to the meeting armed with a resolution passed by South Wales delegates on 13 February demanding a national conference, clearly in the hope of getting a decision to end the strike.

With Scargill now in a minority, the executive rewrote the NCB document, deleting references to an 'economically sound industry', but accepting the Board's final say in closing pits subject to the amended colliery review procedure. The Coal Board now declared their document 'non-negotiable'.

That evening Scargill passed on to Willis the NUM's request that he should have another go. In desperation, Willis requested a meeting with Thatcher herself. On Tuesday, he went to 10 Downing Street, accompanied by the six members of the TUC liaison committee monitoring the strike. It was just under a year since Thatcher had last met the TUC, when she contemptuously rebuffed Len Murray's pleas for the trade unionists at GCHQ.

This time the meeting was 'cordial'. Peter Walker, with Thatcher's support, agreed to modify the NCB document, overriding MacGregor's objections. In exchange the TUC seven made it clear that they were negotiating a final agreement on behalf of the NUM. The **Financial Times** of 21 February reported: 'The "constructive" attitude shown . . . by Mr Norman Willis . . . and his colleagues impressed ministers — including the Prime Minister.' The feeling was mutual. 'What a magnificent woman!' exclaimed one of the TUC seven on leaving Downing Street.

The government were under pressure. A MORI opinion poll published in the **Sunday Times** on 10 February showed Labour and Tories running neck and neck. Only 34 per cent of those polled thought Thatcher 'a capable leader', her lowest rating since June 1981, and 60 per cent thought the government were handling the miners' strike 'badly'.

But the government weren't really offering anything. The substance of the NCB document remained. Ambiguities which seemed to conflict with the NACODS agreement were removed, and the clause referring to the need for an 'economically sound industry' was marginally modified. That was all. But by involving the TUC in making these changes, the government ensured that, should the miners reject the document, they would be isolated from the rest of the trade union movement.

Imagine the surprise of the TUC seven, fresh from their paper triumphs in Whitehall, when they met the miners' executive on the evening of Wednesday 20 February. Far from being congratulated, they were questioned closely. Jack Taylor in particular was nonplussed to learn that what they were confronted was not a basis for negotiation but *a final agreement*.

The executive rejected the document unanimously. The NUM special delegate conference summoned to meet the next day backed them. Even right-wingers opposed the document. 'Quite honestly, I think we have been conned,' said Lancashire miners' leader Sid Vincent. Northumberland president Dennis Murphy summed up the miners' contemptuous attitude to the TUC: 'If you send a boy to do a man's job you've got trouble.'

Faced with the Coal Board's terms in all their harshness, none of the miners' leaders could put their names to a document which gave MacGregor a blank cheque to close down pits. It just wasn't on.

But Walker's stratagem had paid off. When the miners' leaders met the TUC the following Monday to appeal for action finally to be taken to implement the Congress declaration of solidarity passed in September, Willis told them 'nothing doing'. The NUM were on their own.

The soft left engineer a return to work

The miners' special delegate conference voted on 21 February to continue the strike. Ten days later, on 3 March, another conference voted to return to work without an agreement. Why did they reverse their decision so quickly?

It was not because the miners' position had become untenable. The basic calculation behind the argument for hanging on still held true. The Tories were worried about their slide in the opinion polls. The pound was still under pressure on the foreign exchanges. After the decision to return had been made, the **Financial Times** acknowledged on 4 March that

> anxiety about the oil price and the rising dollar may have triggered the sterling crisis earlier this year, but it seems fairly clear that the effects of the miners' strike played an important part.

Had the NUM held firm, the government's nerve might have cracked, and the miners at least won terms which secured the reinstatement of victimised strikers. As it was, the nerves of a section of the miners' leaders cracked first.

There was more to it than that. The final decision to go back was the result of a virtual coup by a 'soft left' current among NUM officials which crystallised during the course of the strike in opposition both to Arthur Scargill and to rank-and-file activists.

Throughout the strike the union bureaucracy were in control. They were able to block any offensive strategy aimed at the steelworks and power stations. Once the strike had shifted onto the defensive, after Orgreave, the activists found themselves in a stronger position where they organised. To sustain a kitchen, visit inactive strikers, picket their own pits, did not involve the sort of dependence on the officials for petrol money and legal representation which had been so decisive in Nottinghamshire and at Orgreave. Twinning pits with support groups and other workplaces or union branches gave the activists a degree of financial independence from the officials. There were, however, definite limits to this independence. Even in the most solid pits, the militants had neither the strength nor often the will to defy the officials.

A South Yorkshire miner summed it up:

> Most pickets recognise the officials will not run things effectively. But the pickets don't have the confidence to take control of things themselves . . . The union officials are in control, but have no answers.

If this was true in militant pits, how much more so was it elsewhere? We have seen how inaction by branch and Area officials allowed the Coal Board to make inroads in the weaker pits. The activists could — and did — hold their own pits together. They could not remedy bureaucratic sabotage elsewhere. Nor could they stand up to a co-ordinated offensive by left officials, who enjoyed a credibility which the right wing lacked, but who wanted to end the strike.

Precisely such an offensive began to develop in the last two months of the strike when a 'soft left' emerged, composed of young and ambitious branch and sometimes Area officials.

There were two meetings of the NUM left on the weekend of 5–6 January. The first, of Communist Party miners, was split between simply continuing the existing, passive strategy, and seeking an end to the strike. A wider meeting of Broad Left officials rejected a strategy of mass picketing 'in case this caused splits on the National Executive'.

The soft left, firmly opposed as they were to mass picketing, seem to have played a key role in engineering the subsequent collapse of the strike. When the idea of a return to work without an agreement surfaced towards the end of January, its key mover was Kim Howells, research officer for the South Wales NUM, and the union's public spokesman. Howells, a former member of the Communist Party, was an articulate exponent of the strategy of relying on public opinion and the churches rather than mass picketing. Although an academic, he was tipped to go far in the union hierarchy.

The idea of going back without an agreement had some attractions. It was a way of stemming the tide of scabs. It also avoided the humiliation of signing a deal which the Tories had made clear would be a licence to close pits. The struggle could continue — there was much talk among the idea's supporters of 'guerrilla warfare' pit by pit.

But these attractions were vastly outweighed by the disadvantages. The point of the strike in the first place had been to use the *national* strength of the union to win on an issue where individual Areas or pits could not — that of closures.

It was all very well talking about 'guerrilla warfare'. After the suffering and sacrifices involved in a year-long national strike, would miners then throw themselves into pit-by-pit struggles to win what they failed to achieve nationally?

Above all, returning to work without an agreement meant throwing away the NUM's main card — that of being able to keep the militant areas out on strike into the summer of 1985. This not only weakened their hand over pit closures. It meant abandoning those miners who had been victimised by the NCB for their part in the strike.

By the end of the strike 718 miners had been sacked. The final total was likely to be higher, as miners came up in court — for example, over 60 Yorkshire miners had been charged with unlawful assembly. Some were sacked even though they had been acquitted, like Davie Hamilton, Monktonhall delegate and a member of the Scottish Area executive. Going back without an agreement meant leaving these men at the colliery gate. In effect, it would give the NCB *carte blanche* to weed out and victimise the militants.

Scargill moved quickly to denounce the idea. The **Financial Times** reported on 7 February:

> Following a radio interview by Dr Kim Howells . . . carefully spelling out the growing feeling in parts of the [South Wales] coalfield that this might be the only way of securing an orderly end to the strike, Mr Scargill hit the telephone to remonstrate forcibly with him. Even if what he had said were true, Mr Scargill insisted it should not have been said.

Scargill was not the only one to oppose the idea. Opposition to a return without an agreement was so strong at the South Wales Area council on 9 February that Howells was stripped of his position as official spokesman.

But the idea had strong backing from the South Wales Area executive, who allowed Howells to keep his job as research officer, no doubt to continue lobbying for the proposal. The South Wales president, Emlyn Williams, stepped up the pressure for an end to the strike at an Area delegate conference on 13 February.

Why did South Wales so strongly support the idea of a return without agreement? Abandoning victimised miners ran against all the magnificent traditions of solidarity in the South Wales coalfield. But the South Wales leadership was living off past glories. The number of miners in the coalfield had sunk from 271,000 in 1920 to only 21,405 at the start of the 1984–5 strike. The left-wing Area leaders did not attempt to organise a strike against the rundown of the coalfield until 1980. The 1984–5 strike was more solid in South Wales than elsewhere — less than 2 per cent were scabbing at the end of the first week, according to NCB figures, compared with 37 per cent in Scotland, 33 per cent in the North-East, 13 per cent in Yorkshire, and 7 per cent in Kent.

The figures, impressive though they were, were misleading. The Area leadership had consistently opposed mass picketing, relying instead on winning support from a 'broad alliance' including such forces as the Wales Council of Churches. To keep the strike solid the South Wales officials relied on the miners' traditional loyalty to their union, and the strength of the pit communities. The result was a dangerous passivity.

A miner at Maerdy, whose lodge officials were among the first to support a return to work, said:

> No union can depend totally on loyalty. This dependence has weakened the strike here. You can't leave workers to what they read in the newspapers and see on TV. You must counteract it.
>
> There's a 1974 attitude among our leadership. They go to the leaders of [other] unions instead of the rank and file . . .
>
> The NUM didn't get solidarity, because the executive kept saying it was a miners' strike and we didn't need other workers on the picket line. At the beginning of the strike I went to Bristol a few times. We got offers from Avonmouth docks and British Aerospace to come onto the picket line. But the union said it was to be miners only. They didn't even like miners' wives on the picket line at first.

The passivity in Wales meant that there had been fewer victimisations — and this made it easier for the Area officials to advocate proposals which meant abandoning victimised strikers to their fate.

In Yorkshire, Jack Taylor's room for manoeuvre was more limited. There was a large group of activists regularly picketing in the Barnsley and Doncaster panels who were likely to oppose a return without an agreement.

But Taylor was provided with an opportunity to undermine the militants when the High Court declared mass picketing at 11 Yorkshire pits illegal on 12 February. The Area executive voted to obey the court ruling, the first instance of any Area formally deciding to comply with a court order. The Area council upheld the decision without discussion or a mandate from the branches. The Area strike co-ordinating committee was disbanded. As far as the Yorkshire officials were concerned mass picketing was over. Miners were instructed to obey the courts' six-man limit.

The reaction from the pickets was anger. One South Kirkby miner said:

> Blokes have died. Blokes have been in nick. Lads have been chased with batons, chased with horses and by riot police. And now they come under a bit of pressure our leaders have bottled out.

The NUM branch at Frickley voted to overturn the executive's decision and continue picketing. The branch officials reacted by closing the meeting and walking out. One miner said: 'They were terrified. They just didn't want to know about defying the law.' The meeting was told that pickets who were arrested would not have their fines paid. Nevertheless, activists organised a demonstration of over 500 men and women which marched through the village of South Emsall on 19 February to picket Frickley colliery.

Elsewhere in the Yorkshire coalfield the attitude was similarly defiant. The day before the Frickley demonstration 1,000 people took part in a mass picket and demonstration organised by Armthorpe women's action group. A similar demonstration took place in Edlington a few days later. Sylvia Arrowsmith, a miner's wife in Edlington, said: 'If the men can't or won't picket because of the injunctions then it's up to us women to show the way. We don't belong to the NUM — there's nothing the courts can do to us.'

Such courage and determination could have been tapped by a leadership that wanted to continue the strike. Instead, the officials used their superior resources to overcome rank-and-file opposition. In the days following the Frickley demonstration, the number of pickets dropped sharply. The branch reversed its earlier decision, and agreed to accept the court injunction 'under protest'. One Frickley miner explained what had happened:

> There are two sorts of problems really. One is money. People from the outlying villages such as Upton, which is two miles away from the pit, aren't getting petrol money to come down to the picket line. The other is the feeling that Frickley can't stand on its own without the support from all the other pits.

Once again, as throughout the strike, the Area bureaucracy had been able to overwhelm rank-and-file militancy. The effect was to weaken the core of activists who had held the strike together since the summer. This made life easier for the officials. It also strengthened the hand of the NCB. They now felt confident enough to move coal from Silverwood, one of the most militant pits in the country, for the first time since the strike began.

These blows to the morale and organisation of the pickets meant that, following the collapse of the TUC initiative, the back to work movement began to accelerate rapidly. Miners who until now had been solid began to wonder what was the point of carrying on, seeing that their leaders were busy running the strike down and talking of surrender.

The NCB claimed that a record 3,807 miners went back on Monday 25 February. The Board's figures didn't bear too close examination. Nationally they claimed 91,000 working miners, but NCB area offices released figures totalling only 78,199. At least 75 per cent of the original strikers were still out.

But the trend was clear enough. The return was especially marked in the solid areas. The South Wales leadership paid the price of their reliance on the passive loyalty of their members. The NCB claimed that 552 South Wales miners went back on 25 February, doubling the number of scabs in the coalfield overnight.

By the end of the week, the proportion of miners breaking the strike in South Wales had, according to the Board, multiplied four-fold to 8 per cent. Nationally, the NCB claimed that more than 5 per cent of NUM membership went back that week.

The pressure to surrender was, however, by no means over-whelming. The Yorkshire Area council met that Tuesday and discussed a motion from four pits in the north of the county, calling for a return to work organised by the Area leadership. It was rejected by seventy votes to three.

What swung the union behind surrender, and cracked the determination of some of the most militant pits, was a coup staged by the soft left, who continued to agitate behind the scenes for a return despite its rejection in early February.

Easington in County Durham was, with 2,169 miners, one of the biggest and most militant pits in the country. It had been the victim of one of the most notorious paramilitary police operations back in August, and the village had been under virtual occupation ever since. As we have seen, the activists had been able to involve 500 miners in regular picketing.

If Easington cracked, the reverberations on the other militant pits throughout the coalfields would be enormous. The soft left set to work on Easington lodge secretary Alan Cummings. He received regular phone calls from South Wales after the national delegate conference.

The constant pressure had the intended effect. On the morning of Monday 26 February the Easington lodge committee passed a resolution demanding a Durham Area conference to organse a return to work without an agreement. The motion also proposed that the overtime ban be continued, that miners should refuse to operate the incentive scheme, and that a levy be organised for the victimised strikers. The lodge chairman and NUM executive member, Bill Stobbs, submitted his resignation, but the committee refused to accept it.

The motion was put to a packed branch meeting attended by 1,500 strikers later that morning, and carried. The militants, taken by surprise, didn't have time to organise against the proposal. Many spoke against it, but the committee carried the day by 60–40. Morale collapsed afterwards.

Alan Cummings tried to justify this *volte-face* afterwards:

> After conference there was an impasse situation. We've got to be realistic about the present situation. People are going back to work in large numbers. People who have been solid throughout the strike. They can't see any end to it . . .

'What way is there?' he asked desperately. With Scargill silent, the wing of the bureaucracy with a coherent strategy, the soft left, were in an increasingly strong position. They played on the fear of many officials over the forthcoming elections in the union to push their call to end the strike.

The NUM executive meeting on Thursday 28 February lasted

eight hours. Much of the day was spent trying to contact Peter Walker or Coal Board officials. Finally the executive listened to a tape-recording of a telephone conversation in which Kevin Hunt, the NCB's industrial relations director, flatly rejected the NUM's offer to accept the NACODS agreement.

Less than a month previously, Thatcher and Walker had said that the NACODS agreement was 'sacrosanct', and that its acceptance would 'immediately' end the strike. But now the Tories, sensing complete victory, wanted their pound of flesh.

Scargill wanted to fight on, but was overruled by the rest. A national delegate conference would meet that Sunday; meanwhile the Areas would be consulted. The next day the bandwagon for surrender rolled on. Area councils in South Wales, Durham, Lancashire, and Northumberland, along with COSA, voted for a return to work.

Three left Areas held out, with differing degrees of enthusiasm. The Scottish Area executive voted for a return conditional on a 'general amnesty' for victimised miners. The predominantly Communist Party leadership in Scotland had moved sharply leftwards in mid-January, for example organising mass pickets of 1,000 men each at Killoch, Seafield, and Monktonhall. Whether an act of desperation or an attempt to regain some of the ground lost with the militants during the Ravenscraig fiasco, this shift showed what could be done so late in the strike.

Only Kent opposed ending the strike. The 2,163 miners of this tiny coalfield faced the threat of extinction if the strike were lost. All three pits were big loss-makers. Forty-two Kent miners had been sacked, including the entire Betteshanger branch committee.

Most important of all was Yorkshire. The Area council met on Friday afternoon, in the wake of a decision to go back in the nearest militant coalfield, Durham. Despite the pressures exerted from outside, and Jack Taylor's refusal to give a firm lead, the delegates voted to continue the strike 42 to 22. But the supporters of surrender refused to accept their defeat. The council was reconvened on Saturday afternoon to allow delegates to consult their branches. This time a show of hands went 38 to 31 in favour of a return to work — then a card vote went the other way, instructing the Area's conference by 571 votes to 561 to oppose a return without an amnesty.

The whole affair was a classic example of Jack Taylor's leadership style. He was not in a strong enough position to campaign openly for surrender like Emlyn Williams — there were too many militant pits in Yorkshire for that. So he opted for passivity, supporting the status quo and leaving it to lower-rank officials to lobby for a return to work.

Appropriately, the national delegate conference of the NUM which ended the strike on Sunday 3 March met at Congress House, seat of the TUC which had so shamefully betrayed it. The three scab Areas — Nottinghamshire, South Derbyshire and Leicestershire, stayed away.

The South Wales resolution — for a return to work on Tuesday and negotiations for an amnesty — was carried 98–91.

Scargill, flanked by Peter Heathfield and Mick McGahey, spoke to the world's press. The NUM would continue to fight pit closures. The miners' president praised the striking communities: 'Men and women have fought a fight that has not been seen anywhere in the world.' And he pointed the finger of guilt at the TUC general council: 'The trade union movement in Britain, with a few notable exceptions, have left this union isolated. They have not carried out TUC conference decisions, to their eternal shame.

The Kent miners' leader, Jack Collins, spoke angrily for many when he left Congress House that afternoon: 'It's a decision that the British miners will live to regret and that the trade union movement will live to regret. The people who have decided to go back to work and leave men on the sidelines, to unload these men, are the traitors of the trade union movement.'

He was right. The miners' strike did not die a natural death. It was helped on its way by those left-wing officials who were not willing to fight on in the militant strongholds in the hope of at least saving the jobs of victimised strikers.

The Tories were exultant. Thatcher, her eyes on the opinion polls, aped magnanimity. Somehow it was worse than if she had cried 'Rejoice!', especially when she spoke of the miners' families 'who have gone through an awful lot of suffering' — thanks to her orders, to the police occupation of their villages, and the attempts of the DHSS to starve them.

Peter Walker twisted the knife in the wound: even if miners were acquitted of crimes they might still be sacked, he told the House of Commons. Neil Kinnock, statesmanlike to the last, agreed that miners guilty of 'vicious crimes' should be sacked. Students at Haringay college of further education showed what they thought of this by pelting Kinnock with rotten tomatoes.

Emlyn Williams tried to justify his treachery by even-handedly attacking both Kinnock and Scargill — the latter had shown 'lack of guts and lack of leadership', he said, for not making a recommendation to the conference. There were signs of revulsion in the South

Armthorpe marches back to work: 8 March 1985

Wales coalfield. Three hundred miners at Trelewis Drift voted to stay out.

The Great Miners' Strike officially ended on Tuesday 5 March in as much confusion as it had begun 51 weeks before. The mass of strikers marched back to work behind their branch banners, sometimes with bands playing.

An estimated 27,000 miners stayed out. Some were Scottish and Kent miners in support of their Area decisions. Half the Yorkshire miners refused to cross picket lines consisting of strikers from Armthorpe and Hatfield and men from Kent. At Trelewis Drift they did the same. These actions were attempts more to wrest concessions from local NCB bosses about the fate of sacked men that to continue the strike. Its back had been broken by Sunday's conference.

Whenever they returned, the miners did so defiantly and with pride. They were beaten, but they had held out for a year against the worst that the state could inflict on them. Like their forebears in 1926, the miners had, in A. J. Cook's words, fought the 'legions of hell'. They, and the women who had endured with them the longest major strike in British history were all heroes, every one of them. They were magnificent. They deserved better than what was in store for them.

The lessons of 1926

The miners had lost. But how big a defeat was it, both for them and for the wider labour movement?

It is worth considering the comparisons which were inevitably drawn between 1984–5 and the General Strike of 1926. There were very obvious parallels between the two struggles. The miners were at the centre of both. 1926 too pitted the trade union movement against a much better-prepared opponent.

The miners were deserted even more flagrantly in 1926, when the TUC leaders called off the General Strike after nine days, leaving the MFGB to struggle on alone for over seven months. The general council made incompetent efforts to negotiate on the miners' behalf, just as Norman Willis did. The scale of state repression was enormous: there were 9,000 arrests in the whole of 1926, compared to 9,778 during the 1984–5 strike. To cap it all, Labour leader Ramsay MacDonald supported the 1926 strike as grudgingly as Neil Kinnock did nearly sixty years later.

The historian John Foster summed up the effects of the 1926 defeat:

The TUC right-wingers, despite all their betrayals, were able to take the offensive against the left. 'Never again' became a by-word for the following generation. Under the 1927 Trade Disputes Act general strikes and most sympathy strikes became illegal. Trade union membership fell by half a million. And parallel to the harassment and victimisation of the left by the government and the employers, bans and proscriptions were launched in individual trade unions. In almost every union right-wing dominance was ensured for the following decade — with all that this meant in terms of neutralising the mass organisations of the working class in a period of acute economic crisis.[1]

Some were quick to draw the conclusion that the same would happen in 1985. **The Guardian** confidently predicted:

The defeat of the miners will be seen as a landmark in the decline of the industrial working class and advocates of political strike action. It is unlikely that the unions will again mount such a general and co-ordinated challenge to the authority of the state . . . Union strength and membership was in decline well before the miners' strike, and that process is likely to accelerate.[2]

But the differences between 1926 and 1985 are as important as similarities. The most important single difference was that there was no general strike in 1984–5. The sectional divisions in the working class were much greater than in 1926: hence the blacklegging in Nottinghamshire and the more general failure of other groups of workers to support the miners. This sectionalism was, of course, a great source of weakness, but it meant that the miners' defeat was not felt so directly and bitterly by other workers.

The very depth of the solidarity in 1926 meant that when the TUC general council precipitately called the General Strike off on 12 May every section of the class was threatened with defeat. Employers in industries other than mining exploited the collapse of the strike to victimise militants. The railway companies, for example, posted notices stating that strikers, having broken their contracts, were dismissed, and would be re-employed only individually.

Rank-and-file resistance (there were more on strike on 13 May, *after* the strike was called off, than the day before) forced the bosses to negotiate with the unions. But the terms were humiliating: the rail unions admitted that, 'in calling a strike, they committed a wrongful act against the companies', and accepted wage-cuts and the sacking of 'persons who have been guilty of violence or intimidation'. Agreements such as this led to tens of thousands of victimisations.

Solidarity in 1984–5 was much more diffuse. Apart from a small minority of brave railworkers and seafarers, few trade unionists put their necks on the line for the miners. However, the financial support given the miners in 1984–5 was far more than in 1926. **The Guardian** estimated that the NUM may have received as much as £60 million.

Another reason why the defeat of 1984–5 was unlikely to hit the working-class movement as hard as that of 1926 is that the miners were a much smaller proportion of the class. In 1921 there were 1,132,000 miners, 6.3 per cent of the working population; in 1983 the deep coal-mine workforce was 231,600, less than one per cent. Coal mining was the biggest single industry, and the main source of energy for British industry, and of heating for ordinary homes till the 1960s, an all-pervasive part of social and economic life. By the time of the 1984–5 strike this was no longer true. In 1922 miners formed nearly 15 per cent of all trade unionists; by 1984 they were only 2.3 per cent.

Nevertheless, the miners still form a sizeable proportion of the working class in certain regions: in 1981 coal accounted for 21.1 per cent of male employment in the East Midlands, 15.6 per cent in Yorkshire and Humberside, 11.5 per cent in the North, and 12.2 per cent in Wales.

If the miners' weight in the labour movement was far less than in 1926, they were still important strategically, because of their past defeats and victories. But they were now a small part of a larger and more diverse trade union movement: there were slightly more than 5 million trade unionists in 1926, more than 10 million in1984. This made it easier for other workers to sustain the mining communities in 1984–5, but it also meant that the NUM's defeat affected a far smaller proportion of the organised working class than in 1926.

Not only was the trade union movement larger than in 1926: it was in better shape. The recession of the early 1920s caused union membership to collapse, from 8.3 million in 1920 to 5.6 million two years later. An employers' offensive effectively gutted workplace organisation; the engineering lockout of 1922 wiped out the shop stewards' movement which had grown up during the First World War. Real wages fell in the first half of the 1920s.

By comparison, although trade union membership fell after 1979, this was the result of mass unemployment and the proportion of union members among employed workers remained steady. Workplace organisation had been eroded by the recession, but not destroyed. The number of shop stewards was estimated at 300,000. They existed in a far wider range of workplaces than twenty years before — notably the civil service, local government, and the health service. Real wages rose during Thatcher's first term in government.

Above all, the mood of the miners at the end of the 1984–5 strike was radically different to their morale at the end of the 1926 lockout. After 1926 they were completely demoralised, with about a quarter of them unemployed, and tens of thousands in the 'Spencer' union in Nottinghamshire, South Wales, Durham and elsewhere. The miners of 1985 went back after the strike with heads held high.

Consequently, the Tories were unlikely to ride roughshod over the rest of the working class in the wake of the miners' defeat. Attacks there would be: after all, Thatcher had deferred struggles on other fronts to deal with the miners. The railway unions in particular were now likely to face a productivity offensive. But there was no reason to believe that there would be no resistance. Indeed, as the miners' strike dragged to its conclusion, teachers launched a succession of selective strikes in support of their pay claim.

There was one respect in which the pattern of 1926 was likely to be followed. The miners were then, as in 1984–5, on the sharp end of a generalised ruling-class offensive. Stanley Baldwin made his aim clear in July 1925: 'All the workers of this country have got to take reductions in wages to help put industry on its feet.'

The sheer depth of support for the General Strike, however, took the government and employers by surprise. Some sections of big industrial capital decided that collaboration with the trade union leaders made more sense than frontal assault. The talks which followed, organised by Sir Alfred Mond, the chairman of ICI, between the TUC and the bosses of 22 big firms, helped to entrench a philosophy of class collaboration among the trade union leaders.

The 1980s equivalent is the 'new realism' that had already been put forward at the 1983 TUC Congress, but then been stymied by GCHQ and the miners' strike. With both safely out of the way, the centre-right majority on the TUC general council could now pursue closer relations with the government and employers.

Indeed, the strike had forced the Tories and the union bosses to collaborate. The **Financial Times** reported after the collapse of the TUC initiative: 'The TUC and the Government — particularly Mr Peter Walker . . . have moved more closely together than they have been.'[3]

The 'new realism' had been the policy of the centre-right — of such figures as Len Murray and Alistair Graham. But the shift towards accommodation with the Tories could be observed on the trade union left as well. One of the government's biggest successes since its re-election had been increasing trade-union compliance with their legislation — first the defeat of the NGA at Warrington, then the abandonment of the NUM to its fate at the hands of the courts, and — last but by no means least — Austin Rover's use of the 1984 Trade Union Act against eight unions for not holding a strike ballot in November 1984.

Now there were signs that the Transport and General Workers Union, anchor of the TUC left, was considering retreating from the position of unconditional opposition to the Tory anti-union laws adopted by the Wembley Congress in 1982. The **Financial Times** reported on 25 January 1984 a strategy conference of TGWU officials:

Mr Ron Todd, general secretary-elect, made it clear in a keynote speech that . . . there was no real pressure on the union to change its present position on the law. But he did say to the conference that if the union were to suffer a large number of blows arising out of the legislation, it might be necessary to reconsider its position . . . He confirmed, too, that he had proposed a much more tactical approach by the union in its present position to the government's labour laws. In particular, the general mood of the conference seemed to be in line with suggestions from key centre-right figures in the TUC that unions and TUC should really support disputes only where there seemed from the outset a strong likelihood of victory.

There had been a similar coming together of left and right on the general council after 1926. Even here, it would be a mistake to exaggerate the similarities with 1926 and its aftermath. Class-collaborationist trade unionism flourished in one form or other from the late 1920s to the early 1960s. Its success depended upon certain objective conditions. Having fallen earlier, real wages actually *rose* by 10 per cent between 1926 and 1935.

The reason was simple. The prices of primary products — food and raw materials — fell sharply during the Great Slump which began in 1929. British capitalism, with its vast Empire, was in an especially strong position to take advantage of this situation. Under the protectionist policies adopted in 1931, the colonies were forced to exchange cheap food and raw materials for British manufactured goods. Traditional industries such as mining and shipbuilding stagnated, but some workers were able to find jobs in new protected industries like cars and electrical engineering. And though money wages fell, the cost of living fell faster, so that those workers with jobs were better off.

In effect, the British ruling class used the Empire to cushion workers from the worst effects of the slump, rather than stage the sort of offensive which led to the General Strike. Cheap food bought social peace. The real price was paid by tens of millions of colonial peasants and labourers. Then the war economy and afterwards the great boom of the 1950s and 1960s brought most workers jobs and rising living standards.

The collaboration between employers and union leaders after 1926 depended for its success on being able to deliver improvements in living standards. But British capitalism no longer can afford to concede such improvements. It is a declining and uncompetitive part of a world system that is itself in crisis. The Empire is long gone, and with it the surplus fat which allowed British capital to ride out the 1930s comparatively easily.

Real wages did rise steadily under Margaret Thatcher's first government. But, though this bought electoral success and limited working-class resistance, it could not be allowed to continue. The need to force down wages and thereby to increase the rate of profit underlay the Tory assault on the miners.

It followed that further attacks on other groups of workers were inevitable. Even quite right-wing trade union leaders may fight back if attacked, if only in a bureaucratic and timid fashion. Their power depends on that of workers' organisations — so they have a vested interest in preserving trade unions' basic strength. The 'new realism' was likely to have an uneasy and turbulent life.

The fate of the trade union movement generally is a matter of speculation. Of the miners it could be said with certainty that the struggle was only beginning. They were likely to face attacks on several fronts.

First, Ian MacGregor would press ahead with his plans to subordinate the coal industry and its workforce to the imperatives of the market. This did not mean merely pressing ahead with closures. Even before the strike had ended, the Board had approved plans to reorganise its structure. The headquarters staff would be dramatically cut, and a large share of power devolved onto the area and pit managers. The latter would be given a share of NCB profits in exchange for increasing output. New markets would be sought in an effort to reduce the

NCB's dependence on the electricity industry. The **Financial Times** summed up the logic of MacGregor's strategy: 'There is no doubt that the ultimate implication is break-up and privatisation.'[4]

Secondly, the NCB were intent on using the gains they had made during the strike to establish much greater control inside the pits themselves. Derek Law, manager of Silverwood in South Yorkshire, told the **FT**: 'We've got a faction of about 30 to 40 real militants and this is an ideal time to sort them out. Before the strike we took a soft line and the result is we have trained left-wingers.'[5]

Colliery managers talked of relying much less on the old system of continuous consultation with the NUM, and of sending full-time branch officials back down the pit. The bosses at British Leyland had done that to most senior stewards after workplace organisation had been defeated in the car factories by Michael Edwardes.

Another technique which Edwardes had pioneered, with the support of his deputy chairman, Ian MacGregor, was that of directly appealing to workers over the heads of their union leaders through letters and even personal visits. The Coal Board had acquired much experience of these methods through their efforts to orchestrate scabbing. Now they would no longer be prepared to talk to miners solely through the intermediary of their union. MacGregor said on 4 March: 'The management of this industry have learned to communicate directly with the people under their control.'

In the same speech he referred to his hope that 'a representative leadership' of the NUM would emerge. This was the third prong of the attacks the miners would now face. The Tories seemed less interested in encouraging a scab breakaway union than in using the blackleg organisation centred on Nottinghamshire to topple Arthur Scargill and the other left-wing union leaders.

The leading article in **The Times** the day after the miners decided to go back spelled out the strategy of the Tory right:

> this strike is about a divided union and the struggle by working miners to rescue their union from the Communists and ultra-leftists who have hijacked its leadership . . . The struggle for control of the NUM will not end simply because all members . . . return to work tomorrow. Indeed, with the strike over, it will enter its most critical though less visible phase . . .
>
> The strike has been defeated . . . But the hard left's grip on the NUM leadership has not yet been defeated. That is tomorrow's struggle within the NUM . . . The moderate miners

. . . deserve the moral support of the government.[6]

The Times has become, since Rupert Murdoch took it over in 1981, an uncritical exponent of Thatcherism. Among its columnists is David Hart, adviser to Thatcher and MacGregor and their contact with the miners who worked through the strike. The same day **The Times** leader appeared, the National Working Miners' Committee announced plans to seek a court order forcing the NUM to hold a ballot under the 1984 Trade Union Act to elect the national executive, with the aim of eventually removing Scargill from the union presidency.

Whether these various strategies came to fruition was a matter for the future. It was clear, though, that the miners would face an uphill battle to protect their jobs and working conditions, and to preserve and strengthen their organisation. Here the experience of the 1920s and 1930s had positive lessons.

For union organisation *was* rebuilt. It grew out of struggle. The very scale of the employers' offensive forced isolated grops of miners to put up bitter resistance. Usually at the centre of these battles was the Communist Party, in those days a very different organisation which, despite its Stalinist politics, sought to lead workers' struggles.

One example was at Lumphinnans in the Fife coalfield, where after 1926 the coal companies drove through modernisation schemes which had previously encountered stiff resistance. Thousands of jobs were lost, accidents and dust increased. But, most important of all, the companies changed their methods of payment from piecework to subcontracting or a simple day wage.

> Disputes in the Lumphinnans pits usually arose out of the new conditions and methods of payment. Deputies were constantly chivvying men to work harder and to continue on past the end of the working day, threatening them that if they refused, there were plenty of men prepared to do so.[7]

Despite the victimisations, pit closures and unemployment in the area, the workers were so provoked that the militants could organise a series of guerrilla strikes. Alex and Abe Moffat, two leading Communist Party members in the Fife pits, fought to become check-weighers, responsible to the men for ensuring that they were paid for all the coal they had cut. They soon won improvements, until the management had them removed by court order.

But the Moffats found a further loophole. They were elected as safety inspectors with a legally enforceable right to inspect the pits. Over the next few years, both they and other Communist safety inspectors carried out regular inspections of both pits, directing attention to dampness, poor ventilation, dangerous machinery, insecure roofing and other dangers. Sometimes the company refused them admission and sometimes it used hooters and water-hoses to prevent meetings at the pit-head, but this basic right, which had been lost in most other pits, was maintained at Lumphinnans.[8]

The re-building of the union in the Nottinghamshire coalfield, which was the stronghold of the scab 'Spencer' union after 1926, would also have been impossible without the work of members of the Communist Party. The Harworth strike of 1936–7 which finally re-established the MFGB in Notts was a product of patient work by Communist Party member Mick Kane, who became the union branch president, and built it up from seven members in 1935 to 302 a year later. Kane paid a heavy price for the eventual defeat of Spencerism. He was sentenced to two years' imprisonment on a riot charge arising from the strike.

It was thus agitation around often small but concrete issues which re-established trade unionism as a fighting force in the coalfields after 1926. The example was very relevant to the miners as they returned to work in March 1985. Coal Board managers would be eager to restore production as quickly as possible. Even though, as we have seen, they planned to establish much greater control over the work process, their need to raise output would give the miners something to bargain with. Especially in pits where scabbing had been comparatively low, and where a fighting spirit was preserved to the end, militants would be able to find issues around which to organise.

There was, however, one last lesson of 1926. It was the activity of *socialist* miners which was central to rebuilding after the lockout. What were the political implications of the great miners' strike?

8

WHAT WENT WRONG?

THE MINERS'S STRIKE has raised some fundamental questions. Some socialists will argue that the miners should never have fought, that they were bound to be beaten, and that their defeat requires a compete re-appraisal of the left's strategy. Others will unconditionally defend the miners' leaders, especially Arthur Scargill, placing all the blame for the defeat on the TUC and Labour Party leadership. In this final chapter, we consider these arguments, and draw what seem to us to be the political lessons of the miners' epic struggle.

Was defeat inevitable?

People have given a number of reasons for regarding the miners' defeat as inevitable. Some simply say that the strike was doomed from the start — that the NUM should not have taken up the Coal Board's challenge, coming as it did in the spring and at a time when coal stocks were at unprecedented levels.

It is certainly true that the strike took place at a time and on ground not of the miners' choosing. The **Sunday Times**, a supporter of Thatcher's policies, admitted: 'There are good reasons for thinking that the timing of the dispute, and the choice of battleground on which it has been fought was deliberately engineered by the government so that it could take place on the government's terms.'[1]

But workers are often forced to fight in less than ideal conditions. The miners' union had in the three years before the strike suffered a series of major setbacks — the 'No' votes in three successive strike ballots, and the failure to prevent pit closures in Scotland and South Wales. Had the NCB been able to force through closures in

Yorkshire, the stronghold of the NUM left, then effective resistance to mass redundancies in the coalfields would have collapsed. The door would have been open to the sort of massive contraction and restructuring of the mining industry which other sectors of industry such as steel and engineering had already experienced.

Had the miners' union not taken up the challenge in March 1984 the result would have been a defeat at least as devastating and demoralising as any resulting from the strike. Had the miners capitulated without a fight, then Thatcher's offensive against the British working class would indeed have seemed unstoppable. The very length and scale of the strike, its political and financial cost to the Tories, revealed the miners' strength, and the impact workers can have when they fight back.

So whatever our criticisms of the miners' leaders, they were absolutely right to fight when they did. Despite their vacillations and the enormous errors they committed, they did something to restore the honour of the British trade union movement after nearly five years of supine acceptance of Thatcherism.

There are some who accept that the NUM had no choice but to fight, but argue that the failure to hold a national strike ballot doomed the strike to defeat. This argument was made from the very beginning of the strike, not only by the Labour right wing, but also in other, more surprising quarters, for example, by members of the Communist Party such as Bea Campbell, and by an ultra-left sect called the Revolutionary Communist Party. These strange bedfellows say that a national ballot would have almost certainly resulted in a 'Yes' vote. This would have re-united the miners and closed down the Nottinghamshire coalfield.

It is important to understand that the argument about the ballot is not about democracy in the abstract, whatever Labour leader Neil Kinnock might say. The Tories support secret ballots because of the *sort* of democracy they involve, one that reduces workers to passive and isolated individuals vulnerable to the barrage of capitalist propaganda launched at them by the mass media.

The most basic aim of workers' organisation is to overcome this atomisation, and to mobilise their collective strength as a class. This involves a different kind of democracy, one based on workers as a collective, in which decisions are taken openly after the issues have been argued out at mass meetings. These two political forms, the capitalist democracy of the state, and the workers' democracy embryonic in trade union organisation, were starkly counterposed during the miners' strike.

In any case, the Tories' attitude to even their own sort of democracy is highly pragmatic. They are in favour of secret ballots when they win them; when they lose, their attitude changes. The courts happily overrode the defeat of the pit incentive scheme in the October 1977 ballot, and Thatcher shamelessly denied the GCHQ workers a vote over the withdrawal of their trade union rights. Socialists should be equally pragmatic about ballots.

The reason Tories demanded a ballot was that a vote taken before the pickets went out in March would have ensured there was no strike — as was shown by the Area votes in South Wales, Derbyshire and elsewhere.

By mid April, a ballot might have gone the other way. According to a MORI opinion poll 68 per cent of miners supported a strike, as opposed to 26 per cent against and only 6 per cent undecided.[2]

But the consequences of a 'No' vote would have been catastrophic. It would have been the fourth successive defeat for the NUM left in a strike ballot — and this after the Tories had thrown down the gauntlet and the overwhelming majority of miners had been on strike for over a month. Such an outcome would have been quite likely — the press and TV campaign for a 'No' vote in the run-up to such a ballot would have been unprecedented. The majority of strikers, who were not actively involved in picketing, might well have succumbed to this campaign, and to the mounting economic pressures of a lengthening strike. In the aftermath of a defeat for the strike in a ballot, even if the more militant Areas had stayed out, the government and the NCB would have been able, in time, to ride roughshod over the industry.

The situation would have been different if NUM leaders had operated differently — if Jack Taylor had not tried to restrain the Yorkshire pickets from going to Nottinghamshire; if Ray Chadburn and Henry Richardson had not denounced the pickets and demanded a ballot during the early weeks of the strike; if Arthur Scargill had not failed to campaign in Nottinghamshire during that crucial first month; if there had been concerted efforts to involve rank-and-file miners actively in the strike, then Nottinghamshire would have been closed down in the same way as other Areas that voted no in local ballots, and the question of a national ballot would have been academic. As it was, Scargill was right not to take the risk.

There is a third argument used by those who say defeat was inevitable: that the Tories were unbeatable because of the power of the state they controlled. This assertion takes a variety of forms. Some draw on the relatively sophisticated analysis provided by the **Marxism Today** team of 'Thatcherism' as a new form of capitalist rule based on direct ideological appeal to the masses, backed up by a strengthened repressive state apparatus. Others have argued, more straightforwardly, that Britain under Thatcher is becoming a police state, or even a fascist state.

The nub of the argument, whatever its forms, is that there has been a decisive shift in the way in which the British ruling class operates, in which mobilising the consent of the ruled has increasingly been replaced by far greater reliance on coercion. The book **State of Siege** by Jim Coulter, Susan Miller and Martin Walker, while collecting much valuable evidence of how the strike has been policed, strongly conveys the impression that there has been a radical change in how the state operates under the Tories.

The truth is more complex. Capital has ruled Britain ever since the defeat of Chartism in the 1840s through a combination of force and consent. The ruling class have, on the one hand, sought to incorporate the workers' movement within the existing order through the intermediary of the trade union bureaucracy. On the other hand, the repressive state apparatus — the police and sometimes the army — has regularly been used against sections of the working class whose struggles threaten this pattern.

The precise balance between force and consent has varied over the years, depending on the level of class struggle and the relative strengths of capital and labour. There were violent confrontations between workers and the state during the Labour Unrest of 1910–14 and the General Strike and lockout of 1926. For a decade or more after 1926 mining communities in Nottinghamshire and South Wales experienced savage running battles between supporters of the miners' union and scabs protected by the police. Brutal punishment was meted out to unemployed marchers in the 1930s.

Nevertheless, at the same time the state relied heavily on the trade union bureaucracy to ensure that militant sections of the class, then led by the Communist Party, were isolated. Precisely the same was true of the miners' strike of 1984–5. As we have seen, the leaders of other unions exploited the NUM's struggle to screw minor concessions out of the Tories, leaving the miners to fight on alone despite all the resolutions passed by the TUC and Labour Party conferences.

The role of the police was primarily to help prevent the miners from picketing effectively. But state repression was not responsible for the lack of real solidarity action. That was the achievement of the trade union leaders. Without the sabotage of the right-wing leaders and the failure of the left leaders, Thatcher could not have beaten the miners.

There is a more specific version of the argument about the role of the state in the strike — namely, that it meant that the methods of 1972 and 1974 were no longer effective. Kim Howells, the South Wales miners' talkative research officer, claimed towards the end of the strike that mass picketing had failed:

> The state is much better organised for taking on mass pickets than it was in the early 1970s . . . It is the hardest lesson any workforce has had to learn since 1926. The whole of the organised labour movement has to take a fresh look in future disputes.[3]

Howell's nerve was staggering. He admitted in the same interview that 'there had been a deliberate policy against mass picketing in South Wales.' Indeed, throughout the coalfields the mass picketing strategy which brought victory in 1972 hadn't failed — it had not seriously been tried.

The leaders of the militant Areas did not concentrate their forces on specific targets until they closed them down, as the Yorkshire pickets did in 1972. Instead they resorted, certainly in Yorkshire, to gypsy picketing, sending miners haphazardly from one site to another. They did not campaign to build the pickets at important targets, relying instead on the secrecy of the envelope system. They allowed coal to leak through the miners' blockade through their policy of dispensations especially for the steel industry. They prevented attempts by militants to involve passive strikers in picketing their own pits once the back-to-work movement developed.

Of course, it is unlikely that even had these mistakes been avoided the miners would have won on their own. The decisive victory of Saltley in 1972 was only won thanks to the solidarity of Birmingham engineering workers. But the precondition of that action was consistent and vigorous picketing by the miners themselves. The miners could not expect to win the support of other workers unless they were seen themselves to picket massively.

The failure of the NUM leaders to organise mass picketing does not absolve the leaders of the rest of the trade union movement from responsibility for the miners' defeat. Of course, there was an argument in their defence — namely, that although some of them, the TUC lefts, genuinely wanted to help the miners win, they were unable to win the support of their rank and file. After all, one might say, the strike itself revealed clearly the scale of the downturn in the class struggle — in, for example, the willingness of miners and other workers to cross NUM picket lines. The trade union leaders could hardly substitute themselves for a passive and divided rank and file.

The weakness of workplace organisation was undoubtedly one of the decisive features of the strike. Nevertheless, a large minority of trade unionists supported the miners, and were prepared to show this by donating food and money, and, in some cases, taking industrial action, even if this was usually of a token nature.

Precisely because of their lack of confidence in their own ability to deliver more decisive action, these workers looked to the left-wing trade union officials for a lead. Had the TGWU and similar unions given such a lead, had they instructed their members not to cross miners' picket lines, and campaigned to have these instructions observed, the outcome of the strike might have been very different. The activists who supported the miners could have been crystallised into a powerful movement for class-struggle methods. As it was, the resolutions of support for the miners remained pieces of paper, and opportunities such as the two dock strikes were squandered.

The end of class politics?

Running through such arguments that defeat was inevitable is a more general theme. In the wake of the strike many socialists are likely to argue that the outcome has exposed the traditional methods of econonic class struggle — strikes, picketing, and so on — as obsolete. This view was put forward even before the strike ended, by Michael Ignatieff in the **New Statesman**:

> There are those on the left who maintain that the miners' strike is a vindication of class-based politics after decades in which the agenda was defined by cross-class campaigns like feminism and CND. Yet the strike demonstrates the reverse: a labour movement which is incapable of presenting a class claim as a national claim, which can only pose its demands in the language of total victory, which takes on the state and ends up on the wrong side of the law cannot hope to conserve its support and legitimacy among the working-class public. The miners' strike is not the vindication of class politics, but its death throes.[4]

Others were not so forthright, but expressed broadly similar views. The most important example was that of the right, or Euro-communist, wing of the Communist Party, and the grouping with which they are associated, the Labour Party 'soft left'. This grouping had a strong influence on the South Wales and, to a lesser extent, Scottish Areas of the NUM. Towards the end of the strike the soft left became more and more openly critical of 'Scargillism' — by which was meant class-struggle politics. The Communist Party's industrial organiser, Peter Carter, complained in **Marxism Today**:

> What has failed to happen is the bringing together in a mass popular movement of those forces within our society that have already demonstrated sympathy for the miners. This development has been restricted because of a view held that the strike can be won by picketing alone, by the miners on their own.[5]

The miners would have won, the soft left suggested, if they had sought to build a 'broad democratic alliance' embracing forces far beyond the working class. Dave Cook wrote:

> The more the miners have expressed their struggle in terms of their defence of the community, the future of youth, the role of women and the need for a new energy policy, and have linked up with other groups, for example progressive church people, the stronger they have been. The interweaving of their industrial strength with other forces and issues broke down their isolation which the media sought to impose on them.[6]

The model of this 'broad democratic alliance' was provided by the strategy pursued by the South Wales miners' leaders.

It is difficult to overstate the disastrous consequences which this strategy had for the strike. Emlyn Williams, Terry Thomas, Kim Howells, and the other members of the Area executive resisted attempts to shut down the steel industry, actively discouraged mass picketing, and relied instead on appeals to the legendary loyalty of South Wales miners to their union. In the end the passive solidarity of the strike in South Wales crumbled very quickly — partly because of the lobbying by some Area and branch officials for a return to work.

If the soft left strategy severely damaged the miners' union, this was partly because their analysis of British society is so flawed. There is no basis whatsoever for the claim that class politics is on the way out. In June 1984 there were 20,913,000 employees in Britain. Of these, at least three-quarters — more than 15 million people — were wage-labourers, compelled, in order to live, to sell their labour-power to capital.

The main effect of the recession has been to change the composition of the working class — to reduce the proportion of manual industrial workers, and increase that of white-collar employees. Many of the latter are, however, routine clerical workers, with no more power over the means of production, and often lower wages, than manual industrial workers. And despite the rundown of manufacturing industry, there were still 5,480,000 manufacturing workers in June 1984 — more than one in four of all employees.

Capitalism has reshaped the working class, not abolished it. Counterposed to this massive proletariat is a tiny capitalist class — one sociologist has estimated that the core of the business class is between 25,000 and 50,000 people, less than a thousandth of the population.

The miners' strike dramatically demonstrated the centrality of the class divisions of British society. The Tories resorted to all the traditional methods of class war — the police, the courts, the mass media — in order to isolate and crush the NUM. Blacklegging was resurrected on a scale undreamt of since the 1930s. The polarisation between labour and capital could not have been starker.

The miners did not fail because they used the methods of class struggle. On the contrary, most of their leaders were opposed to these methods, and often prevented attempts seriously to use mass picketing — sometimes under the influence of 'soft left' ideas. The NUM suffered from too little class politics, not too much.

The soft left justify their 'broad' strategy by invoking the omnipotence of Thatcherism. They grossly exaggerate the Tories' success. Economically, Thatcherism has been a failure — it was the Tories' inability to reduce real wages which forced them to attack the miners. Electorally, they have benefitted from a split opposition, and they have made only limited inroads even on the ideological front so emphasised by **Marxism Today**. Support for the welfare state actually grew during Thatcher's first term. Opinion polls consistently showed between 30 and 35 per cent of the public supporting the miners during the strike.

There were a number of points in the strike when the Tories were pushed onto the defensive — most notably during the first dock strike in July 1984, and then when it seemed as if NACODS was going to strike in October. Determined action by the rest of the trade union movement could have forced Thatcher to surrender. As it was, the Tories were saved, but less through the invulnerability of Thatcherism than thanks to the trade union leaders' refusal to take action in support of the NUM.

Thatcher's decisive superiority over the miners lay only in this

— she was willing to pursue a decisive and coherent strategy on behalf of her class. The trade union leaders were, by contrast, timid and indecisive, ready to sell the miners for a quiet life, while the behaviour of the official Labour Party leadership was beneath contempt.

One side in the miners' strike pursued class politics: the other didn't. Which side won?

The politics of the trade union bureaucracy

The fundamental reason why the miners lost their strike was because they were betrayed by the leaders of the trade union movement. But the leaders of the NUM itself cannot be absolved of all responsibility for the defeat. Above all, the leaders of the main left-wing Areas — Yorkshire, Scotland and South Wales — consistently blocked attempts to use the methods necessary to win the strike.

The role played by Jack Taylor and the Yorkshire NUM leadership was especially important. During the great struggles of 1910–26 the South Wales Miners Federation was the largest district of the union and the pacemaker of militancy in the coalfields.

Since the late 1960s Yorkshire has played a similar part — the largest single Area and the main base of the rank-and-file organisation behind the strikes of 1969, 1970 and 1972. Arthur Scargill epitomised the militancy of the Yorkshire miners, just as fifty years earlier Cook was pushed forward by the struggles in the South Wales coalfield.

Consequently, the Yorkshire leadership's hesitations, vacillations, and sometimes outright obstruction had a decisive effect on the 1984–5 strike. The Yorkshire miners — and their counterparts in other coalfields — displayed sheer heroism in the way they sustained the strike. They deserved better leadership than they received.

But why did the Area leaders perform so disastrously? Was it simply a matter of personal failings on the part of people such as Jack Taylor (dubbed the 'Yorkshire Pudding' by pickets early on in the strike)?

The history of betrayal by trade union leaders is too long to put what happened in the miners' strike down to individual failings. Already at the end of the last century the American socialist Daniel de Leon denounced the trade union leaders as 'labour lieutenants of capital'. 'The Labour leader of today,' he wrote, is 'nothing but a masked battery, from behind which the Capitalist Class can encompass what it could not without — the work of enslaving and slowly degrading the Working Class.'[7]

The miners have had plenty of experience of trade union leaders' betrayals — they were deserted by the other unions belonging to the Triple Alliance on 'Black Friday', 15 April 1921, then, after the TUC had called off the General Strike on 12 May 1926, left to fight on alone for seven months. The pattern was the same in 1984–5, with both the right and the left of the TUC willing, on the whole, to give the miners verbal support, but not to translate it into action. Even when the NUM's assets were sequestered in early December, the TUC leadership refused to act.

This conduct was a consequence of the nature of the trade union leadership as a social group. Trade unions are in a contradictory position. They are the basic defence organisations of the working class, through which workers struggle to improve their wages and conditions, and to protect their jobs. Yet trade unions operate within the framework of capitalism. They strive to make workers *less* exploited, rather than to abolish capitalist exploitation altogether.

Workers thus struggle through trade unions both *against* capitalism, and *within* it. They seek to improve their situation, but within the limits of capitalism. This is reflected in the separation of politics and economics that is characteristic of trade unionism. Workers organise within production to improve their material conditions. Politics is treated as separate from this, as concerned above all with contesting and winning elections. Trade unions do not seek to mobilise workers' collective strength politically, against the power of the capitalist class concentrated in the state.

So long as workers limit their horizons to those set by capitalism, every struggle, however militant, must end in a compromise between capital and labour. Which side the compromise favours will depend on the relative strength of the two sides. Nevertheless, every strike finishes in a settlement and someone has to negotiate the compromises. A division of labour naturally emerges between workers and their representatives, whose time is increasingly spent bargaining with the employers.

So there arises the full-time trade union official. His (or, very occasionally, her) role cuts him off from the workers he represents. He is removed from the discipline of the shopfloor, with its dirt and dangers, from the daily conflicts with foreman and manager, from the fellowship of his workmates, to the very different environment of an office.

The official's earnings no longer depend on the ups and down of capitalist production — they no longer involve working overtime, nor are they vulnerable to short-time or lay-offs. If a plant is closed, the official who negotiates the redundancies won't get the sack.

All these factors place the full-time official in a privileged position in comparison with rank-and-file trade unionists. They also give him the power and the incentive to usurp control of the union. Not only that, but the recognition given to trade union officials by the employers brings with it an increased social status, and the things that go with this — 'executive' salaries, free cars, subsidised houses, expense accounts, lucrative sinecures such as seats on government bodies, dinners with bosses, free trips round the world to international conferences.

Constantly closeted with management, the trade union official comes to see negotiation, compromise, collaboration with employers — class collaboration, as the very stuff of trade unionism. Struggle comes to seem a disruption of the bargaining process, a nuisance and an inconvenience. Because their privileges and power are bound up with the strength and prosperity of the union organisation, the officials identify the interests of the workers with those of the machine. As the great revolutionary socialist Rosa Luxemburg put it, 'organisation . . . from being a means has been gradually changed into an end in itself, a precious thing, to which the interests of struggles should be subordinated.'[8]

All these factors conspire to make the trade union officials into a conservative bureaucracy, whose role is to negotiate the terms on which labour is exploited by capital, and whose interests are therefore different from, and opposed to those of the trade union rank and file.

The miners, as one of the first well-organised groups of workers in Britain, have long had to contend with this bureaucracy. Dave Douglass writes of the early days of the Durham Miners' Association, founded in 1869:

The full-time officials soon developed a particular character. Almost invariably they were drawn from the ranks of the moderate, self-educated, temperate miners. Once elected, they thought their role was to inflict upon the members their own moderation, and lead rather than serve. The members found they were being policed by the men to whom they were paying wages. The officials became more and more preoccupied with arbitration and conciliation as the cure for all ills, and more and more impatient of local action which ran up against it. The leadership rejoiced in the formality of the conciliation machinery

. . . preferring any course of action, 'even simple submission', in preference to a strike.[9]

The bitter conflict between bureaucracy and rank and file during the Cambrian Combine Strike of 1910–11 led a group of militant socialists in the South Wales Miners Federation to produce **The Miners' Next Step** in 1912. They argued that the officials

> are Trade Unionists by trade and their profession demands certain privileges. The greatest of these are plenary powers. Now, every inroad the rank and file make on this privilege lessens the power and prestige of the leader . . . The leader has an interest — a vested interest — in stopping progress. The condition of things in South Wales has reached the point when this difference of interest, this antagonism, has become manifest. Hence the men criticise and are discontent with their leaders. But the remedy is not new leaders.

Even militant workers are, however, reluctant to believe that 'the remedy is not new leaders'. It is natural to think that the betrayals which take place are the fault of individuals. Get rid of them, replace them with good fighters, and all will be well. So arises the struggle between left and right within the trade union bureaucracy. The division reflects the belief of militant trade unionists that by electing left-wing officials they can avoid future betrayals.

The strategy of the Broad Lefts inside the different unions today is based on this belief — the idea that the movement can be won to class-struggle politics by capturing the official machine. The belief is not a new one. In the run-up to the General Strike the TUC fell under the sway of a number of prominent left-wingers — Alonzo Swales, A. A. Purcell, and George Hicks. These made very radical speeches. Purcell told the 1924 TUC that the unions should be transformed into 'an instrument of solidarity capable of challenging the existing structure of capitalism and bringing into being a Workers' State.'

Yet when it came to it, Purcell, Swales and Hicks were as deeply implicated in the betrayal of the miners as such open right-wingers as J. H. Thomas and Ernest Bevin. Even A. J. Cook, the left-wing secretary of the Miners' Federation, vacillated. In July 1926 he held secret talks with Sir William Layton and Seebohm Rowntree over a possible end to the lockout, without informing the MFGB. Cook recommended the resulting compromise, and he appealed to the miners to 'face the facts'. (As it turned out, both the government and rank-and-file miners rejected the proposals.)

Even the most dedicated and militant socialist is likely to become a prisoner of the machine once elected to full-time office. We have seen how the rank-and-file organisation in the Yorkshire coalfield which brought victory in the early 1970s atrophied after the left had come to power.

The change had disastrous consequences once the strike broke out in March 1984. For Jack Taylor and his like the union had indeed become an end in itself. Picketing was restrained, both because it might deplete union funds and because it might cause the courts to seize the Area's assets. In Yorkshire and elsewhere the Area leaders relied instead on their links with other trade union officials, through the Triple Alliance and the like.

Had rank-and-file organisation been as strong as it was in the early 1970s this wouldn't have mattered so much. As it was, ordinary miners, lacking confidence in their own power, looked to the official to give a lead. The result was a slow spiral to defeat.

The limits of Scargillism

Arthur Scargill stands out as the apparent exception to what we have said about trade union officials. From the strike's very beginning it was, as far as Fleet Street was concerned, 'Scargill's Strike'. The miners' president was the victim of a campaign of vilification gross even by the standards of **The Sun** and the rest of the gutter press. Equally, for the striking miners he was a hero, the symbol of their determination to fight. 'Arthur Scargill walks on water', they sang, and many other trade unionists joined them.

As the strike was driven further and further onto the defensive, the Labour right wing began to aim their fire directly at Scargill. The **Daily Mirror** declared on 28 January 1985: 'Arthur Scargill has lost the miners' strike. It is his defeat more than theirs. He has led the crack guards regiment of the unions to disaster. No one else is to blame.'

One of the most scurrilous attacks on Scargill came from Jimmy Reid, leader of the Upper Clyde Shipyard occupation of 1971 and an old friend of the miners' leader. Reid, now a Labour right-winger, told a **Channel 4** television audience that 'Arthur Scargill is the best thing that's happened to Mrs Thatcher since General Galtieri invaded the Falklands.'[10]

Behind Reid's gutter language — 'Scargillism strengthens

Thatcherism', 'Scargillism is the politics of infantilism' — was almost
certainly the hand of Neil Kinnock, who let it be known that 'he will
not be made a scapegoat by his party's hard left for the expected defeat
of Arthur Scargill and the National Union of Mineworkers.'[11]

Attacks like Reid's should be treated with the contempt they
deserve. But what role did Scargill play in the strike, and what
responsibility does he have for its defeat?

We have argued that a strategy of mass picketing could have
brought victory. Throughout the strike Scargill advocated such a
strategy. This led him to clash seriously with the Yorkshire Area
leadership in particular during the summer of 1984. Is Scargill that
exception to the rule, a trade union leader who meant what he said?

There are many who believe that he is. One of them is John
Lloyd, the ex-Maoist labour editor of the **Financial Times**. Early on
in the strike Lloyd wrote: 'Arthur Scargill is the most serious revolutionary socialist in the UK, maybe in Western Europe.'[12] Ten months
later Lloyd tried to explain Scargill to the businessmen (and the odd
socialist) who read the **FT**:

> From the outside . . . the NUM president appears a man willing
> to resort to any ruse, manipulate any fact, use any person, in
> support of his ultimate purpose of maintaining the strike. So he
> is. But he has also been unwaveringly faithful and honest in
> pursuing the policies laid down by the NUM's national confer-
> ence, constitutionally the union's highest body. It prescribed
> complete opposition, through industrial action if necessary, to
> pit closures, no ifs and buts . . .
>
> Mr Scargill was the country's ace activist and *remains one
> still*: he has the activist's absolute fidelity in the outcome of the
> internal process, very little, almost none perceived, of the
> presidential need to balance militancy with caution, rhetoric
> with reality . . . he is the activist's dream.[13]

Undoubtedly, Arthur Scargill is one of the most outstanding
leaders the British working-class movement has had. His performance during the 1984–5 strike was astonishing. The determination
with which he used every resource at his command to prevent surrender to the Tories and the Coal Board should win the admiration of
every socialist. At several junctures, Scargill and the pickets together
stopped the strike from collapsing. There is simply no comparison
between Scargill and most other trade union leaders.

But the qualities which mark Scargill out as an exceptional

individual do not make him an inexplicable genius. There seem to be two crucial ingredients to his political make-up. One is his experience of the struggles of the 1960s and the early 1970s. More than any other leading figure in the British labour movement Scargill believes that the industrial power displayed by the miners in 1972 and 1974 should be used for political ends, as part of the struggle to achieve a socialist society in Britain. He told **Marxism Today** in April 1981:

> Anyone who believes that we can achieve socialism simply by electing a number of MPs is deluding themselves. We will win parliamentary power, we will win working-class power to the extent that we organise people in this country to fight for, and sustain, the alternative socialist system that we want to see. Parliaments do not necessarily reflect the views of ordinary people, and if you have a Parliament that is not being pushed by a working-class movement demanding, expecting and requiring change, then you will not get that change.

Scargill's belief in the creative role of industrial struggle in the fight for socialism draws him towards his hero A. J. Cook. Cook was influenced by revolutionary syndicalism, the idea that the trade unions would be the instrument for overthrowing capitalism. But Scargill remains committed to the Labour Party as the main vehicle of change. He told **New Left Review** in 1975: 'I think that the ideal way that the working class can achieve working-class power is to change the Labour Party.' Scargill does not reject the parliamentary road to socialism: rather, he believes it cannot succeed without industrial action.

The second ingredient of Scargill's politics is the influence of the ideas of 'socialism from above', ideas common to both Labourism and Stalinism.

Scargill's view of the working-class movement is one in which the initiative comes from the top. 'Leadership' is the key word in Scargill's political vocabulary. In 1975 he contrasted the situation in Yorkshire before and after he took over the Area NUM:

> If you have a right-wing leadership in any union, the whole philosophy, the entire ideology, the notions of that leadership will permeate through the union . . . No one will deny that, whether it be a right-wing union or a left-wing union, the fact that you're able to channel out information, ideas, propaganda, is of immense benefit to the membership, or of immense *harm* to the membership . . .

. . . there have been tremendous strides forward in Yorkshire in the miners' union. It's been done because we have a left-progressive leadership that has been willing to stand up and say 'no' to the Coal Board, that has been prepared to fight for those principles and aims we believe in . . . It's precisely because that sort of leadership has been given on the question of wages and conditions that we have won support.[14]

Scargill is right. Leadership *is* important. The real crime of the left-wing leadership of the TGWU is that they have not been prepared to give a positive lead to their members. Scargill has. On the whole, he stuck by his guns. But he appears to believe that 'left-progressive leadership' is the decisive factor in workers' struggles. This is simply wrong.

It was rank-and-file organisation — initiatives from below — which won the 1972 strike, *despite* the right-wing leadership of the national and Yorkshire Area unions. Even in 1984–5, Scargill was sustained by the confidence of the rank and file. Without the support of the active strikers, and their determination to fight, he could not so often have beaten the NUM right and soft left, however skilful his tactical manoeuvres.

Scargill's stress on the role of 'Marxist, progressive, left-wing leadership' leads him to see change coming from the top. His strategy for the left within the unions is essentially an electoral one — socialists should organise to capture the official machine. Scargill's difference from the rest of the Broad Left lies only in his opposition to backsliding by 'progressive' officials. But the betrayals committed by left union leaders is not a consequence of their lack of moral fibre. It is the inevitable result of their position in the social structure.

The only counter to the bureaucracy lies in independent rank-and-file organisation. Such organisation has a history in Britain dating back to the early part of the century. The First World War threw up the Shop Stewards' and Workers' Control Movement, whose attitude to the bureaucracy was summed up by the Clyde Workers' Committee in their first leaflet, printed in November 1915:

We will support the officials just so long as they rightly represent the workers, but we will act independently immediately they misrepresent them. Being composed of delegates from every shop and untrammelled by obsolete rule of law, we claim to represent the true feeling of the workers. We can act immediately according to the merits of the case and the desire of the rank and file.

Scargill's attitude is very different from this. He helped build the Barnsley Miners' Forum in the late 1960s, openly organising the rank and file in defiance of the right-wing Area leadership. But he pursued this strategy precisely because the right controlled the official machine. Once the left had captured the Yorkshire NUM, the Forum was allowed to wither and die. The lesson of 1972 — the decisive role played by unofficial, rank-and-file leadership — was not learned.

This had disastrous consequences in 1984–5. Throughout the strike Scargill operated through the official machine. During the crucial early weeks when Nottinghamshire hung in the balance, Scargill allowed himself to be bound by the constitutional nicety that the strike was a collection of rolling Area strikes, and he did not intervene publicly to campaign to bring out wavering miners.

Again, Scargill found his strategy of mass picketing blocked by the left-wing Area officials in April, May and June. This conflict surfaced, above all, over Orgreave. Scargill did not break openly with Jack Taylor, Mick McGahey and Emlyn Wiliams. He did not publicly call on the active strikers to defy their Area and branch officials and shut off the supply of coal to the big steelworks. He did not encourage the formation of unofficial strike committees under rank-and-file control.

Had Scargill done so, with his enormous prestige among the activists, the story of the strike might have been very different.

Throughout the long war of attrition waged by the Coal Board and the scabs against the NUM, Scargill maintained a public united front with the rest of the left on the national executive. He did not interfere when left branch officials hindered the activists' efforts to counter the back-to-work movement.

When Yorkshire and South Wales officials began to press for surrender in early 1985 Scargill did not openly challenge them. Those outside the executive were left to infer the differences from hints, innuendo, and private briefings.

In the absence of any attempt to develop independent rank-and-file organisation, Scargill sought to sustain the strike and drive it forward through sheer will-power. It is impossible not to admire the determination, courage and tactical skill that Scargill displayed. But it remained the attempt of an individual to substitute for the collective organisation needed to win the strike.

Any strategy which rests on the determination and commitment of individual leaders is bound to fail. In spite of his outstanding performance in the strike, Arthur Scargill cannot avoid his share of blame for the miners' defeat. What matters though, is less to condemn individuals' failures, than to draw the correct political conclusions.

Labourism and the revolutionary alternative

The approach of left-wing trade union leaders — even the best of them — embodies a certain view of how to change society, one in which change comes from above, from the leaders at the top. This view is not confined to the trade unions. Indeed, its stronghold is the Labour Party. Labour's is a parliamentary road to socialism, which supposes that change will come through capturing the existing state machine.

On this view, the decisive agents of change are to be the Labour MPs whose election leads to the formation of a socialist government. The role of the mass of working people is passive — simply to vote these MPs into office. Socialism comes from above.

It is this strategy for change which explains the strange schizophrenia of the Labour Party during the miners' strike — the despicable part played by its leader, and the magnificent support given the miners by many party activists.

There was nothing new about Neil Kinnock's contortions during the miners' strike. Exactly the same pattern of hostility or indifference to workers' struggles has been displayed by every Labour leader. Ramsay MacDonald, the first Labour prime minister, wrote in 1924: 'Strikes for increased wages . . .not only are not socialism, but may mislead the spirit and the policy of socialism.' His government used anti-union legislation to declare states of emergency aimed at the 1924 docks and London tram strikes.

Although MacDonald was also hostile to the General Strike, the Labour Party benefitted from its defeat. Many workers concluded that industrial action had failed and therefore looked to the ballot box as the main means of changing society. Labour achieved its best result so far in the next general election, in 1929, and formed a minority government. MacDonald presided over the opening years of the Great Depression, did nothing while unemployment soared, and then in 1931 broke with Labour and formed a coalition with the Tories.

The 1945 Labour government represents, for left-wing members of the Labour Party, the high-water mark of their history, the era of such social reforms as the creation of the National Health Service. It was also a time when Labour cabinet ministers were prepared to use the army against strikers, not once, but on a number of occasions — for example, during the dock strike of October 1945.

In August 1945 the new Home Secretary, James Chuter Ede, proposed reviving the Supply and Transport Organisation, which had been used by Stanley Baldwin to break the General Strike. This organisation, now renamed the Civil Contingencies Unit, was used against the miners in 1984–5.

The behaviour of more recent Labour governments has been similar. Harold Wilson resorted to crude anti-Communist witch-hunting techniques to defeat the 1966 seamen's strike, and tried to introduce legislation to ban unofficial strikes. The Labour government of 1974–9 used the army against the Glasgow dustmen in 1975, and against the firefighters' strike of 1977–8. In the latter, the Cabinet committee which decided to send in the troops included the Energy Secretary, Tony Benn.

This pattern of strikebreaking is too persistent to be explained as simply a matter of bad leadership. Every Labour government has set itself against workers in struggle. Why?

The answer is to be found in Labour's basic political strategy.

Even the most radical and militant Labour Party member believes that socialism can be achieved only by winning a majority of seats in parliament — though many Labour activists combine this belief with support for workers' struggles, arguing that society can be transformed by combining parliamentary and 'extra-parliamentary' action.

Thus, two leading members of the Labour Co-ordinating Committee, Peter Hain and Jean McCrindle, criticised Neil Kinnock because 'he has appeared to view the [miners'] strike as an embarrassing diversion from the "real" task of winning electoral support.' Instead they argued that 'extra-parliamentary battles' should be 'seen as opportunities to be seized in order to rebuild working-class confidence in Labour.'[15]

There is, however, a profound contradiction involved in socialists seeking to combine what Eric Heffer once called 'the class struggle in Parliament' with active participation in workers' struggles. Large-scale strikes tend to develop into a conflict with the state. The miners' strike illustrated this very well: not only were the police deployed on a massive scale against the miners, but the effective conduct of the strike required the NUM's defiance of the law, as was shown by the interference of the courts at all levels from picketing to seizure of the national union's assets.

The state is not a neutral umpire which arbitrates in the class struggle between capital and labour. The state is the most concentrated form of power of the employing class, and so will inevitably be used against workers' struggles.

This creates a dilemma for the Labour Party as an organisation committed to using this very same state to transform society. Labour is forced to choose between parliament and the 'extra-parliamentary' struggle. Entirely consistently, the Labour leaders have always taken the side of parliament and the state. J. H. Thomas, the railwaymen's leader and a Labour front bencher, put it very well during the General Strike of 1926: 'In a challenge to the constitution God helps us unless the government won.'

Labour's electoralism itself pushes it rightwards. Voting is a passive and individual activity, in which people's preferences are formed under a massive barrage of capitalist propaganda from the press and TV. Parliamentary elections are therefore a most unfavourable terrain for socialist politics. Winning them means playing down any challenge to the existing order and currying favour with a 'public opinion' orchestrated by Fleet Street. Neil Kinnock's evasions and media gimmicks are not simply a reflection of his ambition and political vacuity. They are an entirely logical strategy for a Labour leader to pursue at a time when weakened organisation and mass redundancies have pushed working-class opinion rightwards, when many militants are demoralised, and the Alliance has split the anti-Tory vote.

Whether Labour gains electorally from the miners' defeat, as it did after 1926, remains to be seen. It is certainly likely that many of those active in the strike will be drawn towards the Labour Party, despite Kinnock's appalling performance. They will conclude that the failure of industrial struggle means that the only avenue open to changing society is through parliament. Many miners politicised by the strike have joined Labour in the hope of changing the party.

The Labour left are, however, just as much affected by the dilemmas of reformism as the right wing. They too are committed to a parliamentary road to socialism. This means accepting the prevailing division between politics and economics, electoralism and trade unionism. Tony Benn illustrates this.

Unlike Kinnock, Tony Benn was unequivocally committed to the miners' cause, and worked unceasingly for their victory. However, on the central issue of the strike — the failure of the TUC to support the miners — he was silent. Benn did not use his considerable prestige to campaign for the leaders of left-wing unions such as the TGWU to issue instructions to their members to black scab coal and oil. And more generally, the hard Labour left did not challenge Kinnock's leadership, despite his attitude to the strike. Because their strategy too depends on winning elections, and this keeps the Labour left part of a 'broad church' which embraces right-wingers like Denis Healey.

The miners' defeat is likely to push the centre of gravity of the labour movement further rightwards. Already in January 1985, once it was clear that the NUM was on the ropes, Kinnock took to the offensive against the hard left. He put strong pressure on Labour councils not to defy the Tories' rate-capping legislation, backed an inquiry designed to find ideological grounds for expelling the left-wing **Militant** tendency, and denounced Tony Benn and other Campaign Group MPs, who disrupted the House of Commons to demand a debate on the strike, for being 'wiling to fight to the last drop of miners' blood'.

Sections of the Labour left began to make their peace with Kinnock. Two left-wingers on the party national executive, Michael Meacher and David Blunkett, came out against Labour councils' defying rate-capping legislation. Then, within a week of the strike ending, the Labour group on the Greater London Council split when GLC leader Ken Livingstone argued that the council should obey the law and set a legal rate. Kinnock had the Labour left on the run.

Such compromises on the part of Labour left wingers are nothing new. Time and again socialists have tried to make the Labour Party into an instrument of radical change. Their efforts have always been frustrated by the dominant coalition of right-wing parliamentary leaders and the trade union bureaucracy with their massive block vote. Successive left-wing leaders have usually ended up surrendering to the right wing — Stafford Cripps, Aneurin Bevan, Michael Foot. Those who stood firm, like James Maxton, were driven into the wilderness.

There is only one way of breaking out of this frustrating cycle of right-wing leadership and left-wing impotence and betrayal. That is to reject the fundamental premiss of Labourism, shared by all its factions from far right to hard left — that socialism can be achieved through parliament, by capturing control of the existing state machine.

The state is not a neutral umpire. It is the basic underpinning of capitalist class domination. The flagrant contempt with which police chiefs ignored the opposition of elected local authorities to their strike-breaking activites, the naked class bias with which the courts ruled consistently against the miners' union, the single-mindedness with which the Tory government mobilised all the resources at its disposal to defeat the NUM — all these illustrate the simple truth that the state is nothing but the concentrated power of capital.

The state is the employing class's last line of defence. Usually capital's economic and ideological power is sufficient to head off challenges. The pressure exerted by the world money markets was enough to force the 1964 and 1974 Labour governments to tear up their election manifestoes and attack working-class living standards. But there are always what Lenin called the 'special bodies of armed men' — the army, police, and security services — waiting in the background, as the Chilean working class learned to their cost in September 1973.

Socialism cannot come through parliament, but only as a result of workers organising to overthrow the existing state machine and replace it with their own power. Only the collective strength which workers possess in production — in the factories, offices, hospitals, yes, and in the mines — can defeat the organised might of capital.

Again and again through the present century workers' struggles have thrown up forms of organisation which transcend the limits of trade unionism. These have many names — the *soviets* in Russia 1905 and 1917, the workers' and soldiers' councils in Germany 1918, the *cordones* in Chile 1972–3, *Solidarnosc* in Poland 1980–1. What they have in common is that they began to organise workers on a class-wide basis, transcending the sectional divisions built into trade unionism, and break down the reformist barrier between economics and politics, challenging the power of the capitalist state.

Through such bodies, councils of workplace delegates elected by and accountable to the rank and file, workers can both overthrow the existing state, and create one of their own, based on the most thoroughgoing democracy.

Alas, the 1984–5 miners' strike did not see even the remotest beginnings of workers' councils. But it did provide a glimpse of how workers can be won to socialism. It is through their own struggle that workers develop the organisation and confidence necessary to over-throw capitalism. More than this, involvement in struggle alters workers' view of the world. They are no longer passive and isolated individuals, but part of a collective that is acting to change the world, in however small a way. They also discover the reality of class society.

Of no struggle is this more true than the miners' strike. The men and women of the pit communities began the strike in the main accepting the view of the world given by the mass media: that the police are there to protect us, that black people are unwelcome 'aliens', that women's role is to be passive sex objects and childbearers.

The experience of the strike transformed these men and women. They soon learned the truth about the police — many of them the hard way, under a truncheon or boot. The women began to organise, discovering undreamt-of abilities and challenging the traditional sexual division of labour in the family. Mining men and women travelled the country picketing and seeking solidarity. They began to make political connections. They met black people and discovered that they too were persecuted by the state. Their views about sexuality began to change when they came across lesbians and gays who supported their strike. They started to see analogies between their villages under police siege and the Catholic ghettoes in the north of Ireland.

Perhaps these experiences will have a lasting effect on only a minority of those involved, once the pressures of everyday life re-assert themselves. Nevertheless, the strike dramatically demonstrated the possibilities inherent in workers' struggles — their capacity to transform the working class.

It follows that to achieve socialism requires a different sort of party from the Labour Party. Such a party would focus, not on elections, but on workers in struggle, using every strike as an oppor-tunity to raise the general level of socialist consciousness. Such a party would seek, not to appeal to the lowest common denominator, but to organise the small minority of workers who are at present convinced of the need for revolutionary socialism in order to relate to the vast majority who at present are not.

The crisis in which both British and world capitalism are caught up means there will be more struggles like the miners' strike. Capital can solve its problems only by attacking working-class organisation and living standards. When it does, the larger and better organised the revolutionary minority, the greater the chance of avoiding the defeat the miners suffered in 1985.

The ultimate reason why the miners lost was because capital had a determined, ruthless, highly class-conscious leadership while the working class did not. Fortunately the working class lost only a battle in 1985. But to win the war will require a different sort of leadership, one which builds on every workers' struggle in order to launch eventually an assault on the citadel of capitalist power in the state machine.

The leadership given by a revolutionary party would not seek to substitute itself for workers' struggles. Rather it would seek to make these struggles conscious and directed not just at an individual employer but at the capitalist state that stands behind *every* employer.

Revolutionary socialism is socialism from below, arising from the self-activity of the working class rather than from the initiatives of trade union and parliamentary leaders at the top. Those working to achieve the self-emancipation of the working class can take inspiration from the miners' example. The daring and initiative with which they launched the strike, the courage and endurance with which they waged it, the pride and defiance with which they ended it — all were a powerful vindication of the capacity of the working class to transform society.

The memory of the Great Miners' Strike of 1984–5 will always shine as an example of working people's heroism and determination. We can say of the mining communities, as Karl Marx wrote of the first workers' revolution, the Paris Commune of 1871, after its defeat:

> Working men's Paris, with its Commune, will be for ever celebrated as the glorious harbinger of a new society. Its martyrs are enshrined in the great heart of the working class. Its exterminators history has already nailed to that eternal pillory from which all the prayers of their priests will not avail to redeem them.

NOTES

Notes to Chapter 1

1. Michael Crick, **Scargill and the Miners** (Harmondsworth 1985) page 98.
2. Quoted in **The Scotsman** (7 March 1984).
3. Quoted in the **Financial Times** (7 March 1984).
4. **Financial Times** (7 March 1984).

Notes to Chapter 2

1. Royden Harrison, Introduction to **The Independent Collier** (Hassocks 1978) pages 1 and 2.
2. B J McCormick, **Industrial Relations in the Coal Industry** (London and Basingstoke 1979) page 62.
3. Vic Allen, **The Militancy of British Miners** (Shipley 1981) pages 63–4.
4. L J Handy, **Wages Policy in the British Coalmining Industry** (Cambridge 1979) page 221.
5. Andrew Taylor, **The Politics of the Yorkshire Miners** (Beckenham 1984) page 169.

6. Quoted in M Crick, **Scargill and the Miners** (Harmondsworth 1985) page 21.
7. Taylor, page 88.
8. Allen, pages 139–40.
9. Quoted in 'The New Unionism', **New Left Review** issue 92 (1975) page 9.
10. **NLR** 92, page 10.
11. **NLR** 92, page 10.
12. **NLR** 92, pages 11–12.
13. **NLR** 92, page 17.
14. **NLR** 92, pages 18–19.
15. Reginald Maudling, **Memoirs** (London 1978) pages 160–1.
16. Allen, page 240.
17. Taylor, page 268.
18. **NLR** 92, page 24.
19. Crick, page 88.
20. Quoted in **The Thatcher Government** (Oxford 1983) page 110.
21. **The Economist** (27 November 1982).
22. **New Statesman** (10 August 1984).
23. Crick, page 96.
24. **Socialist Review** (October 1983).
25. Reproduced from the **New Statesman** (23 March 1984).

Notes to Chapter 3

1. **Nottinghamshire Evening Post** (15 March 1984).
2. **Sheffield Morning Telegraph** (15 March 1984).
3. Quoted in the **Morning Star** (14 March 1984).
4. **Financial Times** (16 March 1984).
5. **The Economist** (24 March 1984).
6. Quoted in the **Daily Mail** (31 March 1984).
7. Roy Ottey, **The Strike — an insider's story** (London 1985) pages 81–2.
8. **The Observer** (8 April 1984).
9. Ottey, page 27.
10. Douglas Hurd, Minister of State at the Home Office, **Hansard** (20 June 1984).

Notes to Chapter 4

1. **Financial Times** (30 March 1984).
2. **The Times** (20 March 1984).
3. **NLR** 92, page 13.
4. **NLR** 92, page 22.
5. **Financial Times** (8 May 1984).
6. **The Economist** (26 May 1984).
7. **The Guardian** (21 May 1984).
8. **The Guardian** (4 June 1984).
9. **Sunday Times** (15 April 1984).
10. **The Times** (1 June 1984).
11. **The Economist** (16 June 1984).
12. Huw Beynon (editor), **Digging Deeper** (London 1985) page 145.

13. **Digging Deeper**, page 144.
14. **Marxism Today** (September 1984).
15. **Morning Star** (14 May 1984).
16. **Marxism Today** (September 1984).

Notes to Chapter 5

1. Quoted in the **Financial Times** (13 February 1985).
2. **Socialist Worker** (22 September 1984).
3. **Socialist Worker** (22 September 1984).
4. 'Beyond the coalfields', in H Beynon (editor), **Digging Deeper** (London 1985), pages 151–2.
5. Quoted in the **Financial Times** (8 March 1985).
6. **Sunday Times** (3 June 1984).
7. **Financial Times** (25 May 1984).
8. **The Economist** (7 July 1984).
9. **The Economist** (14 July 1984).
10. **The Economist** (14 July 1984).
11. **Socialist Review** (May 1983).
12. **Socialist Worker** (15 September 1984).
13. **The Economist** (8 September 1984).
14. Quoted in **The Observer** (30 September 1984).
15. **Sunday Times** (21 October 1984).
16. Quoted in the **Financial Times** (20 October 1984).
17. Figures given on **Channel Four** television news (7 March 1985).
18. **Financial Times** (1 March 1985).
19. **Financial Times** (22 May 1984).
20. **The Guardian** (8 June 1984).
21. **Financial Times** (20 September 1984).
22. **Socialist Worker** (24 November 1984).
23. **Financial Times** (1 March 1985).

Notes to Chapter 6

1. A report prepared for Yorkshire NUM on these events is published in Coulter, Miller and Walker, **State of Siege** (London 1984) pages 153–7.
2. **The Mail on Sunday** (29 July 1984).
3. Paul Foot reporting in the **Daily Mirror** (18 October 1984).
4. **Financial Times** (4 August 1984).
5. **Financial Times** (8 August 1984).
6. Crick, page 111.
7. **Socialist Worker** (1 September 1984).
8. **Socialist Worker** (25 August 1984).
9. **Financial Times** (21 August 1984).
10. **Financial Times** (22 September 1984).
11. **Daily Express** (25 September 1984).
12. **Socialist Worker** (29 September 1984).
13. **The Miner** (12 October 1984).
14. **Sheffield Morning Telegraph** (25 September 1984).
15. **Socialist Worker** (29 September 1985).

16. Quoted in the **Financial Times** (5 October 1984).
17. **Daily Mirror** (17 October 1984).
18. **Financial Times** (14 November 1984).
19. **Socialist Worker** (17 November 1984).
20. **Yorkshire Post** (24 November 1984).
21. **The Miner** (21 November 1984).
22. **Socialist Worker** (7 December 1984).
23. **Financial Times** (3 December 1984).
24. **Financial Times** (7 December 1984).
25. **Financial Times** (7 December 1984).

Notes to Chapter 7

1. In J Skelley (editor), **The General Strike** (London 1976) page 45.
2. **The Guardian** (5 March 1985).
3. **Financial Times** (22 February 1985).
4. **Financial Times** (4 March 1985).
5. **Financial Times** (1 March 1985).
6. **The Times** (4 March 1985).
7. Stuart Macintyre, **Little Moscows** (London 1980) page 68.
8. Macintyre, page 68.

Notes to Chapter 8

1. **Sunday Times** (20 May 1984).
2. **Sunday Times** (15 April 1984).
3. Quoted in the **Daily Mail** (21 January 1984).
4. **New Statesman** (14 December 1984).
5. **Marxism Today** (March 1985).
6. **Marxism Today** (February 1985).
7. Daniel de Leon, **Two pages from Roman history** (Glasgow, no date) page 29.
8. **Rosa Luxemburg speaks** (New York 1970) page 214.
9. Dave Douglass, 'The Durham Pitman', in R. Samuel (editor), **Miners, Quarrymen and Saltworkers** (London 1977) page 255.
10. Quoted in **New Society** (17 January 1985).
11. **Sunday Times** (27 January 1985).
12. **Financial Times** (14 April 1984).
13. **Financial Times** (23 February 1985).
14. **NLR** 92, pages 7 and 27.
15. **New Socialist** (October 1984).

SOCIALIST WORKER

the weekly paper of the Socialist Workers Party, with up-to-date news and socialist analysis of workers' struggle throughout the world.
★ 25p every week, or for an introductory subscription, send £2.50 for the next ten issues (postage included) to Socialist Worker Circulation Dept, PO Box 82, London E2.